What Others Are Saying about *Batman's Batman*

"Against all odds, Michael Uslan has done it again! *Batman's Batman* is that rare sequel that is every bit as entertaining, informative, and inspirational as his first book. Highly recommended."

—Mark Hamill, voice of the Joker in *Batman: The Animated Series* and Luke Skywalker in *Star Wars*

"Great enterprises often take an equally great amount of time to come to fruition. The Greeks had laid siege to Troy for ten years, at a cost of many lives, before Odysseus got the bright idea to hide a few men inside a big wooden horse. And Michael Uslan spent an equal amount of time—from 1979 to 1989—on his own personal crusade to get a high-budget, adult-worthy film about Batman onto the big screen. Both men—the canny king of Ithaca and the New Jersey 'Boy Who Loved Batman'—deserve to remembered and celebrated for a job well done!"

—Roy Thomas, former editor-in-chief of Marvel Comics and co-creator of Wolverine

"I loved this book. Overflowing with tales of towering victories and crushing near-misses, Michael Uslan shows us the heart of a writer, the soul of a dreamer, and the burdensome gift of being unstoppable."

—Gail Simone, acclaimed writer of *Batgirl, Wonder Woman, Birds of Prey,* and *Deadpool*

"*Batman's Batman* is an extraordinary tale of courage, tenacity, originality, and heart. It is an emotional roller coaster for anyone pursuing their dreams and finding their identity."

—Howard Deutch, director of *Pretty in Pink, The Great Outdoors,* and *Grumpier Old Men*

“Michael’s passion and vision took a 21st-century no-brainer, where we have half a dozen actors playing Batman in various podcasts, films, and animated series, and forged it into existence in a time when no one believed it was a wise investment. Michael’s shadow looms large over the entire Batman legacy. And from this Riddler’s perspective, I’m very grateful.”

—John Glover, Tony Award–winning actor and The Riddler in *Batman: The Animated Series*

“A fellow New Jerseyian, Michael talks about one of the keys to being a successful producer (and surviving) in this business is ‘passion and storytelling.’ *Batman’s Batman* shows he is one of the best at both. His tales reveal his love for movies and the people who make them, not to mention what it takes to get things done. If you’re a fan of Hollywood stories, as I am, you will enjoy this. As I did.”

—Robert Wuhl, actor, writer, and a star of Tim Burton’s *Batman*

“Michael Uslan’s life is a dream come true. He’s a true fan with an encyclopedic knowledge of comics who also had enough business savvy to become a player in Hollywood. *Batman’s Batman* is an inspiring read!”

—Reginald Hudlin, director and Academy Award–nominated producer

“As a child, my dear friend Michael was fascinated with comics. His fascination turned into a passion. His passion into an obsession. His obsession into a career. The result: millions of transformed happy comic fans. A life well lived!”

—Greg Hildebrandt, internationally known fantasy and sci-fi artist, and designer of the original *Star Wars* movie poster and the Marvel Masterpieces card collection

“Michael Uslan is one of the true legends of Hollywood! Without him, superhero movies would not be where they are today and graphic novel–based IPs would not be dominating the global box office. His decades-long fight to bring the true Batman to the big screen is the perfect example of how ‘persistence’ is that primary talent needed to achieve goals that most would think impossible. I hope this book helps inspire a new generation of producers as much as Michael has inspired me.”

—Dimitri “Vegas” Thivaios, award-winning artist and producer

BATMAN'S BATMAN

MICHAEL E. USLAN

BATMAN'S BATMAN

A Memoir from Hollywood, Land of Bilk and Money

RED LIGHTNING BOOKS

This book is a publication of

RED LIGHTNING BOOKS
1320 East 10th Street
Bloomington, Indiana 47405 USA

redlightningbooks.com

This book is printed on acid-free paper.

MANUFACTURED IN CANADA

First printing 2022

Library of Congress Cataloging-in-Publication Data

Names: Uslan, Michael, author.
Title: Batman's Batman : a memoir from Hollywood, land of bilk and money / Michael E. Uslan.
Description: Bloomington, Indiana : Indiana University Press, 2022.
Identifiers: LCCN 2021034050 (print) | LCCN 2021034051 (ebook) | ISBN 9781684351831 (hardback) | ISBN 9781684351848 (paperback) | ISBN 9781684351862 (ebook)
Subjects: LCSH: Uslan, Michael | Motion picture producers and directors—United States—Biography. | Television producers and directors—United States—Biography. | Motion pictures—Production and direction—United States. | Television—Production and direction—United States.
Classification: LCC PN1998.3.U85 A3 2022 (print) | LCC PN1998.3.U85 (ebook) | DDC 791.4302/33092 [B]—dc23
LC record available at https://lccn.loc.gov/2021034050
LC ebook record available at https://lccn.loc.gov/2021034051

DEDICATION

Once upon a time in the world of Comicbookdom, there was a Marvel family, a Superman family, and even a Batman family. This memoir is dedicated to my own family and extended family from the past, through the present, to the future, all to be carried forward by my granddaughters, Harlie Jade Uslan and Tallulah Joe Duncan, who have progressed from infants to toddlers to Disney princesses to superheroes, and my grandson and Bat-Boy, Finley Morris Duncan. On the pages that follow, my grand grandchildren, you will find your roots. From them, may you find your wings.

Love, Poppy

CONTENTS

FOREWORD

So here's the tagline to the book you're about to read, a book that will be a real page-turner or, in this brave new media tech world, a "scroll-downer":

I'm the boy who loved Batman . . . since I was five years old. I had a collection of over fifty thousand comic books dating back to 1936 and attended the first comic book conventions ever held on the planet Earth. Comic books were my life and superheroes my gods (or at least my inspirations). As a kid in my twenties, I had an idea. I raised some money privately and bought the movie and allied rights to Batman from DC Comics in order to set out on my passion dream in life . . . albeit a geeky dream . . . to make dark and serious movies about Batman and his disturbed villains and show the world the Batman as the creature of the night he was originally conceived as by his creators in 1939. It was a good idea, this idea I had. But *how* could a kid in his twenties buy the rights to Batman, then grow up to be the originator and executive producer of the blockbuster *Batman/Dark Knight/Joker* movie franchise? It's impossible! Unbelievable! Inconceivable! But it's true. I did. That whole story I told in my prior memoir, *The Boy Who Loved Batman*. Did you read it yet? You should.

And that brings us to *this* memoir, *Batman's Batman: A Memoir from Hollywood, Land of Bilk and Money*. The title says it all. The following says more . . .

I was inspired to become both a writer and a storyteller by the master, Jean Shepard, whose radio show I secretly listened to nightly on WOR in New York when my parents thought I was already asleep (after all, the show was broadcast on school nights!). It was Shepard's comedy writing and conversational storytelling that influenced my own creative writing style and the way I would approach public speaking. A recent newspaper (remember them?) reported that of the top ten greatest fears of Americans, "death" was number two and "public speaking" was number one. But when you have a great or fun story to tell, those fears evaporate like a carton of Carnation evaporated milk (and if you remember *that*, you're *really* old!). And that's why I embrace public speaking and writing—I have *stories* to tell! And I can't wait to tell them to you!

Jean Shepard would go on to immortality for his book about his life growing up in the good old days, his cowritten screenplay based on his book, and his perfect narration of it in the classic movie that everyone on the planet has seen more than once, *A Christmas Story*.

I was inspired to write this memoir so I could take you on a journey into the strange adventures that happened to me during my thus-far forty-five years in Hollywood, the land of bilk and money. The direct inspiration for me was *Adventures in the Screen Trade*, the book that I first read in college written by the dean of all Hollywood screenwriters, William Goldman. Bill Goldman's tales stunned me, shocked me, scared me, terrified me, and entranced me as I read of the Hollywood passions, excesses, craziness, ascents and descents induced by power, wealth and fame, and most importantly, the creative process in full bloom. Several generations later, I was lucky enough to meet and work with Bill creatively as the originating producer of a movie franchise called "Shazam!" It was Bill, a self-professed Captain Marvel reader and collector since the first appearance of this great superhero in *Whiz Comics,* who would write the first draft screenplay. I will forever contend that this draft would have been the greatest possible *Captain Marvel* movie of 1943! But several generations after his impactful book on the movie industry, I take pen in hand and follow his lead to tell you the tales of working in that same industry today . . . an industry that is in a state of revolution and is changing by the week, as what we all knew as television gives way to streaming; as the largest number of movie theaters (still in existence) are now in China, not the USA; and as augmented reality and virtual reality make their presence known on the horizon. And the infamous "major" film studios Bill first knew (for comparison's sake, think of Jean Shepard's "major" award from *A Christmas Story*) . . . Warner Bros., Metro-Goldwyn-Mayer, Paramount, 20th Century Fox, RKO, Universal, Columbia, United Artists, and Disney . . . are now down to just five—Warner-AT&T-Discovery, Paramount/CBS, Universal/Comcast-NBC, Columbia/Sony, and Disney/Fox-ABC. And there are those futurists who see a time to come in which Hollywood . . . and maybe the world . . . is owned and controlled solely by Disney and Amazon. Life is funny . . . and scary.

So, as we begin this journey through my years in this nutty business, please understand that this is not a history but rather a memoir. The stories that follow are constructed from what I (and others with whom I conferred) can remember of the times depicted. Names have been changed, characters combined, and events compressed. So there!

In the not-always-best tradition of Hollywood, this book is a sequel. It follows my previous tome, *The Boy Who Loved Batman.* And if you know anything about Hollywood, you can assume it's part of an intended trilogy, so stay in your seats at the end of this book for an "after-credits" scene. Like my previous memoir, the stories within detail my life growing up down the shore in New Jersey and my years at school at Indiana University in Bloomington. They will comingle with tales of my escapades in Hollywood and New York in "the Biz." There's a reason for this. An outsider might call it "cause and effect." A movie industry insider might refer to it as "Ya gotta have a setup in order to have a subsequent payoff," and vice versa.

The secret origin of the title of this book, *Batman's Batman,* comes from a true story, a portion of which I first recounted in my prior book. It goes like this:

Astounding and unthinkable as it may seem, as I notified you above, I bought the rights to Batman from DC Comics when I was still a kid in my twenties. From that moment until my Bat-partner, Ben Melniker, and I were able to get the first dark and serious Batman movie made took ten long, long years. In the process, we were turned down by every major studio in Hollywood. My two favorite rejections included the one East Coast head of production who told me in 1979 that Batman and Robin could never be successful as a movie because the then-recent film, *Robin and Marian,* didn't do well. That was a story about an aging Robin Hood and Maid Marian starring Sean Connery and Audrey Hepburn. His apparent reasoning (if you could even call it that) was that both films would have the word

Robin in the title. The very last rejection we received came from the final major studio to whom I pitched a dark and serious Batman movie. The head of production there was a dapper, silver-haired longtime exec. He and Ben had known each other for decades. I pitched my little heart out that afternoon, and at the end of it, he shook his head and with a "tsk, tsk," told me that Batman would not be a successful movie because Columbia's movie *Annie* didn't do well. When I was so puzzled by his proclamation and asked him if he possibly was referring to that little red-headed girl who sings the song "Tomorrow," he said, "That's right." Shaking my head in disbelief, I asked him what that possibly had to do with Batman. His reply was right out of that entire generation of adults who had been conned into believing comic books were corrupting their children and causing a massive post–World War II rise of juvenile delinquency in America: "Oh, come on, Michael! They're both out of the 'funny pages.'" At that moment, there was simply nothing left inside me and I began to scoop together the Batman comics and the copy of my sample screenplay for *Return of the Batman* and prepared to exit. That's when he turned to his old pal.

"Ben," he said thoughtfully, "you and I go back a long, long time. If you really want to do a Batman movie, we'll consider doing it with you . . . but it has to be the funny, pot-bellied Batman with all those 'Pows,' 'Zaps,' and 'Whams' that audiences will remember and love."

That's when I, without any hesitation, said, "No way."

The exec sat himself down right in front of me and leaned in with lines of experience furrowed in his forehead and a frown of frustration draping his chin. "Son," he said, and I knew that anytime someone addressed me as "Son," I was already in trouble. "Better to have a film than to have no film at all."

And with only a split second of hesitation, I said, "No."

That was it. Another "Pass" and the final Batman rejection from the last major studio. Ben and I found a parklike bench on the grassy grounds of the studio. I sat, despondent with my head bowed into my hands. That's when sage Ben Melniker became a cross between Yoda and Obi-Wan Kenobi.

"It's quite ironic, Michael, that our final no . . . came from you. You know what that makes you?" he gently asked.

"Yeah, Ben, I know. It makes me an idiot," I replied with something just short of disgust.

"No," he countered. "It makes you Batman's Batman!"

"Huh? What?" I inquired as I lifted my head to see where he was going with this.

"You have a vision for Batman based on how he was created . . . this dark and serious thing. And you're refusing to let anyone else come in who might corrupt that or turn it back into some campy comedy. You're forfeiting big money . . . sacrificing everything . . . in order to protect Batman and defend him. Michael, you're Batman's Batman!"

It was a dawning for me . . . an epiphany. This wasn't about getting a movie made. It was about getting *this* movie made . . . *my* movie. And it wasn't about money. It was never about money. It was about passion. And with that, Ben pulled me right smack out of my depression.

"So we failed to get a major studio to understand. Okay. There are other ways to make movies happen and find financing. Let's strategize and pursue every other possibility out there!" he declared.

I jumped up off the bench, suddenly reenergized, and off we went . . . into movie history. Movies to come like *Batman, The Dark Knight,* and *Joker* would forever change Hollywood and redefine how the world culture would perceive comic books, superheroes, and supervillains.

And that is the secret origin of the title of this book.

But there's a backstory to all this.

In the beginning (or, if you're a big baseball fan, "In the big inning . . ."), there was a blue-collar kid from New Jersey. His dad was a bricklayer, his mom a bookkeeper. He didn't come from money and couldn't buy his way into Hollywood. He had no relatives in Hollywood. He didn't know anybody in Hollywood. So, how could he get there from here? And once "there," how did he survive the land of broken dreams, hollow hopes, sharks, predators, egomaniacs, screamers, and entitled, overindulged madmen? The answer would eventually come through passion, perseverance, tightly held hopes, mentors, benefactors, creative geniuses, and true friends with grounded values. It's amazing what they all can mean to one person committed and dedicated to making his dreams come true in a place that can, indeed, be a land of creative milk and honey instead of a clichéd land of bilk and money.

There are eight million stories in the state of mind called "Hollywood." These are a hundred and fifty of them.

MICHAEL E. USLAN,
Sitting on the northwest corner of Sunset Boulevard and Gower,
where two producers from my birthplace, Bayonne, New Jersey,
founded the first film studio in Hollywood in 1911.
2021, one hundred and ten years later.

PRODUCER PROLOGUE

The THIRTEEN *Ps* of PRODUCING

My disguise must be able to strike terror into their hearts. I must be a creature of the night, black, terrible. . . .

—THE BATMAN, *DETECTIVE COMICS* #33

Join me on my first trip to Hollywood (a.k.a. La La Land). It's December 1975: "Michael, I know you want to be a writer, but in Hollywood, a writer is a person who gives up his or her babies for adoption," said the International Creative Management exec as I was on the verge of hyperventilating and as he was transforming before my very eyes into my first mentor in the motion picture and television industry.

Irwin Moss was a king of Hollywood business affairs at one of the premier talent agencies in all of show business. Remember, it's called "show business" because it's 50 percent "show" and 50 percent "business." He was the first one to respond to any of the 372 résumés with cover letters I sent out to people I didn't know in the "City of Broken Dreams." I was finishing school but starting my search for that mystical goal that was as diaphanous and translucent as a mirage in the desert or the eternally elusive Lost City of Gold—employment in the industry of my dreams.

My quest to become a writer of movies, television, animation, comic books, and books was, in the words of my screen idol, Humphrey Bogart, "The stuff dreams are made of." My mom and dad taught my older brother, Paul, and me to dream *big*! However, their teaching came with a stern warning from my mother that the art of making our dreams come true is not quick or easy. It would come at a price . . . a high price . . . the price of commitment and perseverance. It's a price I've paid over and over again in my career and in my life. That price would be long durations of emotional and financial pain. This is my story of that pain and of the nirvana-like exhilaration of reaching the mountaintop the moment my dream came true. For me, that dream was obvious and organic, while deemed impossible by most of the rest of the world as they viewed it within the context of that time.

I dreamed of bringing a serious Batman to the silver screen (ultimately, to the world) in order to restore the darkness and dignity of this superhero without superpowers in line with the intentions of his 1939 creators, Bill Finger and Bob Kane.

And, as detailed in my prior memoir, *The Boy Who Loved Batman,* that dream would in 1979 empower me as a kid still in my twenties to raise money privately and buy the rights to Batman from DC Comics . . . and then to endure the ten tortuous years it would take before we could get that first movie made in 1989.

Batman, as envisioned by genius filmmaker Tim Burton and genius production designer Anton Furst, with the amazing talents of Michael Keaton and Jack Nicholson, would not only be a box-office smash but it would also impact the global culture in that magical summer of 1989. Hollywood would never be the same.

But thirteen years earlier, in a big, shiny marble and glass office sat a kid who was about to graduate and was terrified that his entire future in the movie biz would be determined in the next hour, left in the hands of the one high-powered Hollywood stranger who, for some unclear reason, had chosen to take the time and interest to become his mentor. Irwin's essential, experienced advice began with a command. "Michael . . . Why so serious? Take a couple of deep breaths and sit back in your chair before you pass out."

Irwin encouraged me to consider becoming a producer. It was one way to exert some small degree of control over any screenplay I may write, over any book or comic book I may choose to adapt, and over what happens to each project and when. But he cautioned me that at the end of every day, unless someone is a Steven Spielberg, it will be he who puts up the money and has the clout who will be calling every shot. That, usually, is the major studios and television networks. To quote William Shakespeare (or was it Errol Flynn's masseuse?), "Ay, there's the rub!"

"Once a writer turns in his or her script, it's gone. The producer, director, studio exec, or studio itself determines if a new writer is brought in to rewrite it," stated Irwin matter-of-factly. I later learned that the process of screenplay "development" might include such possibilities as eventually sixteen writers being brought in . . . or the studio deciding to change what the writer originally envisioned . . . such as a science fiction opus for Charlize Theron . . . turned into a western epic for Dustin Hoffman. In the words of Woodstock's Melanie in 1969:

> *"It's the only thing I could do all right*
> *And it's turning out all wrong, Ma!*
> *Look what they've done to my song!"*

WELCOME TO HOLLYWOOD!

What is a producer? I describe my role as boss, father, mother, general contractor, camp counselor, and shrink.

What does a producer do? Try this on for size . . .

In 1984, we produced a truly fabulous miniseries for PBS American Playhouse, *Three Sovereigns for Sarah,* the true story of the Salem witch trials of 1692. We all agreed going in that our production of *Three Sovereigns for Sarah* would be 100 percent historically accurate. We were going to shoot on any locations intact from 1692 and duplicate ones that no longer existed. Our miniseries would focus on three sisters who really lived then. One of them, Rebecca Nurse, was accused as a witch and sentenced to hanging. Rebecca's home and farm were extant and would become a primary location for us. We were given a tour of the place. Her bedroom was pristine from the night they came in and took her away. In her bedroom were her bed, spinning wheel, and dresser, with her glasses still atop that dresser. The guide demonstrated how her bed worked. Like most beds then, the frame had holes in it to allow ropes to pass through to hold up the mattress. Wooden knobs on the end of the ropes held them in place. The mattress was stuffed with hay from the barn. A pillow and blanket were on the bed. Every night's sleep caused the ropes to sag by morning, so every evening, Rebecca had to tighten each rope by twisting the knobs until the ropes became taut and able to support the mattress well. This is where the expression "sleep tight" comes from. When I asked our guide about the rest of that expression, "and don't let the bed bugs bite," he said the mattress was stuffed with straw, the straw came from the barn, and bugs were in the hay. Aha! A historical epiphany!

Although we had the Rebecca Nurse estate, the Salem Village meeting hall no longer existed, and that was where the witch trials took place. What to do? In the basement of the Peabody Museum, our historians unearthed the original plans from 1672 for that meeting house, and we rebuilt it, offering to sell it to the town for $1 when we were done filming so it could be used as a tourist attraction. We received lots of media attention when it became known we would be doing the first oak post beam construction in the United States in some 170 years. It was only a few short weeks later that my phone rang at seven o'clock one morning. We had a crisis at the construction site. Our construction crew was working night and day to finish the set before shooting began, and a local official ordered workers to cease work on the basis that our reproduction of the 1672 meeting hall wasn't "up to code." We pointed out this was a movie set on private property that was being donated to the town at the end of production. We had immovable resistance that reminded me of the days on his home-building jobs when Grandpa Uslan would start swinging his two-by-fours at deserving city bureaucrats. One of the wonderful young actors in our production was John Dukakis, son of the governor of Massachusetts (and later, candidate for president of the United States). I spoke to John and told him what had happened and that we faced the possibility of having to shut down and move to another state. He called his dad. Forty-five minutes later, we were no longer being stopped from proceeding with our work.

As a bonus, the good governor wound up attending and emceeing our wrap party and was kind enough to provide this Yankees fan with his tickets for a Yankees / Red Sox series at historic Fenway Park. I'd shoot in Massachusetts anytime!

As one of the coolest things to happen to this history major, my production office wound up on the second floor of the House of Seven Gables! We hired the two leading historians on the subject to be our historical advisers and gave them the power to halt a scene from being shot if there was any actor's costuming, jewelry, or other such details that were not correct. Our famed director from British cinema, Phillip Leacock, was thrilled with the cast we had put together, led by Vanessa Redgrave, Kim Hunter, Phyllis Thaxter, and Patrick McGoohan. Patrick had not been our first choice. We were trying to entice James Mason out of retirement to play the chief magistrate. His agent was helpful and had me call James at his house in Switzerland to discuss the role directly. I had a thrilling conversation with one of my favorite actors that day (his Alfred Hitchcock movie *North by Northwest* remains one of my all-time favorites), but it was unlikely he'd schlep across the world to do this role. The next day, I was listening to the car radio when they announced that James Mason had died the previous night. It dawned on me that I might have been the last person to whom he ever spoke.

I was thrilled to be working with Patrick, as a fan of his British TV series *Secret Agent* and in the belief that his TV series *The Prisoner* was (along with *The Twilight Zone* and *The Adventures of Superman*) the best TV series in history. The first day we met on set, I made Patrick an offer. I'd take him to dinner at the best restaurant on the north shore if he would agree to listen to me tell him what every detail in the symbolism-laden *The Prisoner* really meant or stood for. He agreed, and that night I regaled Patrick with such pronouncements as my fact that the Prisoner, who was never addressed by his name but only by his number, Number Six, was actually John Drake, Patrick McGoohan's famous spy character from his previous TV series. To prove it, I quoted from Johnny Rivers's theme song to the *Secret Agent* TV show . . . "Secret Agent Man, they've given you a number, and taken away your name." Patrick listened to my entire diatribe and then said, "That was fascinating, Michael! But totally wrong!" I was crushed. And then he turned my world upside down. "Why are you so sure the Prisoner had been a secret agent? Why couldn't he have been a scientist with the secrets they were trying to wrest from him being scientific ones?" asked a cunning Mr. McGoohan. I was blown away! The thought of him having been a scientist never occurred to me. As soon as I got home, I pulled out my VHS tape collection of the original seventeen episodes of *The Prisoner* and rewatched all of them in order from the perspective of Number Six being a scientist. And that's when I realized it made no sense. Patrick was just screwing with my head! And he did such a good job! This joke was on me.

Working with the Academy Award–winning actress Vanessa Redgrave was a privilege. She is truly one of the great actresses of a generation. Her performance in *Three Sovereigns for Sarah* was magnificent, and she, like the entire crew and cast, was so passionate that this production remain totally accurate at all costs . . . albeit on a diminutive PBS production budget. How totally accurate? One of our historians approached me on set one day and asked if I was really serious about our being accurate about everything? I assured him I was. Well, he informed me that in next week's shoot when Vanessa walks her cow through a field of cattle, the cattle in 1692 did not look like cattle does today. I wanted to know if we had to have the script rewritten or if there was any alternative. That's when he told me about Plimoth Plantation out by Cape Cod. It was a re-creation of an authentic village from that era, populated by actors who never break character when questioned by visitors or when tourists try to interact with them. Plimoth Plantation had been crossbreeding cattle, and theirs did, indeed, look the same way cattle did in 1692. I jumped into my car and drove there. I explained to the officials what we were doing and that it was for PBS American Playhouse and assured them of our commitment to accuracy. The deal was made, and we wound up having a cattle drive up Route 1 through Saugus en route to Salem, Peabody, and Danvers. Just a typical atypical day in the life of a producer.

OMG! I'm working with my idol, Patrick McGoohan, the star of *The Prisoner* and *Secret Agent* during my teen years!

And if you think that was a strange producer's day, how about the time we were filming in a certain state and our production manager was unexpectedly visited on location in this beautiful right-to-work state by two burly men who "suggested" we hire their men instead of the people we had already started working with. They even offered us a bargain rate of twice as much as we were paying our dedicated current crew. Our unit production manager (UPM) thanked them kindly but refused their offer. They suggested we all think it over before our sets accidentally caught fire and people got hurt. They would come back the next day for our final response.

What to do? How should a producer deal with a so-called problem like this, where there didn't initially appear to be an option of considering multiple creative solutions? Luckily (?), I had already witnessed a similar situation as a boy growing up on the Jersey shore.

It's amazing how your experiences as a child or teen or college student and the people who waltz in and out of your life can relevantly contribute to what makes you, "You" as

Me, circa age four, with my family, as Dad does his best imitation of New Jersey's Tony Soprano.

an adult. I was eight when hell erupted on earth . . . or at least on my little portion of it. Once upon a time in New Jersey . . .

My dad had his own small mason contracting business in the Asbury Park Shore area, Joseph Uslan, Inc. He had two trucks, a van, and a car that he would drive till the odometer broke somewhere north of 250,000 miles and the floor of the car rotted away into a contemporary version of Fred Flintstone's foot-powered putt-putt. My brother and I worked summers for him, and it was *awful*! We worked in 95°F New Jersey humidity tarring foundations, carrying bricks and bags of cement, and (my personal specialty) going for coffee for everyone twice a day.

A job came up for bid on the foundation and masonry work on a new house going up in Deal, which is halfway between Asbury Park and Long Branch, the latter well known as the center of the Mafia on the Jersey Shore way back then (and the subject of famous wiretaps that resulted in a state warrant out for Frank Sinatra, which prevented him from coming back to his hometown of Hoboken for many years). My dad, who had a great rep on the Jersey Shore as a top mason, won the bid. The owner, Willie Lawrence, would pay a third to start, a third halfway through, and a third immediately upon completion. My dad's work was amazing. The fireplace and chimney were magnificent, and the stone and brick veneer were done to perfection. My dad got his first two payments as agreed. When he finished the job, Mr. Lawrence raved about what a beautiful job it was and heartily congratulated my father as my dad handed him the final invoice. Mr. Lawrence thanked him and said he'd send him a check.

Thirty days went by and no check. Pop called him and asked if there was any problem with the job. Mr. Lawrence said no and reiterated that he loved the work. My dad reminded him about the check, and Mr. Lawrence said he'd send it right away. Another thirty days passed and no check. My dad called him again and explained that he was a small outfit and couldn't afford to carry a job; he needed to pay for the materials they used as well as for the men who had done the work. He reminded the man that he had been promised a check over two months ago. Mr. Lawrence was annoyed and yelled, "I told you you'd get your check, so stop bothering me about it!" He slammed down his phone. Another thirty days later—no check. My dad called him one more time, insisting he make payment or my dad would have to turn it over to an attorney. Mr. Lawrence exploded, "If you do that or bother me again for money, your wife's gonna wake up one morning and find you in cement on the bottom of a river and your kids disappeared off their school bus!" My dad was shocked and said, "Are you insane? How dare you threaten—" but Mr. Lawrence hung up. My dad called his attorney and told him to institute suit against Mr. Lawrence. Two days later, the lawyer called back with very scary news. He had both my parents get on the phone, and he asked Pop if he knew who he was dealing with. My father was puzzled by the question until the lawyer explained what his investigation had turned up. Mr. Lawrence was supposedly a Mafia lieutenant, and anything he had said was to be taken seriously.

My mom freaked! It was bad enough some maniac was threatening her husband—but her *children*!?! Mom was strong emotionally, mentally, and—we once found out—physically.

My mom and dad had taken me and Paul to Storyland, where Route 66 and Route 35 converge off the Asbury Circle (traffic circles were all the rage in New Jersey for decades until someone counted how many millions of people died in one every year). It was our own local Disneyland, later torn down with most of the rest of my childhood and converted into a humongous Sears until it was transformed into a makeshift movie studio where Woody Allen shot several of his pictures including *Stardust Memories*. Inside Storyland, we visited the Three Bears' home, of which Goldilocks had made a shambles; "Grandma's House," which was a little kid's delight (until my brother whispered to me that a wolf had just eaten Little Red Riding Hood's grandma on the premises and pointed out what he called "Grandma's murdered blood" in a puddle on the floor that I believed was, indeed, Grandma's murdered blood, until my mom overheard this and made everything right again by overruling Paul and declaring the puddle actually to be the result of Three Little Pigs with the runs); and the homes of those now-notorious Three Little Pigs. Uh-oh! There were great big signs posted on the fence around the three real pigs mulling about in the mud in between their model homes made of straw, sticks, and bricks, respectively. These signs all read: Danger! Do not feed the pigs! If you knew my brother Paul when he was growing up, you'd know what happened next: he slipped his little hand through the fence and offered some of his popcorn—and fingers—to the Three Little Pigs. The one who lived in the straw house, who, going back to the original fairy tale, obviously had issues and was mentally challenged, promptly bit down on my brother's entire hand, and when Paul screamed and shrieked and hollered blue murder to the point where even I, the daily target of his fists of fury (he was like a nine-year-old Bruce Lee with anger management challenges) felt badly for him, my mom moved like lightning to instinctively protect her cub, tearing through the fence and grabbing the entire snout of the pig in what years later scientists would explain as an adrenaline rush, forcing the jaws of the pig apart just like Johnny Weissmuller did to the alligator in *Tarzan Unchained* and extracting Paul's bleeding hand from this living, breathing, painfully oinking sausage-meat machine. Paul was so thankful and relieved that he remained on his best behavior for over an hour. I was impressed with my ma and have never been so impressed by anyone since! Word spread on the school playground like wildfire, from the swings and the jungle gym to the seesaw and the merry-go-round. All the boys started referring to my mom as "Mrs. Uslan—Pig-Fighter!" I was never prouder of anyone in my whole life! But I digress . . .

So under what they thought was a mob threat, my mom freaked for only the second time ever. A worrier by genetics, she sat my dad down and pondered what had to be done to protect her cubs. Oh yeah, and her husband too. This was a Mafia guy! That meant there was only one solution. In movies, you've known him as Obi-Wan or Yoda. In comic books, he's the all-seeing, all-knowing Watcher or the Ancient One or the Supreme Intelligence. In New Jersey, he's known as "Uncle Izzie."

Uncle Izzie, like some of my great uncles in Bayonne in the 1910s and '20s, was an "entrepreneur," a more socially acceptable term for someone in the rackets. In Bayonne back then, it usually meant booze during Prohibition, bookmaking, and the numbers. Knowing the lingo was important. For example, when Uncle Max had to go to jail for a short while, he was never "in jail." He was "sitting." His friends on the force made sure he had all the comforts of home in his cell or on the roof of the jail while he was there. It was in jail that he had the opportunity to fine-tune his pinochle game in addition to hearts and poker. His father-in-law, my great uncle Sam, owned Botwinick's, the ultimate Jewish deli and restaurant on Avenue C across from Langella's (Bayonne-born actor Frank Langella's grandparents) fruit stand. It was in the back room at Botwinick's that the biggest card games outside New York City took place. On those occasions when, as a little kid, I wandered through the heavy curtains and into that back room, my hands were immediately filled with half bagels and chopped liver or whitefish and I was sent off with a little *potch in tuchas* back into the restaurant where my Aunt Lil and cousin Henrietta would quickly hand me a Dr. Brown's black cherry or cream soda, my favorites to this day. (Although everyone in the family swore to me when I was five that *potch in tuchas* meant "smack in the tush," I was convinced it was an Indian term and started referring to myself as Chief Potchintuchas. I got belly laughs from this tough crowd, which may have been the start of my interest in show business.)

Truth be told, we already had a Hollywood star in the family—my dad's aunt was a silent film star named Anna Luther. Whenever she'd come back home to Bayonne for a visit, she'd pick up my dad and his sisters and brothers, have them pile into a "big, big car," and take them all clothes shopping. Her mother, Mrs. Luther, was the Jewish midwife in Bayonne who not only brought my dad into this world but also (eerily, coincidentally) my *Batman* producing partner, Ben Melniker, just two years after my father was born. Anna was most famous for being the first actress/stuntwoman to leap from a cliff on horseback down into

Ausable Chasm in upstate New York. She was also the best friend and sidekick to Pearl White, who had starred in the famous *Perils of Pauline* serials; roommate of Mabel Normand and Mae Busch; friend of Mack Sennett and Fatty Arbuckle; and wife of one of the biggest stars in the history of vaudeville, Eddie Gallagher of the comedy team Gallagher & Shean. "Shean" was Al Shean, the uncle of the brothers Groucho, Chico, Harpo, Zeppo, and Gummo Marx. Check the MGM movie vault for the 1941 Busby Berkeley film *Ziegfeld Girl*, with about every major MGM star of its day. It's all about Eddie Gallagher and his daughter! Al Shean and Mae Busch are in it, along with Judy Garland, Hedy LaMarr, Lana Turner, Jimmy Stewart, Jackie Cooper, Eve Arden, Edward Everett Horton, and Tony Martin. (If you don't know who any of these people are, you need to strap yourself into a chair in front of Turner Classic Movies and not move until 2031.)

So, my folks called Uncle Izzie. He was one of the few "entrepreneurs" who had survived in Bayonne after the Italian Mafia came in to take over the rackets in the 1920s under the watchful eye of Longy Zwillman. Instead of resisting, as others had done before mysteriously disappearing off the face of the earth, Uncle Izzie bowed and waved them in, offering them anything they might like from his business. They liked it all. But because he was so pleasant to deal with and cooperative, they agreed to take care of him—in a nice way. He opened Irv's Liquors uptown on Avenue C. Drive by—in a nice way—and you'll see his big sign. It's still there. It's still Irv's Liquors, although it's now really Ahmet's Liquors. Uncle Izzie's newest friend was a fellow named Anthony Russo. In New Jersey, he was better known as "Little Pussy" Russo, and eventually "the Godfather"—for real. As my mom and dad explained what happened and the threat from Mr. Lawrence, Uncle Izzie told them to sit tight while he made some calls. A couple of days later, he called back and instructed my dad that at 3:00 p.m. on the following day, he was to get dressed in a suit and tie and go to an office above the Flame restaurant by the Hollywood Drugstore on Ocean Avenue in Long Branch and meet Mr. Russo. His only other instructions to his nervous nephew were to tell Mr. Russo exactly what had happened and be polite and respectful. And with that, my dad was on his own!

He followed Uncle Izzie's instructions, showing up right on time, and was ushered in by two men he would later describe as "having presence." Mr. Russo was puffing on a cigar behind his desk when my dad entered. There was no small talk, no pleasantries. "Joseph," he began. My dad got more nervous. He was "Joe." The only time he heard "Joseph" was when his mom was angry with him, like when he was sent to the rabbi to study for his Bar Mitzvah one cold winter afternoon and threw firecrackers into the rabbi's pot-bellied stove and had to jump out of the temple office window to escape the man's wrath and wound up never being Bar Mitzvahed. But I digress. . . .

"Joseph, your Uncle Izzie and I go way back together. He tells me you have a problem," Little Pussy mused (or mewsed?). "What is your problem?"

Pop told him the whole story. Most of the time he spoke, Mr. Russo had his chair swung around so he was smoking his cigar while looking out his window toward the ocean, just past Mac's Ember, Max's, and The Windmill, homes of the best hot dogs on the Jersey Shore so long as you also include the infamous Syd's in Avon, infamous because it was the greasiest grease pit known to man and his hot dogs were cooked in the same grease that had been coagulating there since 1952. Like what seemed to constitute half the population of Jersey, Syd was a cousin on the Uslan side. (I have hundreds of aunts and uncles and thousands of cousins. People who know me swear that everyone in the world but them is related to me. I run into cousins everywhere. When I was ten, my mom and dad took us to Broadway to see Sammy Davis Jr. in *Golden Boy*. On the way into New York, we stopped at a toll booth on the turnpike and the toll collector turned out to be a cousin. We parked at the Port Authority and ventured out onto Eighth Avenue in an era when Eighth Avenue was part of Hell's Kitchen and the Port Authority was the home of every homeless person in midtown, though back in those politically incorrect times they were sadly and tragically referred to as hobos, bums, derelicts, and drunks. Pop hailed a cab at the corner of Forty-Second Street and Eighth Avenue. The hack driver was our cousin. Get it now? This weird shit happens *all* the time! Cosmic.)

So, Syd was a cousin. But the really interesting thing about Syd was the big sign that said Syd's in daunting wooden letters over his hole-in-the-wall little building. One day Syd died of a heart attack amid his hot dogs and fries and onion rings. I guess his fryer and the slippery seats my brother slid off of and the wet walls really were all part of a restaurant made out of cholesterol. It did in Syd. As Frankie Valli and the Four Seasons said, "'Grease' is the word" . . . just not the word you'd expect to see listed as someone's cause of death.

Sam Warner, who had worked for Syd doing most of the really hard work, took over the joint but didn't want to lose Syd's reputation. He had new wooden letters mounted on top of the sign, so it now was even higher on the roof and read, "Sam Warner's Syd's." Sam died within six months. Two college business students bought the place and didn't have enough money to take down the rooftop sign, just enough to add some letters to it. So above "Sam Warner's" they placed the towering words "Stan and Ed's." Now the one-floor building had about six stories of signs calling out to Avon, Bradley Beach, Ocean Grove, Asbury Park, and assorted Shore Points, "Stan and Ed's Sam Warner's Syd's." The next year it was bought by Schneider's, which lacked the sense of humor they'd have needed to make it "Schneider's Stan and Ed's Sam Warner's Syd's." It just became "Schneider's." Nobody went there anymore. But I digress. . . .

When my dad finished telling his tale, Mr. Russo swiveled around in his chair and said, "Mr. Lawrence has a big mouth. This is not the first time he has opened that big mouth. Joseph, I'd like to ask you a favor."

Omigod! This is *exactly* what would happen one day in *The Godfather*!!! My dad held his breath in fear of what was about to come.

Little Pussy Russo continued, "Forget about this. Go home and be a good husband to your wife, a good father to your boys, and please give your Uncle Izzie my kindest regards."

And with that the two "presences" in the room helped my father up and out the door. This audience was over.

As soon as he got home, my mom asked him what had happened, and honest-to-God, my dad didn't know. They called Uncle Izzie and reported what was said for his postgame analysis. Uncle Izzie was pleased.

"Did he or did he not tell you to forget about it?" quizzed the venerable Irving Botwinick.

"He did," replied my dad.

"Then go about your business and forget about it," Uncle Izzie strongly suggested. This matter had been taken care of, Jersey style.

Two weeks later, my dad came home from work, showered, and sat down in his favorite living room chair, waiting for my mom to serve dinner in the kitchen. (We didn't have a dining room. No one I knew growing up had a dining room before sixth grade. In fact, the whole concept of having some different place to eat besides the kitchen was totally alien to me. Still sorta is.) He opened the *Asbury Park Press*, and buried there (no pun intended) in an interior page was a squib of a story, "DEAL MAN MUGGED." It reported that Willie Lawrence of Deal was mugged the previous night as he got out of his car in his driveway. He suffered a broken arm and broken leg and was taken to Fitkin Hospital. The apparent motive was robbery. Ten days later, Pop drove by the house, and it had a for sale sign on it. Word on the street was Mr. Lawrence was out of the hospital and had moved to Florida. Two weeks later, my dad got a check in the mail for the final payment.

So, my parents had taught me an important lesson about standing up for myself and not bowing to pressure, even from burly guys who looked like the supporting cast of *The Godfather*. In my case, those two men did return the next day, reiterating what they considered their unrefusable offer, which had gone up a bit, and restating clearly, graphically, and in no uncertain terms their fears for the production's regretful imminent and certainly threatening disruptions. They knew their business. But what they did not know was that our UPM was wearing a wire, which they learned as the local FBI greeted them on their way out with an offer of their own. That offer was not refused. Another atypical day in the life of a movie producer.

So then, what does a movie producer do, besides pretend to be Eliot Ness taking on what Hedley Lamarr generally described in Mel Brooks's *Blazing Saddles* as "rustlers, cutthroats, murderers, bounty hunters, desperados, mugs, pugs, thugs, nitwits, halfwits, dimwits, vipers, snipers, con men, bandits, muggers, bushwhackers, hornswogglers, horse thieves, train robbers, bank robbers, and ass-kickers"? In the pages that follow, we'll take a close but fun look at producing, focusing on thirteen important aspects of the job, each beginning with the letter *P*. As you'll see, producing isn't just something to be learned on the job. You also need to bring to the table the things that shaped your character growing up, along with the lessons learned from your past (maybe even long past) experiences. Like my parents' crisis inspiring me to stand up to the forces of evil on a movie set, I'll share a litany of stories and tales of the colorful and wonderful people from my own past who helped me become the person I am today, as well as the producer.

For a history buff like me, the greatest part of working at a major movie studio and being a movie producer is that I sometimes rub elbows with history. Sometimes that means finding myself unexpectedly at a particular historic event (how about the Secret Service having me shake hands with Boris Yeltsin in front of the White House?) or in the presence of someone whose contribution to society will far exceed that of most celebs (like meeting every astronaut who walked on the moon or lunching at 21 with Walter Cronkite at Richard Nixon's table as he revealed behind-the-scenes, off-the-record analysis of the Clinton impeachment). Sometimes it means being invited to a place that few people ever get to see (like the command shack for security in the basement of the White House or the internal security workings of a major Atlantic City casino). And sometimes it's having someone unexpectedly walk into my office or confront me under a lamppost in a deserted cul-de-sac in the Hollywood Hills at 1:30 a.m. only to reveal a story with a secret of historic significance known only to the smallest handful of the most powerful people on earth—*if* that person can be believed! And every so often, it's just simply a thrilling moment of meeting and interacting with someone I've idolized, reminding me why I was so impassioned to get into this silly business to begin with . . . like that bittersweet night in 1992 while having a late dinner at Matteo's in Westwood, the restaurant that was a home to Frank Sinatra, Dean Martin, and the Rat Pack. We were the only ones in there when, suddenly, the Italian music stopped playing over the speakers and Dean Martin's greatest hits came on. A limo pulled up and, very slowly, out shuffled Dean Martin at the very end of his incredible life. I was saddened to see him so fragile and moving like an old man. But I knew he had recently experienced the death of his son, and our waiter said it destroyed him. He was there eating dinner by himself. Off I went to the men's room. When I came out and passed his table, I slowed to smile and say hello. He was cordial and warm. Just then, over the restaurant's stereo system came Dean singing, "Everybody Loves Somebody." I said to him, "Dean, you *have* to sing it to me!" He smiled at me and replied, "Son, I already sang that song! Now *you* sing it to me!" And so, despite my lack of ability to carry a tune, at the top of my lungs I belted out "Everybody Loves Somebody" to Dean Martin. He cracked up. I was thrilled. There is magic . . . beautiful magic . . . to be found in the world of producing if I don't let the special moments pass unseized and if, on the appropriate occasions, I pause to let ten-year-old Michael out to bask excitedly in that magic.

Ready? You're about to read of my adventures and misadventures in Hollywood and New York (and even such places as Salem, Massachusetts) during my career, which is now on its path toward five decades. You'll also read of the people and exploits who got me to where I needed to go (including such characters as my Uncle Izzie), from childhood to high school to college to law school and beyond. Enjoy the ride! I have for well over forty-five years.

My final destination? I'm still not sure. It could be Hollywood: the Land of Milk and Honey. Or it could be Hollywood: the Land of Bilk and Money.

In the immortal words of my idol, mentor, creative associate, and friend, Stan Lee, "I've been very lucky. . . . Money's OK, but what I really like is working. . . . I don't know where the hell I'll be in five years. Maybe I'll (still) be producing movies, maybe I'll be on a corner selling apples. I don't know. But I'm having a hell of a lot of fun!"

M. E. U.

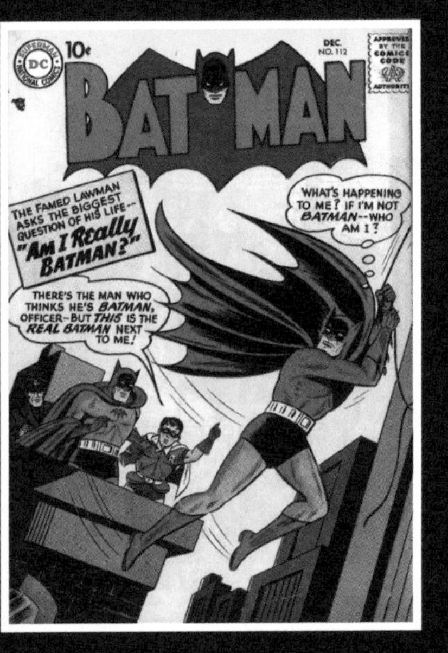
10¢
SUPERMAN DC NATIONAL COMICS
DEC. NO. 112
APPROVED BY THE COMICS CODE AUTHORITY
BATMAN
THE FAMED LAWMAN ASKS THE BIGGEST QUESTION OF HIS LIFE-- "Am I Really BATMAN?"
WHAT'S HAPPENING TO ME? IF I'M NOT BATMAN--WHO AM I?
THERE'S THE MAN WHO THINKS HE'S BATMAN, OFFICER--BUT THIS IS THE REAL BATMAN NEXT TO ME!

CHAPTER ONE

The PASSION

There is no viable movie, no viable project, no viable pitch unless it comes from the passion of a producer and only if that passion is ably and sincerely communicated to the financial and distribution sources as well as to the talent needed to come aboard. This then is the starting point for producing.

Maybe that's what he's about. Not winning. But failing, and getting back up. Knowing he'll fail, fail a thousand times, but he still won't give up.

—BATMAN: ZERO YEAR

LEFT: Batman! He inspired me, helped mold my own code of ethics, and made me either want to be him or be like him.

Why did I fall in love at age eight with the character Batman? Why did he immediately and forever become my favorite superhero, even though he had no superpowers but for his humanity? I can talk about his primal origin story, his rogues' gallery of supervillains, and his car. But on the most basic level, the reason is the simple fact that I could identify with him, relate to him, and be inspired to personally adhere to his moral code involving no killing, no guns, and maintaining honor, integrity, and fairness.

No matter which Batman is your true Batman, in a time of crisis, whether global or personal, follow my lead and live by his code.

When my dream became to make dark and serious Batman movies back in 1966, it dawned on me that I had three big problems:

1. I didn't have any relatives in the movie business.
2. I didn't know anyone in the movie business.
3. I didn't come from money, so I couldn't buy my way into Hollywood.

So, what then do you do when you have a dream . . . when you're burning with a passion that you can actually feel coursing through your veins? How do you jump a Grand Canyon? How do you make your dreams come true?

It was my passion that carried me far . . . far enough to buy me the time to find each and every door in my career path that I saw was barely open a crack. Then, it was up to my drive to propel me, to shove my foot in that door, then to squeeze my way in.

I was lucky enough to discover my passions early in life. As a baby boomer raised in the 1950s and '60s, my world was a globeful of television programs, cartoons, movies, and comic books. This clearly did not follow in the footsteps of a child preordained to go into his father's business. As a young man, my dad was fortunate because of a catastrophe of all things. Sound like Bruce Wayne? It was the Great Depression of 1929 that forced him to bow out of high school in order to go to work for my grandfather as a mason to help his family economically survive what would become sixteen years of Depression replaced by World War II. Yet that's exactly what allowed him to discover his own passion in life: masonry. He realized he was an artist at heart, and as my grandfather taught him his craft, he brought creativity to his stonework. He now had two loves in his life—his work and his girlfriend since age thirteen, Lillian, who in 1932 would become his wife (and two decades later, my mom).

If Dad's lesson setting me on my path through life was to follow my passion, then Mom's was her mandate for commitment and her high standards of perseverance. She cautioned the need for a high tolerance for frustration. That same quality would not only see me through a kid's jigsaw puzzle to completion but also would later empower me to find the inner resolve to last the ten years it would one day take to make the first serious Batman feature film. As she consistently advocated knocking on doors again and again until my knuckles would bleed, I can unequivocally say today that the *Batman/Dark Knight/Joker/The Batman* movie franchise was built upon my bloody knuckles.

So how do you discover your passion in life? The answer is simple: get up off the damned couch! If you are in your twenties, you still have the precious element of time on your side ... time to walk down different paths without sacrificing your future ... because it's just as important to learn what you don't like at this stage as what you do like. As I have traveled the world, speaking at universities, comic cons, and business conferences, I've met young people from all over. And in my own nonscientific sampling, 85 percent of young people have chosen not to get off that couch, preferring to sit back cozily, waiting for the world to come to them. If you jettison any misguided sense of entitlement, get off the couch, and become proactive searching for your passion and then charging forward to grab it, your competition becomes 15 percent, not 100 percent, and your chance of success just sky-rocketed!

Sometimes, passion rears its head in the least likely of all places or circumstances. Case in point: I was delighted and proud when I was informed that I had been chosen for the Trailblazer Award by the highly respected organization Cine and was to be honored along with the great composer Marvin Hamlisch, whose transcending artistry included the classic films *The Sting*, *The Way We Were*, and *A Chorus Line* and the song "California Nights" in 1967 for rock 'n' roll star Lesley Gore, who would sing it on the *Batman* TV show where she played the minion of Julie Newmar's Catwoman. Two weeks later, the song BATtled its way into the top twenty hits of the day.

The award show and dinner were held at the French Embassy in Washington, DC, so you know the food was sublime. I was enthralled meeting and spending time with Marvin. But the biggest thrill for me came when I was introduced to the man who would be introducing me on stage and presenting me with the award. There, with his trusty aide, I met Senator Patrick Leahy, president pro tempore of the United States Senate.

I told him that I first heard of his appearing at Washington DC Halloween parties dressed as Batman from the esteemed former secretary of state Madeline Albright when we met her in London during the filming of *Batman Begins*. It was she who tipped me off what a Batman fan and comic book collector the senator was. (And you can see him in his cameo-plus roles in several Batman movies ... sort of like the secret Stan Lee.)

As Nancy and I were introduced to the senator and his aide, he presented me with his ultimate challenge. "Michael, I have the toughest Batman trivia question for you. Nobody has ever been able to answer it correctly in all the years I've asked it." I accepted Senator Leahy's challenge as Nancy and his aide looked on. No bets were placed.

"What is the only correct date on the giant penny in Batman's Hall of Trophies in the Batcave?" asked the senator.

Without a moment's hesitation, grand comic book geek that I am, I rattled out, "Doesn't everyone know that it's 1947, because it first appeared in the story, 'The Case of the Penny Plunderers' in World's Finest Comics #30 published in 1947?"

I then laid down an equal challenge. "Senator, I have a question for you: What was the original last name of Batman's butler, Alfred ... and it's *not* 'Pennyworth'!"

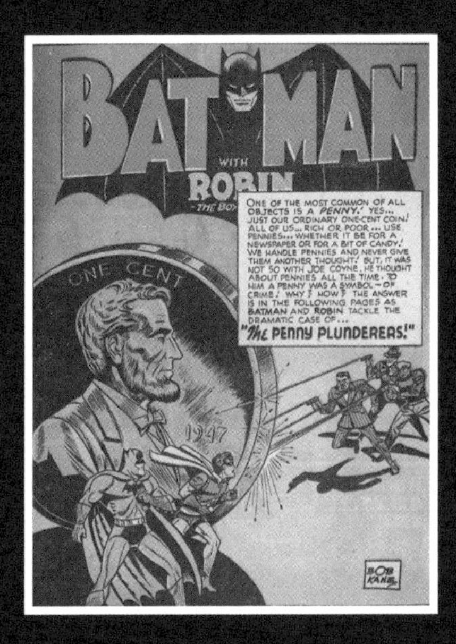
BATMAN
WITH
ROBIN
ONE OF THE MOST COMMON OF ALL OBJECTS IS A PENNY! YES... JUST OUR ORDINARY ONE-CENT COIN! ALL OF US... RICH OR POOR ... USE PENNIES... WHETHER IT BE FOR A NEWSPAPER OR FOR A BIT OF CANDY! WE HANDLE PENNIES AND NEVER GIVE THEM ANOTHER THOUGHT! BUT, IT WAS NOT SO WITH JOE COYNE. HE THOUGHT ABOUT PENNIES ALL THE TIME. TO HIM A PENNY WAS A SYMBOL -- OF CRIME! WHY? HOW? THE ANSWER IS IN THE FOLLOWING PAGES AS BATMAN AND ROBIN TACKLE THE DRAMATIC CASE OF...
"The PENNY PLUNDERERS!"
ONE CENT
1947
BOB KANE

"No, it's not, Michael, because his original last name was 'Beagle.'"

With that, Nancy and the senator's aide rolled their eyes and headed for the hors d'oeuvres, with Nancy saying, "Come on! Let's let these two boys have a playdate!"

In subsequent chapters, you'll read about how passion either won the day for a project of mine, or at least allowed me to sustain until the final outcome materialized, good or bad. Whether it was my quest to bring an entertaining yet educational children's show to network television by acquiring the rights to the computer game *Where in the World Is Carmen Sandiego?* and succeeding; acquiring the rights to make a prime-time, live-action TV series based on Mr. Potato Head and failing at the last minute; or having a moment in time where I might be able to buy Marvel or DC Comics if I could just persuade one major financial institution to back someone they merely saw as an overgrown kid wanting to buy a "funny book" company, passion always was the one irresistible force that saw me to the end of each unfolding story.

But along with passion for a project or production, there must also come a clear and enthusiastic passion for movies and the industry. The most appalling experience I have far too often as a producer is when film or telecom students wind up in my office vying for an internship or a job and don't know who Frank Capra or Michael Curtiz were, have never seen *Citizen Kane* or *The Maltese Falcon*—but admit they've heard of them—or have the audacity to announce shamelessly that they "don't watch black-and-white movies." I will chase them out of my office. They will never succeed in this business. They will never be respected in this business, this art, this craft, if they don't respect its past. Film and telecom schools must share the blame for turning out a generation of college students who can't pick out Errol Flynn or Alfred Hitchcock or Katharine Hepburn in a lineup.

Nightmarish case in fact: A bright young development veep in his twenties whom I worked with on a project became an important exec at one of the studios. We wanted to work together again, and he asked me to bring him a project. I had come up with a way to remake the film *Charade* with a modern-day creative spin that I was convinced was cool and contemporary without denigrating the integrity of the original property. I went to his sprawling office to pitch this to him and was shocked when he admitted he not only had never seen the movie but he had never even heard of it. Patiently, I explained that it starred Cary Grant and Audrey Hepburn and featured some of the greatest "heavies" in the history of American cinema, including James Coburn and George Kennedy.

"George Kennedy the comedian?" he asked me.

I was puzzled. "Oh, you must be thinking of George *Kirby*. No, this is George Kennedy, the scary bad guy in so many films," I replied.

"No," he corrected me. "George Kennedy, the old comedian from *Naked Gun*." He had no idea that Kennedy had had a career before that film. Regrouping and continuing my pitch,

LEFT: Batman's giant penny materializes in *World's Finest Comics* #30, "The Penny Plunderers."

I started talking about the original and how my take would be different. I saw confusion in his eyes when I mentioned the Audrey Hepburn role.

I paused. I didn't want to insult him, but I had to ask: "Uh . . . do you know who Audrey Hepburn is?"

The reply will live forever in Hollywood Hell: "Is she the actress whose head shakes?"

I was totally confused by his question. Then it hit me. *"Noooo,"* I said gently. "You're thinking of *Katharine* Hepburn, and her head only started shaking when she was like ninety. This is *Audrey* Hepburn." The words I used after that—such obscure terms like *Breakfast at Tiffany's, Sabrina,* and *Roman Holiday*—might as well have been in the language of ancient Rome for all they meant. It was at that moment that I first wondered if life had passed me by and if I wouldn't be better off at home, rather than in Hollywood today, secluded with my Turner Classic Movies collection.

When I started in this business in 1976, studio production execs all seemed to have extensive backgrounds in literature and English and mythology and the literary classics and the craft involved in screenwriting. Today, more and more, I'm stumbling across very young execs whose qualifications for the jobs appear to be that either they have watched tons of movies and TV or they are some important Hollywood person's dentist's son. The trouble then becomes exacerbated when they spend all their time looking over their shoulders, afraid of who might be coming up behind them to take their jobs, rather than looking forward and being daring or different or innovative in backing new projects from creative filmmakers. After so many decades in the business, I've found that small group of forward lookers and thinkers who are so great to work with and desperately try to avoid the others.

P is for Passion. It's the seed of life in every movie project. It is the superpower that singularly brought my vision of Batman to the movie and animation world.

CHAPTER TWO

The PRAYER

If you realize that movies like *Batman* and *Constantine* and *National Treasure* each took some ten years to get made from start to finish, the producer benefits from faith in his or her project against all odds and what seems like some unnamed force of nature akin to gravity that continually works against a movie ever happening. But how do you inculcate faith, commitment, and perseverance in a person? For every producer, it must begin with belief . . . an immutable belief in himself or herself and an immovable belief in his or her work. Without that, you don't have a prayer . . . and you need one.

The scope of one's personality is defined by the magnitude of that problem which is capable of driving a person out of his wits.

—SIGMUND FREUD

All people have limits. They learn what they are and learn how not to exceed them. I ignore mine.

—THE BATMAN, *KNIGHTFALL*

What do you do . . . what can you do . . . when over a course of some ten years, it seems like everyone is telling you "no," "your idea sucks," "you're wrong," or simply, "you're crazy"? Ten years of repeated rejection? It tests your mettle as a human being. You have to look deep inside yourself and ask the only true core questions: Do you believe in yourself? Do you believe in your work? Each time I was forced to confront that reality and ask myself those two questions, I kept coming up with the same answer: I am not just being stubborn! It doesn't matter if everyone else believes I'm wrong. I believe I'm right. I believe in me.

But how does a person develop that ability in the face of a wall of rejection to remain adamant in the belief in oneself? For me, it was a simple answer. It's all I knew. It's all my mother told me, taught me, and reinforced in me. If I was fantasizing about being Bruce Wayne, I had to stop and absorb the realization that my mom was the first Batman. She was my first superhero in my life. She was also the most honest person I have ever met. The rest of my life was devoted to doing what I could to emulate her and live by her strong code of ethics. My brother has felt exactly the same way since the day he officially matured at age forty. And it's this belief that's critical to being a producer in the celluloid jungle every single time Hollywood takes aim at you, fires at you, or besieges you.

Growing up in the 1950s and '60s, I had as glorious a group of superheroes surrounding me as the Justice League or Avengers. Better, my superheroes were all real. My mom and dad, grandparents, aunts and uncles, brother, older cousins, best friends, and some of the greatest teachers ever all either subtly or directly drilled in me the most basic and incalculable need to begin every quest in my life with a steadfast belief in myself and my work.

My mom used to tell me and my big brother, Paul, when we were growing up on the Jersey shore that the older you get, the faster time passes. We had *no* idea what she was talking about. But we do now. What's the simplest way I can possibly explain what she said? I know. . . . In the early days of my life, Mickey Mouse lived through Walt Disney. Today, Walt Disney lives through Mickey Mouse. I hope that makes sense to you. It does to me now.

As our parents' generation began to vanish around us, and with it our "buffer," my own philosophy evolved from the teachings and examples set by both my dad and my mom. My dad was truly a philosopher-king, though he never finished high school. His knowledge and wisdom came from his life's experiences, from the people he met, as well as from the endless newspapers and books he loved to read. He not only collected sayings, quotations, and meaningful stories but he also memorized them and quoted them at every chance he had to stand up and speak in public or to any family assemblage. His favorites included Emerson, Thoreau, and the Roosevelts (Franklin and Eleanor). His ultimate philosophy boiled down to his favorite quotation:

From Ralph Waldo Emerson:

> *"What lies behind us,*
> *And what lies before us,*
> *Are tiny matters*
> *Compared to*
> *What lies within us."*

Mom's most basic philosophies included be honest; once committed, remain committed and endure; believe in yourself; market yourself; the two greatest gifts we can give our children are roots and wings; and most importantly, as she taught us so long ago, family first.

To understand my lifelong story with Batman, you need to understand what we refer to in the movie biz as my "backstory." Therefore, we begin in 1956, a time when Mickey Mouse was still living through Walt Disney, and my thirst for superheroes began with Superman and Walt Disney's Zorro. My lifelong idols, Zorro, the Lone Ranger, and Batman taught me to believe in myself and to never give up. Case in point:

Thank God I was reading lots of comic books in second grade! It helped me solve the most disturbing mystery of my life. We came back to school after Christmas vacation and our cute and nice and sweet and kind teacher, Miss Siciliano, dropped the bomb on us—we were from now on to call her "Mrs. Slover." It made no sense! I never heard of a person suddenly changing her name. It was upsetting and confusing, and I felt angry. I elected not to participate in this charade. So I kept calling her "Miss Siciliano." She kept correcting me, and then one day when she was being really cranky for no apparent reason whatsoever, she yelled at me about it. I wanted to cry . . . but couldn't . . . wouldn't . . . in front of what my dad would call my peers and Uncle Phil would call "little pishers."

My teacher was a bright and wonderful young woman who understood the total belief I had in my Zorro fantasy and how much I equated myself to my TV hero. I recognize it today as a grandpa with my granddaughters, Harlie and Tallulah, who between the ages of three and six could dress daily in different Disney Princess gowns and become Elsa or Anna or Jasmine. When I acknowledge their fantasy and join in, I'm welcomed into their fantasy world and watch them developing inspired ethical codes and evolving concepts of "self."

That's why I was lucky to have Miss Siciliano as my teacher. A minute after she scolded me that fateful day in second grade, her smile came back and she came over to me, speaking in her real, soft voice like she used to in the old days when she called herself by her real name. She was sorry she'd snapped at me. I kinda understood she had some kinda problem. Then she explained it to me . . . and *only* me . . . so no one else could hear. She said she'd tell me the true story about her name if I promised never ever to tell anyone. Yes, she really *was* still Miss Siciliano, but now she had something very secret and very important to do. To do this thing, she needed to be like Zorro, whom I think she knew I drew pictures of every day in class on unused portions of arithmetic paper. She needed a secret identity! I would know that she was Miss Siciliano, but the world would know her only as "Mrs. Slover." Of course! I never even bothered to ask her why. Who cared? I had a teacher with a secret identity! And only I knew it! I was so excited and called her "Mrs. Slover" at every opportunity from then on. My teacher was a female Zorro!

Zorro? He was my life. I got to stay up till 8:30 p.m. on Thursday nights to watch his TV show *if* my teeth were brushed and *if* I was in bed and in my Zorro pajamas. I had a Zorro lunch box; a Zorro Pez; all the Zorro comic books; a Zorro puppet; a big Zorro figure on his big horse, Tornado; a Zorro book; all eighty-eight Zorro trading cards (including that one showing him dressed as Zorro but with his mask down so you could see he was really Don Diego); a Zorro pencil box; a complete Zorro costume with a fancy Zorro sword; and an entire Zorro playset, which inside the real tin walls of the garrison had little black cannons that actually shot out little black cannonballs, which one day, for reasons I can't explain or justify, I pointed at my mouth and fired right down my throat. Crying hysterically, I ran downstairs to my mommy ("Mom" always became "Mommy" in moments of panic), who was watching Art Linkletter's *House Party*, which came on just before *Queen for a Day*, and I screamed that I had swallowed a cannonball!

Now, my mom was frightened. She knew something traumatic had just happened to me, and, fearing time might well be of the essence in this crisis, she tried to get the accurate story from me. She made me repeat two more times what had happened. "I swallowed a cannonball!" I wailed in utter distress. "I swallowed a cannonball!" My mom, as always, maintained her cool in any crisis. She pulled me into the kitchen and gave me a glass of water to wash down whatever it was I thought I'd swallowed. Then she made me eat a piece of bread . . . I think to push it down in case it was stuck somewhere in my windpipe or lodged loosely in my larynx. She then calmed me, holding me as she dialed Dr. Goldstein on our brand-new phone that actually stuck to the wall. He made her repeat two more times what had happened to me.

Twenty-six years later when this subject came up during family stories time at dinner one night, my mom confided in me that she felt like a complete idiot telling Dr. Goldstein I'd said I had swallowed a cannonball. If he didn't know her as a rational and intelligent woman, he would not have told her to bring me right over but would have spent a few valuable minutes questioning her sanity. Before she loaded me into the Packard, my mom tried once more to understand what I thought I had swallowed. By now, I was together enough to show her my Zorro cannon and the cannonballs. She told me to bring them to Dr. Goldstein, sighing that it could have been worse. The only thing worse I could think of was my cousin Howard being allergic to chocolate, which I learned every time I heard his mom, Big Aunt Shirley (who had that classic mom's radar sense whereby she always seemed to know when, anywhere in North Bergen, Howard was just about to bite into a chocolate), grate out a gravely yell, "Howard! Don't eat the chocolate!" To me, that would be a fate worse than death. Far worse than when his sister, Nancy, thought she was Peter Pan and sprinkled sprinkles on her head, convinced it was "fairy dust," and tried to fly by launching herself off her toy chest to the sounds of her collarbone breaking in three places. To my knowledge, Nancy has never flown since.

So in we rushed to Dr. Goldstein's office all the way over on Grand Avenue in Asbury Park across from my mom's hairdresser, Cortez. Grand Avenue was still grand back then

RIGHT: Never could have dreamed that one day I'd be writing *The Lone Ranger*!

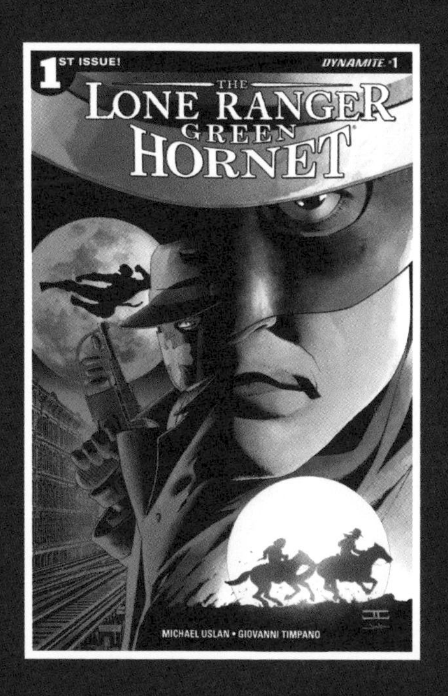
1ST ISSUE!
DYNAMITE #1
THE
LONE RANGER
GREEN
HORNET
MICHAEL USLAN • GIOVANNI TIMPANO

but never intimidated me the way Dr. Goldstein's small office did. The second I walked in I could sniff that pungent smell of the kind of alcohol his nurse, Anita, smeared on my tushy right before Dr. Goldstein whipped out from behind his back the shot the size of Zorro's sword. I started crying, begging my mom not to let him give me a shot. She promised he wouldn't, and though she never lied to me, I was still a little suspicious. But all he did was place me behind his fluoroscope (one of the first ones made and one of the last ones still in use) in what were my originally all-white underpants and fluoroscoped my body through the wonder of science and a massive amount of radium sure to locate the little Zorro cannonball in my stomach and contaminate half the Jersey Shore with enough radiation that scientists will still be getting clicks on their local Geiger counters twenty thousand years from today.

For being so brave, my mom took me to the Wanamassa five-and-ten to pick out some small toy as a reward. I selected a magic trick. It was a small wooden rectangle that could magically transform a penny into a nickel and it really worked! Excited, I took it over to one of my best friends, Harvey Civins's, house across from the lake in West Allenhurst. He had a tire swing! I showed Harvey the trick. It still worked great, which some tricks don't when you get them home from the store. Harvey didn't believe it. He claimed it wasn't a real penny. I indignantly said, "Is too!" He dared me to prove it. I was stumped. "How?" I asked the little naysayer. Harvey said to prove it by balancing the penny on my tongue. Somehow . . . some way . . . that seemed to make sense. So perched on his porch, I perched the penny on the tip of my tongue. Four seconds later, I swallowed it.

Starting around age six and with no other comic book superheroes available to me on TV, besides Zorro and Superman, I found that the Lone Ranger sufficed. He had a sidekick, just like Batman and the Green Hornet. He wore a mask, just like Batman and the Green Hornet. He rode around on a speedy conveyance, just like Batman and the Green Hornet. He never killed, just like Batman and the Green Hornet. And he was a hero, though most people wrongly believed he was a villain, just like the Dark Knight and the Green Hornet. It would take me years to learn that both the Lone Ranger and the Green Hornet were created by the same man who created the Green Hornet to be the modern-day urban version of the Lone Ranger. Even more astounding, writer Fran Striker made it increasingly clear that the Green Hornet was, in fact, the grandnephew of the Lone Ranger. Incredibly, due to complex legalities, it would take eighty-five years before the Reid family saga could be told. The tale of the passing of the hero torch from the Lone Ranger to the Green Hornet was finally able to be told in the Dynamite graphic novel *Lone Ranger/Green Hornet: Champions of Justice* . . . and I got to write it! And so, I scratched another line off my bucket list!

In the interim, my passion for the Lone Ranger that began by watching him on TV as a child resulted in my producing two other Lone Ranger media projects over the years.

RIGHT: Thirty-five years after writing *The Shadow* for DC Comics, I was back with my favorite fedora fighter for Dynamite Comics.

THE SHADOW GREEN HORNET
DARK NIGHTS
DYNAMITE #1

Circa 1990, post the 1989 *Batman* hoopla, I approached the owners of the Lone Ranger, an IP/brand that had been "resting" since its epic misfire as a feature film back in the super seventies. In that one, two of the more looming problems that helped torpedo the venture included the following: (a) the sad fact that all the dialogue of the lead actor had to be dubbed by actor James Keach to remove all traces of star Klinton Spilsbury's Canadian accent; and (b) the sadder fact that the company behind the film, with guns blazing, went after the man it perceived to be the villain of the story, heralded and beloved actor Clayton Moore, who *was* the Lone Ranger to an entire generation of baby boomers (yeah, yeah, yeah, except for that one season the "fake" Lone Ranger replaced Moore during a rather nasty contract dispute . . . a tale to be saved for the next book)! In those days, an older Clayton Moore was making many public appearances as the Lone Ranger before clamoring crowds of college coeds, kids, and their clans. The movie company took the poor man to court to stop him from appearing in public in his (authentic) Lone Ranger mask. Its legal bullets overwhelmed "our" Lone Ranger, forcing him to get by wearing a pair of sunglasses rather than a mask whenever he appeared. I paid specific homage to Clayton Moore and that specific incident in my graphic novel *Lone Ranger/Green Hornet: Champions of Justice*, when a city cop sees the maskless older Ranger trying to stand up to the bad guys and offers his hero his state trooper–style sunglasses.

In the early nineties, I felt it was time for a new Lone Ranger to gallop onto the world's TV screens. On the heels of our enormously successful first *Batman* movie, I pitched a serious and somewhat darker and more realistic version of the show that would be written as alternative history. I used carefully researched locales, true incidents, and real historical figures—both good and bad—with which the Lone Ranger and Tonto would intersect. I wrote and produced what we call a "sizzle reel," which was about three minutes long and backed by one of the great world philharmonics playing the loudest and most stirring version of Rossini's "William Tell Overture," the classic theme song of the Lone Ranger since his days on dramatic radio. Working with the two great owners of the brand, by the end of that year's huge NATPE television convention, where new shows and reruns were sold to stations all over the country and globe, they had good news and bad news for me. The good news was that they had sold my series to enough TV stations to be able to green-light it for production. However, the bad news was that they were declaring bankruptcy. My version of the Lone Ranger died with his boots on. Welcome, yet again, to Hollywood.

My heroes' lessons had sunk in—I would never give up! But, damn . . . it would take so many more years. . . . But like my idol, my mom, I dug another bunker, put on my army helmet, and hunkered down for one more Hollywood siege. This one lasted until 2008. You count the number of years. I can't bear to.

Eric Ellenbogen and I both learned the ins and outs of the movie business at the feet of our mutual sensei, Benjamin Melniker. Eric would go on to an illustrious career in the industry, at various times the president of Marvel, Lorne Michaels' Broadway Video, and Classic Media. It was at Classic Media that we would intersect again. Eric's company had bought and accumulated the rights to many, many great brands, including Lassie; Turok and the characters of Gold Key/Dell Comics; Richie Rich, Casper, and all the Harvey Comics characters; Sergeant Preston of the Yukon; and the Lone Ranger! We reconnected in the early nineties and talked about creative ways we might work together. I suggested that rather than going the "old man in a worn sweater" old and quaint version of Lassie, we do the equivalent of a *Home Alone* movie with Lassie, the protective family dog, proving smarter than the two bad guys looking to burglarize the house. That idea wound up playing dead. More than a quarter century later, I still think it's an awesome idea for rebuilding a once-mighty global branded franchise.

The two projects we wound up targeting began with a Dell / Gold Key comic book character I had loved as a kid, Turok, Son of Stone. Turok had make a resurgence in popularity thanks to a hit video game from Acclaim and a corresponding comic book series. At Classic Media, working with Eric and his development and production topper, Evan Baily (importantly, whose grandfather Bernard Baily cocreated and drew the Spectre and Hourman for DC Comics in the Golden Age), we decided to produce a budget-conscious, direct-to-home-video animated movie based on the earlier comic books, but R-rated. Why a hard "R" for graphic-animated violence? Turok was a dinosaur hunter in *The Lost Valley*, and when you have humans going directly up against dinosaurs, you're going to have some savagery and bloodshed. Just ask that guy on the toilet in *Jurassic Park*. Or that guy being mushed under the toes of a giant gorilla in *King Kong* (the *real* one, not the big guy from remake 1, 2, 3, 4, 5, or 6).

Upon the completion of *Turok*, Eric, Evan, and I set our sights on producing a Lone Ranger movie that would be based on a great screenplay, whether it was produced in animation or was in live action on a blockbuster budget. It brought our hero into contact with an exiled Samurai warrior as they set out together on a noble, yet nearly impossible quest in the days of the Old West. And it *was* a great screenplay by the talented Tony Bedard with input from Evan; my head of development at the time, F. J. DeSanto; and me. We were pushing hard toward beginning production when word came. Classic Media was bought by Dreamworks, and there was no interest there in an animated or live-action Lone Ranger feature. Not again! Yes, again. Hooray for Hollywood!

Years later, a very big budget Lone Ranger feature film was made with Johnny Depp as Tonto. There was some severe dabbling with the IP. While Clayton Moore was busy turning over in his grave, I was watching this movie and determined that it would be the first movie I would walk out on since I'd walked out of the St. James Theatre in Asbury Park about halfway through the unbearable *Barabbas* with Anthony Quinn when I was ten. I got out of my seat, walked back up the aisle, and, just before leaving, realized I was on an airplane. I trudged back to my seat and switched the in-seat entertainment center lodged in the back of the bald guy's seat in front of me to a different movie, *The Green Hornet*, with Seth Rogen. This time I didn't hesitate. I jumped. At least in my mind. Look, I understand what can happen in Hollywood. If some studio or money source becomes intent on making a movie a certain way or with a certain star or director, all a producer can do is kick and scream once logic and passion fail. No one intends for a movie to fail or violate the integrity of a well-known character or brand. But there are hundreds of creative, technical, and corporate cooks orchestrating the dinner. Sometimes, even though Sherlock Holmes was created to be the ultimate cerebral superhero, turning him into the Batman of the nineteenth century may be embraced by the modern, young audience. Other times, not so much. I should know. I lived through four of 'em. Painfully. I'd show you the scars, but they're not particularly visible. Just four more Hollywood whippings.

But it was far more than TV stars that prepared me for what life doles out, since we all know that nobody promised that life would be fair. Besides superhero parents, I had two superhero teachers . . . and one other who became my Joker.

One year with Mrs. Rita Friedman as my teacher in eighth grade was all I needed to excel as a writer. By the end of that school year, I knew how to write and deal with sentence structure—all stuff I get to ignore here and now while writing this book . . . unless she shows up tonight like Jacob Marley and marks up my manuscript with her slashing red pen. I'm scaring myself. Excuse me while I pause to make absolutely sure I have split no infinitives.

Mrs. Friedman and my seventh-grade English teacher, her sister-in-law, Mrs. Elinor Stiller, who uncovered a creative writing ability in me and nurtured it, kept track of me all throughout junior and senior high school. They were there to talk with whenever I needed help, a bit of tutoring, or moral support. They insisted I submit one of my creative works to the national creative writing contest sponsored by *Scholastic* magazine in my senior year of high school. Since I was not a fan of a certain other English teacher from high school who read symbolism into every book, story, and poem till I thought it became extreme and out of control, if not wacky, I decided to satirize her sort of overanalysis. I took a Mother Goose nursery rhyme, "Little Jack Horner," and did my own Freudian analysis to prove it was actually a case history of a deeply disturbed young man in desperate need of psychosexual therapy.

> *"Little Jack Horner" and the "ID" Complex*
>
> *Little Jack Horner*
>
> *Sat in a corner*
>
> *Eating his Christmas pie.*
>
> *He put in his thumb*
>
> *And pulled out a plum*
> *And said, "What a good boy am I!"*
>
> *A surface analysis of this poem, which borders on the line of pornography, exposes the fact that the central character called, suspiciously enough, Jack Horner, is suffering from a deep emotional and mental condition resembling isolated cases of paranoia. This, obviously, stems from a depressing childhood. Not once in the entire passage is there reference to his parents. Divorce, separation, or perhaps just a depraved socio-economic environment was the reason he did not want to mention his family. After*

all, would a normal mother permit a boy as young as Jack to sit in a corner with a whole pie, stuffing himself before dinner? Not unless she, herself, suffers from a manic-depressive insanity. When one is deprived of love and is bent on releasing his emotions, he often resorts to eating a great deal. Here again, Jack's emotional instability is revealed. The epitome of insecurity is thumb-sucking. Unknown to even Jack, he subconsciously keeps putting his thumb in his mouth. One can only conclude that he is afflicted with functional disintegration, which can lead to aberration of the mind, or worse, to total mental alienation.

At this point, one may wonder how it can be assumed that Jack is evidently nearing puberty. This hypothesis seems readily proved by his immature eating habits (re: use of the thumb). This support of such a theory may well be contradicted, however, by the fact that he was psychotic, and his mother, also being of demented mind, noticed self-destructive tendencies in his behavior. Thusly, she refused him such possible weapons as a knife or fork to prevent him from inflicting wounds on his body. This, therefore, leads to the proposal that the boy was masochistic and a latent sadist. Why else would he be sitting in a secluded corner mutilating a pie?

"Horner," according to Webster's College Dictionary, is suggestive of being strong or having strength. Perhaps the "unique" sexual tendencies of his became more dominant when he realized that he was not the strong person he desired to be. Quite the contrary, due to his excessive overeating, an established emotional problem, he was most certainly obese, and as the selection admits, "Little . . ." Deeply rooted in his subconscious, he may have recognized his effeminate traits in stature, walk, varied idiosyncrasies, et al. In rebuttal, he hostilely attacked the nearest object—a Christmas pie.

Christmas is traditionally a time of joy. Jack, however, spends the day as a recluse in the corner. Again, this exemplifies the fact that he was exceptionally self-conscious and, perhaps, ashamed of his own body. This being true, it would seem that his psychosis is also part neurosis. To fulfill his sexual needs and relieve the inhibitions which he so wantonly repressed, he rejects heterosexual love, homosexual attachment, and even (the result of childhood experiences) spurns the Oedipan dream. Instead, these outlets of emotion are, in his degenerating mind, incorporated in his thumb. In his precorner adventures, he thrives on these previously recessive needs by sucking feverishly on his thumb. By Christmastime, however, he is content with putting his thumb in the pie and obtaining satisfaction.

The plum is symbolic of the usually pseudo-intellectual "ID" complex. For the layman, this term refers to a belief in super egotism of oneself. Jack did not expect to pull out a plum while probing the pie, which was representative of his subconscious mind. There, though not realizing it, he found the easy, weakest answer to his emotional problems and self-consciousness. He then pulled out the plum, or took on the mental guise of conceit. Outwardly, he became egotistical, so people would not know him for his true self. This is similar to the case of Lord Byron, the famed poet, who also suffered from such social difficulties. Jack's decision to use the "ID" complex as a cover reached its apex when he excitedly proclaimed: "What a good boy am I!"

In this stage of self-deception, Jack was able to publicly conceal his psychotic state, yet all the while he was being spiritually torn apart by a raging conflict between his consciousness and his subconsciousness. It seems inevitable at this rate that Jack will become a human vegetable by the time he reaches physical maturity.

I entered this into the big contest, and I won a national prize. By the time I got to college, *Scholastic* had a national creative writing contest just for college students in North America. So I entered that one, too, this time doing my Freudian analysis of "Little Tommy Tucker" and "Baa, Baa Black Sheep." If you thought Little Jack Horner was depraved, you should see what I did to this guy. In the end, I changed the overall title to "Mother Goosed."

I won the college contest, one of only four people at that time ever to have won both contests. As a result, *Scholastic* gave me a major award (There's that word, *major,* again! No, not a lamp in the shape of a stockinged woman's leg!) by publishing me for my first time in an anthology of "the best creative works from colleges and universities in North America." When my published copy arrived in the mail one afternoon, I stared at it until I couldn't see through my tears of joy. If my mom made me believe in myself, it was Mrs. Friedman and Mrs. Stiller who made me believe in myself as a creative writer. I owe the three of those great women everything.

In 1989 when our first *Batman* movie opened and was such a huge hit, we had a premiere screening in New York City. The theater was packed, and I was fortunate to have several minutes to speak to the SRO crowd. I had tracked down Mrs. Stiller and Mrs. Friedman and, fulfilling a fantasy I had harbored since eighth grade, sent a limousine for them and brought them to the night's festivities. I told the assembled audience all about them. I spoke of the power and importance and influence a good teacher could have on the lives of her students. And I specified that no one would have been in that theater that night and that there would have been no *Batman* movie but for them and the impact they had on my life and on my work and on my dreams. I had them stand up and they received a standing ovation. They honored me by their presence that night. And in my own attempt to do the same for them, I think the two best things I have ever written have been their eulogies, which I delivered as the representative of all their students over their lifetimes of teaching. So if you're reading my book right now, this very second, please stand up and clap for Mrs. Elinor Stiller and Mrs. Rita Friedman, my teachers.

But I also told you there was a Joker in my high school deck. Another teacher . . . the antithesis of Mrs. Stiller and Mrs. Friedman. Let's call her . . . Miss Jacqueline Napier. (Names have been changed to protect the innocent . . . namely, me!)

We may have been in the same high school but were never on the same wavelength. She didn't understand my writing, like the time she gave me a C for a piece I wrote that the class loved. It was Mother Earth talking to mankind and decrying what it had done to her. My teacher's comment was, "I don't understand this. Who are you talking to, Mike?" Or, "Who is talking to you?" I couldn't have been more frustrated for an entire school year. If the writing wasn't cookie-cutter crap, she didn't get it and didn't like it. She wanted everyone writing and thinking the same. She was Spiro Agnew in a dress. Look him up on Wikipedia. Despite her best efforts, I still aced every lit test and every English test she tossed at us. And then at the end of the school year, brand-new Ocean Township High School announced it would be starting honors courses in each subject the following year and that the teachers would determine who would go into honors. The problem boiled down to the administration's poor choice of the word *determine* rather than *recommend*. Earlier in the day, I was given a notice by my history teacher that I'd be going into Honors History. I now expected the same from my English teacher, as I had all As the entire year. She passed out the notices, and I didn't get one. So, of course, I went up to her desk and told her that I didn't receive my notice. She said I would not be getting one. She did not place me in Honors English. "But I got straight As!" I said, alarmed. "But you don't know how to write," she answered back. I debated her, challenged her, argued with her, parried her thrusts, and kept fighting on behalf of my keen desire to learn, which she was denying me. Finally, she heard enough and told me the discussion was over. And so, I stormed out of the classroom and went straight upstairs to the English Department Office. I found Mrs. Friedman and Mrs. Stiller and told them what had just happened. They calmed me and told me she wouldn't hold me back. The two of them would talk to her and set her straight. I was tremendously relieved . . . until the next day, when they informed me the woman had told them she knows better than they do and to butt out of her business. They then arranged a meeting for me with the head of the department. I made my own case and showed her my writings for the school year along with the teacher's clueless comments on them. Supported by Mrs. Friedman and Mrs. Stiller's recounting of my work in their classes, the department chairwoman said she was absolutely convinced I should be in Honors English and would talk to my teacher. But, she cautioned me, she had to convince Miss Napier to make the change. She could not just override her unilaterally, because the policy was clear that each teacher could solely make this determination for her students. The next day at the end of English class, just as the bell rang, my teacher said, "Michael Uslan, please stay after class for a few minutes." *Yes!* Her boss spoke to her!

As the last student exited the room, a snarl appeared on my teacher's face, and her eyebrows furrowed. I was watching that scene from *The Wizard of Oz* the moment Miss Gulch transformed into the Wicked Witch of the West right in front of Dorothy's eyes. "If you think by going over my head you're going to get me to change my mind about your getting into Honors English next year, you are sadly mistaken! Think about that the next time you consider going over a teacher's head!" she screamed at me.

I walked out of the room and upstairs to the English Department triumvirate who believed in me as much as I firmly believed I deserved to be in Honors English. The chairwoman was upset that she was unable to convince my teacher to change her mind. I asked if I had any other recourse and was told I could try the principal and then the Board of Education. (This was the '60s. Kids didn't sue their schools and boards and teachers back then. It just was unthinkable.) So I went to see the principal and pleaded my case. He was amazed at the lengths I was willing to go because of faith in my own ability and being so goal driven . . . just to try to get the best opportunity to learn. He was puzzled that no one had yet been able to resolve this. He told me not to worry. I worried. And, as it turned out, deservedly so. The next day, at the beginning of English class, the Wicked Witch of the West didn't even bother to try disguising herself this time. She walked over to my desk and hissed, "You stay after class!" I narrowly dodged the fire she was breathing. And later, she . . . well, *ranted* and *raved* won't cover it. *Screeched* and *cackled* are better word choices. "I see that Mr. Big Shot doesn't like to listen to his teacher and goes over her head, this time to the principal of the school! Well, let me tell you something . . . you will *never* get into Honors English. I will never budge on this!"

I didn't enter Honors English until one entire year later. But I was, indeed, infected with a poison in my system that wanted nothing more than to wreak vengeance on my English teacher someday, and to me, that meant proving I *am* a writer—getting published, going back to school one day with a published work in tow, and confronting her about the evil she had done. I spent hours daydreaming about it or, just before I'd fall asleep at night, fantasizing about all the ways I would one day show her! I eventually had rehearsed in my head exactly what I would say to her on that day. I refined that fantasy to perfection. In my freshman year of college, after winning my second national Scholastic Magazine Creative Writing Contest and being published in book form, I could not wait until I got home over Christmas break. My first stop was Ocean Township High School. The Wicked Witch of the West was still teaching English there, four years after the doomsday trap she had sprung on me. I clutched my book and waited outside her classroom door until the bell rang, ending seventh period and the school day. As her students filed out, I slipped inside. She was organizing her papers at her desk as I called out a hello to her. She looked up. It only took her a couple of seconds to recognize me. I began my revenge . . . the same revenge that had been pushing me and pushing me to succeed as a creative writer.

"I brought you something to see . . . and you really need to see this," I taunted as I slapped the book down before her on her desk. "You're now talking to a published author!" I proclaimed. "A published author that you said didn't know how—"

She drowned me out with a sudden and boisterous, "Oh, Mike! I'm so proud of you!"

Huh?

"I always knew you'd go on to great things!" She droned on with excitement, but my ears were starting to clog. A trick! This is some trick!

"And Mike, I can't help but feel pride, myself, because I feel that I'm partly responsible for this as one of your teachers who always knew you were special!"

I just wanted to throw up. Not from the bs. Not from the disconnect. Not from the delusion. But from all these years of a perfect planned revenge . . . and now she even took that away from me. Revenge, clearly, is not all it's cracked up to be. And so I never said another word. I stood there in a sad daze, picked up my book, turned around, and walked out of that cursed classroom, out the door of my high school, and took a fresh step forward into my future. Years later, as I was battling incessantly for my dark and serious Batman movie, facing a new round of bad guys in the process, I was able to remember what I had learned the hard way back then . . . revenge is not so sweet. Batman, himself, even figured that out the day he was able to stop his mission of vengeance to get the guy who murdered his parents and was then able to devote himself to a mission of justice to get all the bad guys.

A story I love telling over and over again is the one that happened a few years back when my agency asked me to a meeting to hear straight from this horse's mouth how, at this stage of my career, I perceive myself. I told them I saw myself as a Hollywood proctologist . . . someone trying to cut every asshole out of his life in the Biz.

P is for Prayer. It was the one thing everyone in Hollywood told me I didn't have in thinking I could buy the rights to Batman and make dark Batman movies. But I did. I believed in myself, would not let go of my dream, and I did it!

CHAPTER THREE

The PREP

Passion is essential. A prayer can't hurt. Packaging is important, and pitching is key. But if you don't come to the pitch, the meeting, the Zoom, the set, or the office with sufficient preparation, you will not succeed. In the movie industry, "prep" or "preproduction" is how you adhere to the business part of "show business." Good prep helps a producer deliver a picture to the financier/distributor on budget and on schedule.

That moment, that perfect moment you let go of your rigid concepts of what was possible. When there was nothing left to do but step beyond anything you learned before. . . . Empowering!

—BATMAN: ZERO YEAR

Professionally speaking, this chapter should be the shortest and in the least need of explanation.

"Be prepared!"

It was my Cub Scout motto. It is universal and eternal. Nothing beats prep . . . doing your homework or due diligence before taking that meeting, writing that memo, or showing up on a set. Every corollary to it is simple and global:

Better to be an hour early than five minutes late.

Dress how you wish to be perceived.

Whenever you encounter new people, walk up to them, look them in the eyes, give them either a firm elbow bump or a firm socially distanced handshake, and introduce yourself.

Anticipate. Strategize. Think. Reason. Plan. Collectively, it's all preparation, with little difference whether in your professional life or private life.

Case in point:

I was so fortunate to grow up where I did when I did. My mates were neighborhood kids I went to school with from kindergarten through high school. We were in Cub Scouts together, Little League together, clubs and after-school activities together, and class trips together. We knew each other's siblings, parents, and grandparents. That is a very warm and fuzzy bond. So when the time came for our thirtieth high school reunion, like most of what Archie, Betty, and Veronica would call my "pals 'n' gals," I wanted to see as many of us back together, including our great teachers. That was the moment I decided to actually "produce" our thirtieth reunion—a feat that would take ten months of planning and prep with the partnership of a platoon of my old friends to make it all happen on a grand scale. Maybe the key for us was that we were, together, kids of the surrealistic sixties.

What we all now refer to as "the sixties" did not start on January 1, 1960. In reality, the sixties started on November 22, 1963, with the assassination of President Kennedy, sinking my generation into darkness, doldrums, and our first dip into depression, only to be lifted up like never before on February 9, 1964, live from the stage of *The Ed Sullivan Show* with the arrival of the Beatles in America. Then, on April 22, 1964, the sixties next transported us en masse with the exclamation, "I Have Seen the Future!" at the opening of the New York World's Fair. But let's go back to the moment the sixties was born . . .

I can't tell you the story of our thirtieth high school reunion—the greatest high school reunion in history—without providing the backstory. If I were Batman, we'd all slip into Professor Nicholl's time machine and journey together back to those swingin' sixties. Since none of my professor friends either have built or own a time machine, the magical device of storytelling will have to suffice.

Starting around seventh grade, something happened. It was the caterpillar-to-butterfly effect that burst some pubescent cocoon, allowing the emergence of what we boys would start referring to in high school as "The Big Three." These were the three smartest, prettiest, in-a-class-by-themselves girls in what would soon become our high school class of '69.

(No, that's just the year we graduated!) In no particular order, they were Barbara Levine, Wendy Preville, and Ronna Berman.

Barbara rose to prominence at about the same time we boys did during the summer of '63 at the Colony Surf Club on the beach at West End, New Jersey. Her boyfriends included the kid who abused Magic Markers and Spirit Masters by sniffing them and the guy with whom she became entrenched in the biggest-ever seventh-grade scandal at Ocean Township School. Our science teacher, Mr. Ryan, taught a unit on astronomy and had us all report to the school playground bordering the woods one night while he set up telescopes and binoculars for a "Star-Gazing Party." But this guy wasn't gazing at stars when he nudged Barbara out of her orbit and behind the backstop. (Kissing. It was all only about kissing back then. Don't forget. And lest I forget, the boy in question was an officer of a high school fraternity made up of cool Jewish guys at a time called "the awkward years" when *cool* and *Jewish guys* were largely incongruous terms of art. I can verify this because I qualified as both Jewish and not cool. The schoolboy frat was called "The Ulps" and one member was referred to as an "ULP." Fellow comic book readers: do not be confused by this. I know that in comics, when a superhero says, "ULP!" it means "Surprise! Oh no! I screwed up!" When that superhero swallows hard in fear in the comics, that's "GULP!" But in Ocean Township High School, "ULP!" meant "a not necessarily cool member of a Jewish male high school fraternity on the Jersey Shore.")

Ronna Berman. A cheerleader! Every boy in the class of '69 was smitten. And there was much to be smitten with. All I ever hoped was that one day she would take all that "smitten" she received and smite me . . . or whatever the correct word is for someone actively doing the smitten thing rather than someone passively feeling the smitten thing. I can go on and on as to how beautiful and smart this girl was. But on the other hand, she had been romantically linked to a few known so-called bad boys who, back then, we collectively referred to as "hoods" or "greasers." (See the movie *Grease* for more information.)

Wendy Preville. Halloween night, 1962. Arlene Singer's make-out party in Deal Park, home of that Fast Crowd. Wendy looked like a Greek statue. Even her hair did. No kidding. Look at her picture from our high school yearbook. Her boyfriend from Deal rallied everyone to play spin the bottle in a circle with Wendy and many others. He smiled slyly, spun the bottle, then stopped it and pointed it at Wendy (which is *strictly* against the rules!) and kissed her. And didn't stop. After a while, all the guests started counting the seconds. They locked lips till sixty! Jeez . . .

So while every boy pined for Wendy, none of us ever considered for a moment there'd be a chance for any other boy in the class. Except me. One time. In my senior year. I took an uncalculated risk and worked up the nerve to come up to the plate for one at bat with Wendy as if I was in the World Series of dating. The two words that gave me a ray of hope: *Vanilla Fudge*. And I'm not talking about ice cream!

Vanilla Fudge was a psychedelic rock band that had the number-one album of 1968 featuring the best-ever rendition of The Supremes' "You Keep Me Hanging On." The band rode high atop the rock charts, and its lead singer and organist was the massively talented Mark Stein from Bayonne. The Steins were related to the Uslans, and I can still recall my dad talking about Stein cousins he grew up with who all had street names like "Shifty." Well, this made the lead singer of Vanilla Fudge my cousin. My senior class needed to raise money for its upcoming senior prom. I contacted Mark through yet another Uslan cousin and got him to bring the group to Ocean Township High School to put on a concert to raise the money my class needed. And they came! And performed a full-blown concert! And brought their roadies and groupies, the latter of whom commandeered the OTHS Spartans football team's portable whirlpool baths and were playing kamikaze in them topless! And it was all under the nose of our principal, Colonel Klink of OTHS! For this night, I was the hero of the class and of any cool-enough kid in the school who was into psychedelic rock.

Leading up to that night, the school was abuzz. Everybody was talking about it. Two weeks before the OTHS event, in order to show me what the concert would be like, Vanilla Fudge invited me to see the band perform at a nearby college. Two comped front-row seats and backstage passes. And that's when I had the brainstorm! If I ever in life had one sliver of the slimmest chance to get one of The Big Three to actually go out with me, this was the bait for the hook. I knew they each loved Vanilla Fudge's music. But which one of The Big Three would I attempt? Barbara Levine was out. The Fudge tickets could make me cooler but not better looking, and she only dated the best-looking guys around Ocean Township and Deal. Ronna Berman had an under-the-radar eye for troublemakers, older guys, and members of the two high school fraternities—the Barnstormers and the Ravens—always starting fights at teen dances at the Asbury Park VFW. Think the Jets and the Sharks only not as cool, not as nice looking, not as good of dancers, and not able to star in a movie like *West Side Story* because they were all in eternal detention. So Ronna Berman was out. I was many things. A "bad boy" wasn't one of them. That was my brother, Paul's, department.

That left The Big Three's Wendy Preville, who miraculously was no longer dating the Kisser. I worked up the nerve to make the call. I could do this. After all, I was that Jughead all the girls felt "comfortable" talking to . . . dammit! I finally convinced myself I could call Wendy. I did call Wendy, and she said yes. Let me restate that . . . *she said yes*! If my life was a movie, this would be the moment you'd see the clips of rockets launching, barns raising, and fireworks going off! It was already the greatest date ever. Ultimately, it became the greatest date that never was. The Fudge canceled that college gig.

It was an hour before I was supposed to pick her up. *This could still work*, I thought. *It can be even better*, I convinced myself . . . kinda. I just needed to prepare enough for this landmark phone call. I tore through the day's *Asbury Park Press* and found a great movie to go see; I'd sacrifice my eight-track tape fund and take her to a fab restaurant. I'd even give her the choice between the Asbury Park area's ultimate thin crust, burnt-around-the-edges pizza from Freddie's; Vic's; Memory Lane; Mom's Kitchen; Freida's; or Sacco's. My friends and I still debate this question today: Who had the best pizza on the Jersey Shore? In fact, at our premiere for *Batman Forever,* I got into this exact discussion with Asbury Park native and former Penguin, Danny DeVito. For fifteen minutes, we were locked in an intense analysis and debate as we were surrounded by cameras and microphones from *Entertainment Tonight* and all its clones. They couldn't imagine what the Penguin and the executive producer of the Batman films were talking about so passionately. I was a Freddie's guy all the way (pepperoni suggested). Vic's was Danny's choice, though a very vocal bunch of my classmates still firmly stood by Mom's Kitchen. I wondered which one Wendy would choose. The answer? D. None of the above.

With fifty-five minutes till pickup time, I called and broke the news, offering instead my creative fallback position commonly referred to as plan B. She simply and sweetly replied, "Oh . . . no . . . that's all right. You don't have to do that. Too bad we can't see Vanilla Fudge, but they'll be playing at the high school in a couple of weeks. So . . . see you in school Monday. Thanks! *Click*!"

Wendy didn't say *click*. Or if she did, I was screaming, "*Shit*!" so loudly I drowned her out. That's what I felt like. Zero. Or less. Hasta la vista self-confidence. Hail and farewell self-esteem. I reached for the stars but reached too far and grabbed stardust. There was a saving grace, however. I wisely never told a soul I had asked Wendy out. Not even my closest pals, Barry and Bobby. I would not have to endure ridicule on top of the embarrassment.

But now *this* night, I decided to have it out with Wendy and confront her face-to-face. Now, I started to feel like a man again. Only this confrontation happened at our class reunion thirty years later.

Before having it out with Wendy—if she would even remember who I was—I worked up the nerve to finally confess to Barry what had happened that night in high school. We were all now forty-eight. He listened to my whole tale and my plan for when I saw Wendy at the reunion. His response? Barry called me a big baby.

Well, that went well. I could only imagine how my Wendy encounter would fare. But I was resolved to do this. Barry warned me. He said I'd been carrying this baggage for thirty years and she wouldn't even know what I was talking about. Why would she ever remember maybe two minutes of her life three decades ago? He reminded me that to The Big Three, we were insignificant. "Forgetaboutit!" he advised. He was right. But I did it anyway. But only because I had a very specific plan of action in mind!

Everyone had already had a drink or three at the reunion when I spotted Wendy at the bar. I went marching up to her and did a turn on a dime when I noticed she was talking to Barbara and Ronna. Jesus Christ! The Big Three ride again! Now here's where everyone wants to know how fat and slovenly they all got. In all honesty, each of them looked better than I remembered them. Stunning. Full of life. Successful. Still with their seductive smarts. Killer smiles. Intact bodies. The Big Three live!

Fearing nothing, having sacrificed my dignity to the drink of the Beefeaters, I said to Wendy, "By any chance, do you have any recollection of me asking you out to a Vanilla

Fudge concert before they played our high school?" She looked at me as if I were crazy. Damn! Barry was right. "Duh," she said sarcastically, "of course I remember. They canceled at the last minute and we couldn't go." Well, at least I had a moral victory this night.

She remembered it. "Well, it's nice you remember," I said as I started to move on to greet my best friend from fifth grade, little Henry Schneiderman, who looked none the worse for those days of inhaling his Magic Marker and sniffing the Spirit Master off the mimeograph machine. Wendy kept talking.

"So you were sweet enough to offer to take me to dinner and a movie, and I felt terrible that you were trapped having to take me out anyway even though there was no concert." Amid a spate of unintelligible sort-of words like, "Huh?" "Wha—?" and a machine-gun burst of "buts," Wendy added that she knew I was stuck and, being the nice guy I was, she just knew I must have felt obligated to go out with her anyway.

Eliminating the next two rounds of "Huhs," Wendy challenged the basic tenets of my existence. Everything I knew about her as a third of The Big Three was illusion and misperception. She suddenly revealed that no boy had ever asked her out in high school. She never dated. She constantly wondered what was wrong with her that put off every guy. She thought I was only asking her to a movie and dinner to be nice. Then she asked me how I liked the senior prom. I said I loved it. Didn't she? Wendy confessed she didn't know because no one asked her. Nor to the junior prom. The girl I—and every boy in the class—thought was untouchable and out of our league and, to some, a snob, was . . . lonely, and her own self-esteem had been run over by a steamroller in high school. Oy! Where was "Instant Replay" when I really needed it?

Shaken to the core, I trotted over to Ronna Berman, who'd left the conversation and was sitting on a barstool while class DJ Steve Huntington was in the background playing "Can't Take My Eyes Off You" by the Four Seasons.

"Ronna, do you remember our senior year? No, of course you do! What I mean is, do you remember the Vanilla Fudge concert?" I asked.

Bemused at my apparent incoherence, she humored me. "Yes, Michael. How could I forget?"

"So, Ronna, *if* back then, two weeks before that, I had invited you to go with me to see them play, remembering who you were dating at that exact time, would you have considered going with me?"

"I'd have loved that," she responded sweetly as I tried to determine if she was lying through her teeth.

"OK. OK. And if the Fudge canceled that concert and I offered instead to take you for pizza and a movie, would you have said yes or no. And be honest. You have to be absolutely honest here!" I begged.

"Freddie's?" she asked. I beamed.

"Yeah," I said, melting all over her bar tab.

"I'd have loved that," she said with that magic thing called sincerity.

I was on a roll and settling debts that had been piling up since I was thirteen. "One last question, Ronna," I said with a total inability to stop being annoying . . . especially with Barry standing behind us now and witnessing this life epiphany. "When we were at Dow Avenue School in seventh grade, if I asked you to go somewhere . . . Palace Amusements on the rides or playing pinball on the boardwalk or bowling at Shore Lanes . . . would you have gone with me?"

Now she knew she had the upper hand, and the well-deserved teasing began. "Hmmm . . . me . . . you in Dow Avenue? Trying on rented bowling shoes together? Sounds utterly romantic! Absolutely! I'd've been right there," she tortured me from my soul to my soles.

"Big baby," muttered Barry as he walked away to embrace the aging members of his Cub Scout Troop 43, Den 4. (I was in Den 2, and, just for the record, not that it was important back then or matters today, but we did beat Den 4 when we played them in "steal the bacon.") After high school graduation, I didn't see Ronna again until a party at her house when I was back home for the summer in between freshman and sophomore years of college, putting in a final summer at Oakhurst Day Camp as a camp counselor, albeit now as a senior counselor. My cousin Brucie went with me that night. He was soon to leave for his freshman year at Wisconsin. The booze was flowing, and lots of people I knew from our high school days were flitting in and out.

Ronna, Bruce, and I wound up in what was the first real, in-depth conversation I had ever had with her, suddenly no longer feeling that crushing intimidation of The Big Three. I couldn't get over our commonality of interests, likes, and dislikes! I turned to Bruce and said, "This is so bizarre! It's like Ronna and I share the same brain! What do you think I should do?" I would never know his opinion, because that was the moment Bruce barfed up an entire six pack of Budweiser onto Ronna's living room's shag carpeting. I don't want to exaggerate this, but any bugs that might have found their way into that carpeting that night were now most certainly building an ark and rounding up two bugs of every species to load on board. It was horrid! While Bruce found a nice quiet place to lie down and relax in the gutter in front of the afflicted house, I did what a cousin had to do and went on cleanup duty . . . my last opportunity to impress a girl. Not cool. Pretty downright disgusting, actually. Did it kill the moment between me and Ronna (if there really was a moment)? The next time I saw her was at our twentieth high school reunion, where she looked like Jackie Kennedy on her best day and proceeded to show me pictures of her two gorgeous daughters, then to ask me how my cousin Brucie's stomach was, and to finally inform me that her mom had to replace their living room carpeting the following week. I started realizing that life—or at least *my* life—was made up of lots and lots of turning points . . . and that there are always consequences, not only for my actions and my words but also for my failures to act and my lack of words. Sometimes no matter how much prep you do, you're powerless if someone just happens to throw up at the wrong time. I started to realize how people throwing up have impacted my life, from Barry heaving on the Rock 'n' Roll twisting, spinning ride at Asbury Park's Palace Amusements to Bruce upchucking at the party and even to the loss of one of my favorite rock stars, Jimi Hendrix. The guy on the radio said he had died choking on his own vomit. I wondered if anyone ever died choking on someone else's vomit? Ugh! Where was I?

Oh, yeah. I had no choice now after learning at my thirtieth high school reunion that both Wendy and Ronna *would* have gone out with me in high school had I only persisted and asked them. *Two* of the untouchable Big Three. I needed to shoot for the trifecta. I found Barbara Levine. She and I had kinda remained in touch and been friends over the years. I posed the same question to her.

"Barb, truthfully now, if in our senior year I invited you to go with me to see the Vanilla Fudge in concert, front-row seats plus backstage passes, would you have gone out with me?"

"Nope," she said matter-of-factly before turning back to the makeshift court she was holding with our former class president, the former president of the student council, the former high school basketball star, the former Magic Marker sniffer, the former class heartthrob, and the former high school rock musician.

Well, two out of three ain't bad! It was the greatest high school reunion in history. Except for my wife, Nancy's, twentieth, in Cincinnati.

Spouses are supposed to have God-awful times at their mates' class reunions when they didn't grow up together. Could you conceive of a more boring evening if you tried? I was determined to have the best time ever at Nancy's reunion, even though I wouldn't know one person there. To be forewarned is to be forearmed. I spent the afternoon of the affair with her high school yearbook taking careful notes. Research and preparation would be essential if I was to fulfill my goal. That night, I was ready, ready, ready to rock 'n' roll!

No sooner did we arrive at the hotel where the dinner event was being held when Nancy was rushed by a group of "kids" now thirty-seven and thirty-eight years old. She was concerned about me, but I told her to go have a great time and not to worry about me. I'd be fine. As the group made off with her, I went to the check-in desk and surreptitiously checked my notes against the list of people who'd signed in and picked up their "Hello! My Name Is" stickers. The guy I targeted as my number-one choice did not come this night; so, I registered as him and was handed my very own sticker to smunch onto my sport jacket over the front pocket, which proclaimed in big letters, "Hello! My Name Is Richard Anderson." For the next few hours, I cast myself as . . . no . . . I would *be* . . . Richard Anderson of Woodward High School's class of '69. And the fun began almost at once!

I sidled over to the crowded bar and positioned myself in between two groups of alums while I ordered a Sapphire and tonic and listened closely to everyone around me. Once I heard enough names and stories recounted by people to each side of me, I struck. I turned around suddenly to the five people to my left, smiled wildly, and yelled with excitement,

"Oh my God! Oh my God!" They all smiled back at me, searching my face and praying for some dormant brain cells to kick in. They didn't, and so they all went to plan B and started shooting sly, quick glances down at my "Hello" sticker. One daring redhead made the first move in our sudden chess game.

"Richard?" she stammered.

"Yes!" I screamed. Remembering what I had just heard from the group on the right, I threw my baited line in the water. "Mr. Romig's tenth-grade biology class?" I asked.

"Of course!" reacted two of the five.

Having memorized photo captions from some of the big photos in the sports section of Nancy's yearbook, I pushed the envelope. "Remember when we all sat together at the championship game against Moeller?" That did it. All five now remembered going with me . . . even though my name really wasn't Richard Anderson and despite the fact that in 1969 I lived in New Jersey and had never been to Cincinnati. But these people were friendly, nice, and hospitable Midwesterners. They would go out on any limb to avoid my thinking they had forgotten me. Once I had more great names and stories, I excused myself, took my drink, and walked in search of the next group to bs with. I was there for over six hours and just lied the entire night and had an absolute blast! Finally, at 2:00 a.m., Nancy found me sitting in the lobby with over a dozen "classmates" having them in stitches with old high school stories. I didn't want to leave. But Nancy was tired and dragged me out of there. Who said a spouse can't have a great time at his mate's high school reunion? Bruce Wayne so knew what it was really all about—having a secret identity was the coolest thing ever, even if only for one night!

The Saturday afternoon before my thirtieth reunion, I had the Township open up our old elementary schools for my class so we could stroll through our old classrooms, try to break into our old lockers, and reminisce together. The strongest common memory we all had was the afternoon of November 22, 1963. The school's switchboard operator extraordinaire, Mrs. Kierstedt, made an unscheduled announcement over the school's intercom system. Her voice cracked rather than boomed like it usually did when she made her student announcements. She said she was putting the radio on over the intercom so we could all listen to the latest news of the attempted assassination of President John F. Kennedy in Dallas, Texas. Within minutes, the word *attempted* faded with all our hopes and dreams. Kennedy was dead. Classes were canceled, and the school buses were ready to take us home early to be with our families. It was a moment forever frozen in time.

Thirty-six years later, the most staggering cosmic moment of my lifetime occurred. It still gives me the chills when I think of it. The prep that went into our thirtieth class reunion was akin to a Hollywood production, as if it was a movie project. I worked with a super committee of "kids" I had been in school with from kindergarten to twelfth grade: Sue Saltzman, Susie Kruse, Wendy Sloter, and other happy volunteers. We set up a class website and for ten months bombarded the 325 survivors of our 333-member graduating class with nostalgic emails, trivia quizzes, and memorabilia. No suits and gowns, no fancy sit-down dinner, no loud orchestra . . . instead, I rented a riverboat for Friday night and organized a jeans- or shorts-only dinner cruise with 1960s music by pro DJ, our own Steve Huntington, for years the voice of Jimmy Buffett's "Radio Margaritaville." For three hours, I trapped everyone on a cruise whereby all ice had to be broken as everyone was forced to talk to each other with no distractions. Old cliques dissolved in minutes as kids met kids as adults for the first time. For Saturday night, I rented our old high school, had a committee decorate the gym like it was our prom, set up a memorabilia museum display, and hired the cafeteria ladies with their hairnets to serve us dinner. For 35 cents, each person could load his or her tray with Salisbury steak, french fries, apple crisp, a milk carton, and a vanilla/chocolate ice cream Dixie cup. I coaxed the guys who played in the hot high school rock band that performed at most of our school dances to re-form, practice, and re-debut at the reunion, and they were great! But on this Saturday afternoon, as we were all roaming the halls of Ocean Township School, one by one, a bunch of us filtered into Mr. Carelli's history classroom. It was virtually intact. The desks looked shockingly similar to ours from 1963. The wall clock and the intercom were unchanged, trapped in low-tech heaven. I went over and sat at my sixth-period desk from seventh-grade history. Then in trickled Arlene Singer, who knew she sat behind me. Gradually, about sixteen of the thirty-one baby boomers in our history class came in and sat in their original seats. We all knew where they were and who sat next to us because we were there all together when we heard that Kennedy was dead. Now, we all got into a discussion about that day so long ago and how every detail was still so sharp in everyone's minds.

And that's when Gary Oppito came rushing into the classroom.

"Hey! Did you guys hear? Kennedy's dead!"

We smiled bravely and told Gary to come in, as we were talking about that whole experience just then. Gary looked at us, puzzled.

"No," he said. "John Kennedy is dead. *Junior*. His plane went down!"

I still get the chills . . .

And speaking of the dead, John Constantine, Hellblazer, was, to me, the James Dean of the occult world. He was kind of like that kid in *The Sixth Sense* but all grown up and able to do something about all those dead people he was seeing. One of the more enigmatic, textured characters ever presented in comics, he was crafted by incredibly talented writers, such as his creator Alan Moore, Neil Gaiman, Garth Ennis, and Jaime Delano. And because he first appeared in the pages of *Swamp Thing*, Ben and I owned the movie and other rights to him. I knew that making a film out of this stunning material would be challenging. It wasn't like trying to sell a comic book like *The Incredible Hulk* to a studio, where I could just walk in, hold up one issue, and the exec would exclaim, "I get it! Guy gets mad . . . turns green and strong!" With *Hellblazer*, I could have given him two hundred issues of the comic books to read and all I'd get in return would be one great big, "What the—?" To get this movie made, I knew I'd have to walk in with the *A* to *B* to *C* of the scene-by-scene, three-act story. And in order to do this, it would take an incredible amount of preparation.

JOHN CONSTANTINE
HELLBLAZER
VERTIGO
DIRECT SALES
GARTH ENNIS
STEVE DILLON

The first challenge would be to find exactly the right writer. It took me six months working with many agents and managers to find Kevin Brodbin. Intelligent and perceptive, Kevin had a passion not just for comic books but also for this character in particular. Together, we worked on the story for almost six months until we agreed it was nailed. Ben and I then made arrangements to pitch it at Warner Bros. to the right exec for this type of project, our *Batman* production veep, Tom Lassally. Tom was enthusiastic about the character and our story from beginning to end. He asked if there was anyone in the Warner lot Ben and I would like to work with; I quickly told him it would be an honor to work with the director of *The Omen*, Dick Donner. Fifteen minutes later, Dick and his wife, Lauren Shuler-Donner, were in the office and Tom asked Kevin and me to do the pitch all over again. We did, and the Donners' response was as great as Tom's. This movie was going to get made. As we were walking out of the office, Tom gave Kevin a pat on the back for a job well done and told him how much he looked forward to working with him on this film. Then Tom mentioned that Kevin looked familiar to him, and he wondered if they had ever worked together before on a film. That's when Kevin revealed, "Actually, Tom, one year ago today, I was temping here for you for two weeks." It was a classic Hollywood tale, and it unfolded right before my eyes. Last year's secretary was this year's golden boy studio screenwriter. Hooray for Hollywood! No, really this time!

Always remember that *P* is for Prep. It can make all the difference in the world. If you're dealing with nice people, you will be appreciated and respected for it. If you're dealing with assholes, *P* is for Preparation H. Keep one nearby, and then break glass in case of emergency.

LEFT: John Constantine, the James Dean of the occult world.

CHAPTER FOUR

The PROCESS

The studio process of developing a script and bringing a project to the moment it will green-light a movie for production can take ten years or more, with studio execs, writers, directors, and actors coming and going in Hollywood's own version of a revolving door. This is why the often-interminable process has been dubbed "Development Hell" by producers and virtually everyone else in the Biz. Kinda sounds like life in general, at its worst.

I have to find another path. Divine my own future. One uniquely mine.

—BATGIRL: YEAR ONE

The process of development in Hollywood is hated across the board. It's antiquated, broken, and too-often anticreative or at best creative by committee. Independent producers have to grin and bear the process year after year after year, either without any pay or recompense at all or, perhaps, with a producer development fee of $25,000–$50,000 upon which to live while tearing calendar pages off his or her refrigerator for the development years as they pass.

Development can, on occasion, also be spectacular and energizing, like when a writer and director and maybe even a studio or network exec are all on the same page, creatively and budget-wise, with the producer. At those moments, all the other pain and suffering somehow recede into carefully suppressed and well-trained brain cells. That's a critical talent for a producer to master while developing a script and project, generally. It's arguably a matter of self-survival for the duration.

In reality, is our own development from child to teenager to young adult to evolved adult to learned, sage, and experienced adult any different a process? It's simply uncanny how often one's life experiences intersect with what becomes one's later career experiences! Take, for example, the most basic principle in the Biz that the best producers live by, the ten rules for making a successful motion picture:

1. Story
2. Story
3. Story
4. Story
5. Story
6. Character
7. Character
8. Character
9. Story
10. Story

What does that have to do with *my* life and my own development process? Let's journey back in time to the nifty fifties on the fabulous Jersey shore . . .

One person who helped me—maybe forced me—to evolve as a human being (or at least to start learning four-letter words) was a member of that special group created to serve, defend, protect, and drive with unparalleled esprit de corps, who valiantly served the baby boomer kids going to school five days a week in them good ol' days . . . the school bus drivers!

Every time I write or develop a treatment for a feature or for streaming or prepare to write a screenplay, comic book, graphic novel, or animated episode, I think back on our elementary school bus driver, Crossbones, and his fellow bus-driver gang and turn them into characters in my stories. They make it so easy! Crossbones was the world's oldest, grouchiest, and most toothless throwback to a former stage of evolution, uncannily resembling Popeye's pappy, one open eye and all! I never even thought about this before, but the guy my mom entrusted to drive me and forty-nine other kids to school every day had only one open eye! And the way his almost-toothless mouth shrunk back into his jaw made him appear to us (and we had bets on this) that he was in immediate danger of swallowing his own face. All the Wanamassa School bus drivers had names that were right out of *Treasure Island* or *Peter Pan*: Crossbones, Bones, Skipper, Whitey, Tucky, Peg-Leg. The last five drivers were the salt of the earth. But Crossbones was just salty. Crossbones hated children. Hell, Crossbones hated life itself! At age 132 (to six-year-old me, at least), I guess he had a right to be bitter. After all, the guy always was griping about his awful pains from lots of ailments strange to the ears of us kids in first to fourth grade . . . ailments like "lumbago," "malaria," and "clap." Whenever he started rambling on about this, Ira Byock (Of course! Who else?) would always yell out to the hard-of-hearing Crossbones, "What was that last one you said?" Crossbones, who *never* should have trusted a kid like Ira (who—did I tell you?—once in first grade jumped off the seesaw while I was sitting on the top), would always scream back at him, "CLAP!" Which we did. All fifty of us on the school bus, while bouncing on torn seats with busted springs, burst into wild applause. We didn't know of any other meaning to the word *clap* but "to applaud." We loved teasing this ancient geezer who increased our vocabulary on every ride by introducing us to his own personal vocabulary list: "friggin'," "frickin'," "damn," "Gol'-damned," "bastards," "rat-bastards," "A-holes," "screw," "screwed," "screwed up," "screw-ups," and "screw 'em." Even better, he opened our minds conceptually to the previous unimaginable visual of a person who somehow had "his head up his ass." How can good ol' Crossbones *not* propel me into the creative process like . . . like . . . a careening school bus out of control?!

You have to respect Crossbones. Give him credit. First of all, he never used the F-word around us and could have been even more bitter if he had let all his physical ailments get to him . . . his glaucoma, arthritic hands, catarrh, or what he claimed to us was the world's longest-running (or "not running") case of constipation. Instead, despite being virtually blind and with almost useless hands, Bones continued five days a week to be responsible for the lives of fifty local children on his bus. We loved him. We hated him. He detested us. He loved us. And we made each other's day, long before Dirty Harry would co-opt that concept in a famous Clint Eastwood movie.

I always thought that Clint Eastwood in his prime would have done a great job portraying one of my all-time favorite heroes, The Shadow. Daniel Day-Lewis would have been another great choice in his prime. And I still would have loved seeing Eastwood play Bruce Wayne at age eighty while serving as the Obi-Wan Kenobi / Yoda of the Batman of the next generation of superheroes, *Batman Beyond*.

The Shadow was the primary influence on Bill Finger and Bob Kane in the creation and early evolution of the Batman. Finger admitted he "borrowed" an earlier Shadow pulp magazine story from November 1936, "Partners of Peril," and converted it into the first Batman tale as presented in *Detective Comics* #27 in May 1939. Meanwhile, Bob Kane was tracing and swiping artwork from that very same issue of *The Shadow* to insert into his first drawn Batman adventure! The creative force behind The Shadow was a close friend of the all-time greatest illusionist and magician, Harry Houdini, and was, in fact, a magician himself. I was a huge Walter Gibson fan and read his Shadow work voraciously. The first comic book I ever wrote back in the 1970s, when I was still in school, was *The Shadow* for DC Comics, all as detailed in the permanent record of my prior memoir, *The Boy Who Loved Batman*.

I would continue to write adventures of The Shadow in the form of graphic novels well into the second decade of the tumultuous 2000s. Masterful director Sam Raimi and I teamed up to make a blockbuster Shadow live-action feature film in this era. Despite a long time in gestation and a great start with an early draft screenplay by Siavash Farahani featuring The Shadow, his agents, the lovely and potentially deadly Margo Lane, and the villainous Benedict Stark, sometimes known as Mr. Remorse and other times acknowledged as the Prince of Evil, we were on our way . . . until . . . a studio exec declared we had a great script in progress with a top director and an exceptional actors list (among the half dozen actors being considered was my personal favorite, Daniel Day-Lewis), but the "facts" were that we were doing it as a period piece and "everyone knows that a period piece doesn't sell." Losing my patience as well as my filter (an issue for many of us as we grow older), I shot back, "What about *Titanic*?" He fired a shot back across my bow, "That's different. That's history." So I retorted, "What about the Indiana Jones movies?" He countered, "That's different. They were Steven Spielberg projects." The studio abandoned our project as stillborn. Six months later, *Captain America: The First Avenger* opened to huge Marvelous success. I called back that studio exec, and when he answered the phone, I simply said, "What about *Captain America*?" and hung up. Welcome to Hollywood, a place where nothing works and nothing is successful . . . until it works and is successful. That's when the rules change and everything is thrust into reverse.

But let's return to the exciting eighties, when I seized the chance of a lifetime to work with Walter Gibson.

My wife and I had taken a little time off to road trip up to Niagara Falls, the highlight of which for me was the Harry Houdini museum, which gave me an idea for a cool movie someday. I was fascinated with magic and particularly Houdini. Walter, who, by the early 1980s, was Houdini's last living associate, had written the best books of magic. I decided to write a magic-themed movie and produce it. My writing partner, Tom Seligson, and I needed the professional consulting of a master magician who knew how Houdini had accomplished all of his greatest tricks and illusions. I hired Walter and spent both quality and quantity time with him.

When my dad was young, he was at the Hippodrome Theatre on Sixth Avenue in New York when Houdini made an elephant disappear on stage right before my dad's wide eyes. He never could fathom how Houdini did it, so the first thing I had to do with Walter was get the secret to this illusion. He explained it to me clearly and simply, and I raced home to Jersey that night to show Pop (it took props) how Houdini did it. It was so incredibly simple, but that was the magic that made his illusions work so well. Walter told me how Houdini walked through a brick wall and made a woman in a movie emerge from the screen and onto the stage—a living, breathing, real human being. He also revealed to me that he was with the master magician the one time Houdini was trapped and could not escape. The way I recall it, Walter's secret story began on "a dark and stormy night." There was a torrential downpour this particular evening in New York as Walter and his wife were heading to a Broadway show with Houdini and his wife, Bess. Walter rode in the front of the touring car while Houdini rode in the back compartment with the two ladies. When the driver pulled up to the curb under the marquee, Houdini went to open the car door, but it wouldn't budge. Try as he might, the back door was stuck. Nothing he could do worked. Houdini was trapped in the backseat of a car. Walter, meanwhile, got out of the front and, in the rain, opened Houdini's door from the outside . . . no problem. As Houdini got out, he grabbed Walter jokingly by his lapels and made him swear he would never tell anyone! Sixty years later, Walter blabbed it to me. In the words of actor Orson Welles (and several others) who played him on the radio, "Who knows what evil lurks in the hearts of men? The Shadow knows!" But so did Walter Gibson!

I had a deal with DC Comics to cherry-pick six DC properties that were always under the radar at Warner Bros. and come up with a pitch to set each project up elsewhere, but it still had to be a company under the wings of Warner. The A-list was off the table. I made my picks: *Shazam, Metal Men, The Spectre, Space Cabbie, Adam Strange,* and *The War That Time Forgot.*

I became the first producer to take a DC property and not set it up under Warner proper. Instead, I set up *Shazam* at New Line with a pitch from my heart due to the fact that the principal writer of Captain Marvel in his Golden Age career was the man who mentored me into the history of comics and the creatives who worked within that world, Otto Binder. Otto cocreated Mary Marvel, the Marvel Family, Black Adam, Supergirl, Brainiac, Krypto the Superdog, the Legion of Super-Heroes, and the list marches on and on. He put me in touch with the cocreator of Captain Marvel, C. C. Beck, when I was in seventh grade. I began a weekly exchange of letters with C. C. as he told the story of Captain Marvel from his unique perspective. Otto also put me in touch with the two top editors of those comic books from the 1940s to '50s, Wendell Crowley and Will Lieberson. I amassed a fortress full of knowledge from these men. They were all long done by the time I set up the Captain Marvel movie, which would be titled *Shazam* (although I had the studio convinced for a while to float past the marketing people the Harry Potterish title *Billy Batson & The Secret of Shazam!*).

As the originating producer of *Shazam,* I worked on that film for over ten years, having the privilege of spending many hours with the dean of Hollywood screenwriters, William "Bill" Goldman (*The Princess Bride, All the President's Men, Butch Cassidy and the Sundance Kid*), who sought the writing job because in his youth he collected every issue of *Captain Marvel Adventures, The Marvel Family,* and Whiz Comics. He could still recall exactly in which candy stores he bought his issues. Bill wrote a movie that would have been the very best Captain Marvel movie of the World War II years, but the studio wanted something reflecting the contemporary way that comic book superhero films were being made. Five writers later and year upon year of development hell, while working in the trenches with two great studio veeps, Mark Kaufman and Chris Godsick, I was finally able to get the studio to agree to giving a comic book writer a shot at the screenplay. I had been campaigning for Geoff Johns for years, but because he was "only a comic book writer" and not a proven Hollywood feature film writer, there was resistance from somewhere on high. The first step was to get him in as a "creative consultant." Eventually, his talent became obvious to certain powers that be and he was able to join in on the screenwriting. A lot of good things started happening the day the studio hired Pete Segal as the director along with his producing partner, Michael Ewing—two nicer guys you could not find in the industry. Pete had directed such fun films as *Tommy Boy, 50 First Dates,* and *Anger Management.* At one meeting, I showed them some comic books showcasing the villain Black Adam and told them Dwayne "The Rock" Johnson *looks* like this guy. He'd be our perfect villain. They both were excited, and Pete reached out to the star and got him interested in joining the fold. At about that time, a new screenplay draft came in and we all felt we were now a draft away from having a shooting script. Then came the day Pete informed me that the studio was suspending *Shazam* because it was going forward with *Man of Steel* and felt the two characters were too similar. I tried explaining how Captain Marvel is closer to Harry Potter and magic than to Superman and super-science. I went back to my original pitch that opened the door at the studio: Captain Marvel is *Big* meets *Spider-Man.* It would be a few years before *Shazam* became unsuspended, but representing over a decade of my life, I remain proud of being the originating producer.

As for *Metal Men,* we were in the process of deciding if we would do it in live action or as a 3D-animated feature (leaning heavily toward live action) when I received a call from DC. It turns out someone at the studio promised *Metal Men* to Lauren Shuler-Donner and would I consider accommodating all parties by substituting some other DC property for *Metal Men.* Wanting to be a team player and having nothing but the utmost respect for Lauren, I consented. Then I shocked everyone at DC by choosing next *Sugar & Spike.* My idea was to develop it into a franchise paralleling the success of the *Look Who's Talking* movies. Talking babies! We could take the technology used in the film *Babe* and make it work with babies!

I had been talking to the topper at HBO, as it was owned by Warner, advocating that it be the first of the pay cable services to get into the comic book superhero business. He told me to pick two and we would be on our way. I pitched *The Spectre* as the first truly horror/superhero movie with one of my all-time favorite DC characters. My one-line pitch was, "The Spectre is the Freddy Krueger of the superhero world." One for one! For the second series, I went back to the characters Ben and I had acquired under our *Swamp Thing* deal and pitched the Vertigo miniseries *American Freak.* A young man turns (choose: eighteen or twenty-one) and starts to slowly morph . . . but into what? Pieces of his skin are begin-

APPROVED BY THE COMICS CODE AUTHORITY
12¢
MYSTERY IN SPACE
MAR NO. 90
ONLY A MOMENT LEFT TO AVERT A COLLISION BETWEEN EARTH AND MY ADOPTED PLANET RANN!
ADAM STRANGE and HAWKMAN IN A DUAL ADVENTURE... "PLANETS in PERIL!"

ning to crack and fall off. He's changing and the clock is counting as he races to learn what is happening to him. He soon discovers that his entire life up to this point was a lie and his parents were not really his parents. Next, shady people are after him and he goes on the run. Mob? FBI? Black ops? As if a fugitive on the loose, he soon encounters a strange girl who becomes the only one he trusts. Becoming increasingly desperate as the changes accelerate, in the end he learns who is chasing him and why and then discovers the answer to who he is. At that moment, he quits running from it and fighting it and allows the change to overwhelm him, allowing his true self to emerge. And that final answer is a *shocker*!

The next week, there was a management change at HBO and that was the end of that.

After meeting with Bruce Willis's people and running material by the star who was then in his *Die Hard* era, they reported they were all interested in both *Adam Strange* and *The War That Time Forgot*. They set up a lunch for me and Bruce. I met him in a restaurant in Santa Monica, and his first question to me was, "They told me you were a Jersey boy like me. That true?" I said it was. Suspicious, he asked me where in Jersey I was from. I replied as anyone from Jersey would reply, "I grew up down the shore at Exit 105 but then moved to Exit 145." With that, he beamed and said, "Only a real Jersey boy would speak like that!" I asked him where he was from. He said, "Exit 2." I replied, "Exit 2?! That's not really New Jersey! That's like Delaware!" On that note we began a fun, creative session over lunch.

I had given him the very first Adam Strange story from Showcase #17 before he wore his superhero costume. I pitched it as the "Indiana Jones of outer space," which got a great reaction. I pitched *The War That Time Forgot* as *GI Joe* versus *Jurassic Park*. He would play the wooden-legged Captain Storm in a film set in the South Pacific in 1943 as an America PT boat and a Japanese cruiser were warring with each other. We learn that the Japanese commander and Captain Storm had grown up a world apart but in similar military families and were truly just different cultural versions of the same kind of person. When a top-secret A-bomb test rips a hole in the very time/space continuum, the two boats and their crews must turn from trying to destroy each other to trying to destroy a far bigger common enemy as dinosaurs start pouring through the rift, attacking them. In the end, only Storm and the Japanese commander are left and are fighting off the dinosaurs back to back. In the end, the rift is closed and the two men lie in a small raft drifting aimlessly in the South Pacific. Then a ship appears on the horizon. They can't tell if it's American or Japanese. Initially elated, the two men who have become blood brothers realize that one of them is about to become a prisoner of war and that tears them up. As the ship comes to their rescue, the two dehydrated men look up and see Japanese faces. Storm is doomed. The commander is hoisted aboard first. When Storm arrives on deck he sees Japanese and American and British and German people all together. That's when they inform Storm and the commander that the year is 2020 and that World War II shit doesn't matter anymore.

LEFT: Adam Strange travels twenty-five trillion miles between Earth and the planet Rann, but apparently the only important thing is whether he was originally from New Jersey.

It was a very expensive period piece, and we got a pass. Everyone seemed to love the story but were scared off by the combination of the above factors.

Regarding *Adam Strange,* we just ran out of time. This was before streaming. I contend it would've made for an intense and fun series.

I pitched *Space Cabbie* the same way they must have pitched *Guardians of the Galaxy* later at Disney/Marvel. I envisioned Danny DeVito in his prime as the Space Cabbie who picks up his fares on worlds and at places like the *Star Wars* cantina to drive them home to their own planets and then winds up in the middle of every intergalactic mess imaginable. Couldn't get Danny's interest, and this was in the years before the Seth Rogens and the newer generation of comedian actors. I asked DC if I could substitute for *Space Cabbie,* and they could not have been nicer. There was a graphic novel I wanted called *The Golden Age.* Here's the Wiki description: "It concerns the Golden Age DC superheroes entering the 1950s and facing the advent of McCarthyism." It was a great story, just a bit too far ahead of where Hollywood was at that particular time. Today? It could be a streaming masterpiece in the hands of the right director and writer. As for why this specifically didn't happen . . . don't ask. I'll throw up. Welcome to Hollywood.

In my own development, I received my BA degree in history, which was always a passion of mine. Whether world history or American history, I soak it up at every opportunity through reading, documentaries, and most importantly, by visiting historical sites. As a dad, wherever possible, I dragged my kids along until they developed their own love of history and started leading the charge. One of my wife's and my goals was to take our kids to all fifty states and throughout Canada before they graduated high school, and we succeeded in that quest. It was the greatest kind of family bonding parents can do with their children as a family unit.

So you can just imagine how very, very desperate I was to use my history degree in my work. One of those times came when I developed a project that targeted one of my favorite topics in American history, the Alamo. Neither John Wayne nor Fess Parker got the true story right. Inspired by a brilliant scholarly book, *Roll Call at the Alamo,* we'd talk about the fact that the defenders were a melting pot, not just a bunch of Texans. We'd examine the true character of Generalissimo Santa Anna (Was it true he may have been a coinventor of modern chewing gum via a business deal with the Adams Gum Company?). We wondered what drove Congressman Davy Crockett to tell his Tennessee constituents they could go to hell because he was going to Texas!? We had a marvelous script by one of the top miniseries writers and one of the top miniseries directors committed to direct. We set it up with the television powerhouse, Lorimar, and worked with veteran Malcolm Stuart and that bright newcomer, Les Moonves, on the project we set up at CBS. Then we got "an order" from CBS and all systems were "Go!" We would shoot on location in Brackettville, Texas, in the reproduction of the Alamo John Wayne built for his 1960 film. We were assured that once an order was given, it was never rescinded. Production was less

RIGHT: Hailing a taxi, Space Cabbie style!

LOBO
21
TAXI
TAXI!
7Y33
DIRECT SALES
ALAN GRANT
KEV O'NEILL

than ninety days away. Ben and I had a huge producer fee due and cleared our calendar for the upcoming year so I could head down to Texas for the preproduction and production of this prodigious undertaking. And then, as can only happen in this cockamamie business, on the same day, one of the heads of Lorimar left Lorimar and our CBS head of miniseries programming left CBS. We got the call that CBS was freezing all its projects until new management was installed. Meanwhile, Lorimar was regrouping. We were told not to worry. An order is an order! Only it wasn't. The new management came in and killed all the projects of the old management. A friend on the inside told me our producer fee had been in a stamped envelope in an out-box when the ax fell; it was never mailed out. Only trouble is, I already started spending it. Oh . . . and Ben and I cleared our schedule, so we now had one long blank for the next year staring us in the face. Welcome to Hollywood or, as it looked more to me at that moment, welcome to hell, development or otherwise.

But I learned the hard way in life that there are many levels of what we often generically call hell. How often did I think I had reached the fiery flames fanned by my fiendish foes of filmland (See: *Catwoman*. Better yet, don't.), only to encounter far, far worse hell in the course of life itself?

This is exactly the reason why if you are going to be a producer in Hollywood, you must be Johnny Appleseed. You must come up with the ideas for many projects that can form your slate. You must option the rights to various comic books, books, screenplays, plays, articles, or video games (commonly called "Intellectual Properties" or "IP") and package them with screenwriters, directors, and stars in the development process. You must toss out creative seeds left and right as you walk along that yellow brick road (known locally as Hollywood Boulevard's Walk of Fame) because you will never know for sure which projects will take and come to pass and which will unexpectedly at the very last minute wilt on the vine.

If *P* is for Process, I had to process this, because becoming Johnny Appleseed would quickly become unavoidable.

CHAPTER FIVE

The PARTNERS

Making a movie amid the Hollywood landscape is not what I naïvely envisioned it would be that day in Irwin's office. I pictured it as a war, and every day I would go forth and fight a battle for my project. No, it is actually a siege, and the most important thing a producer can do is dig a foxhole, put on a helmet, and hunker down for the long haul, with the understanding that the most important decision to be made is who you allow into that foxhole with you to watch your back.

Swear that we two will fight together against crime and corruption and never to swerve from the path of righteousness!

—THE BATMAN, DETECTIVE COMICS #38

The concept of partnering—choosing partners and learning how to play nicely together in the sandbox—is critical to successful moviemaking but begins and is molded while we are children, prepubescent, pubescent, and whatever comes thereafter.

I wasn't Archie in junior high school or even pre-driver's license in high school. I was Jughead. I didn't date the most popular girls and have them competing for my attention. I was the guy they all felt comfortable talking to. My friends were all jealous, thinking there could be more to it than friendship, but I knew better (at least until my senior year when I dared try crossing the Rubicon, only to have met the same fate as Caesar . . . the emperor, not the salad).

My best female friend and I met in eighth grade. Her name is Ellen Genick. She wanted me to make up a fake name for her in this book, so I'm going to call her "Helen Benick."

By the start of high school, Helen possessed the world's perfect body. (Wait a minute! This is so silly! I'm calling her "Ellen"!) But as any boy at Ocean Township High School could tell you, *no* guy ever possessed it. Ellen was pure, disarmingly naïve, and like most of the girls in our class—in Ocean Township and generally at that time—untouchable. In order to put Ellen in proper perspective, please permit this New York Yankees fan to bring up Robinson Cano for a moment. Robinson Cano, though a .320 hitter during the 2009 baseball season, had a terrible postseason, unable to drive in the Yankee runners on base. Well, Ellen Genick stranded more men at first base than Robinson Cano ever did.

The guys had a hard time comprehending how I could be doing what few eighth-grade boys would ever dream of doing . . . talking to a girl. I quickly discovered that by actually talking to a girl, you could get to know her. It was an epiphany. I quickly learned Ellen was more beautiful inside than out. By talking to her, I had made a friend for life—and had a great place to hang out at most days after school because she also had two of the coolest parents in town.

Throughout high school, Ellen dated Dickie. I didn't learn until our high school reunion many years later that boys who grew up being called "Dickie" *never* acknowledge it as adults and correct you every time that they are "Richards" and definitely *not* "Dickies." Speaking of "Dicks," the biggest Dick in all our baby boomer lives was from the "Dick & Jane" reading books that we all grew up with in elementary school. We learned to read starting in first grade by following the adventures of Dick (who was about our own age), Jane, toddler Sally, and their pets, Spot the dog and Puff the cat, as they all learned to "See," "Go," "Jump," "Work," and have "Fun" in a series of scintillating books with such catchy titles as *Friends and Neighbors*, followed by the gripping sequel, *More Friends and Neighbors*, and supplemented by phonics books and think-and-do books. (If only the politicians of the world read the latter!) It was all so educational and innocent that only when I went back and reread these books as an adult did I realize the colossal joke they were playing on my entire generation. Here are just a few samples (*you* decide if I'm reading too much into them):

"Oh, see Dick!" said Jane.

"Work, Dick, work!" said Jane.

"Jane is fun. Dick is fun," said Sally.

"Sally is little. Jane is big. Dick is big," said Sally.

Ladies and gentlemen of the jury, I rest my case.

Like everywhere else in the USA in the 1950s, at our two neighborhood grade schools, Wanamassa School and Oakhurst School, we were profiled and separated into three distinct classes of human beings called "reading groups." The teachers and administrators thought they were pulling the wool over our eyes—the same thing we boys in the class would be trying to do to the sweaters of the girls in the class ten years later. Not so! The powers that were tried to mask the fact that they had broken us up into one group made up of excellent young readers, another group of average readers, and a third group consisting of the slowest readers in the class. So to avoid the stigma of being branded "smart," "average," or "dumb," they named each group after a bird. The smart group was called "The Bluebirds." The average group was called "The Robins." And the slow group was called "The Buzzards." Their ploy failed. Once you were labeled a Buzzard, you were *always* a Buzzard for the remainder of your days at Wanamassa School. You had no hope whatsoever of anyone acknowledging your perhaps delayed progress and then changing you into a Robin or a Bluebird. And don't kid yourself... every single six- and seven- and eight-year-old knew what those labels really meant. Reinforced on a daily basis, each kid accepted the fact that he or she was either smart, average, or dumb. In the 1950s, once a Buzzard, always a Buzzard. It just wasn't right. Some of my best friends were Buzzards.

At Ocean Township School, which ran from fifth to eighth grade, they never used the nomenclature of "junior high school," but judging by the physical changes that took place during those couple of years, something big was happening. To me, it was like watching the scary old movie *The Wolfman* with Lon Chaney Jr.... except that the transformation, hair and all, was happening to me, not him. Hair was growing in places that had never before even been places. Even the way we dressed began changing. The fashion for boys was the bleeding madras shirt (featuring on the back a small loop, commonly referred to as a "locker loop" that, for whatever reason, attracted girls who would come up behind you and tear it off), white socks, penny loafers (these were laceless shoes with a leather slot on the front you could fit a penny inside if you wanted to be cool), and skin-tight white Levi's. The skin-tight Levi's exacerbated an already-growing problem for the boys. How many times boys in the class went up to the blackboard while clutching their notebooks in front of them, well... it's kinda like the Masonic Lodge. We never talked about it. No one else is supposed to know.

This pubescent rite of passage in New Jersey culminated with every guy's getting his driver's license at age seventeen. It was having my own car, albeit a creaking 1961 Impala SuperSport covered with hippie flower decals, thank you very much, that I suddenly was able to move successfully from just being friends with girls to actually taking them out. It's an open question if it was the car that did the trick or the self-confidence the car inspired in me. In 1968, it set back my dad $400 when he bought it from his carpenter pal, Lester Schlessinger's, aged father. To give you the value of a buck back then, Dad strenuously bargained old man Schlessinger down from $420 and considered that $20 saving a major coup. But with or without my car in my senior year of high school, all roads led to Candy, my first true girlfriend of my driver's license era. Candy was sweet. We used to double with my cousin Brucie . . . no, not the New York rock 'n' roll disc jockey, but my real cousin Brucie, the cousin who threw up on Ronna Berman's shag carpeting. We were clone-like growing up. If I was any closer to him, I'd've been behind him, as Groucho Marx might say. Believe it or not, but this is the God's honest truth . . . when I was dating Candy, Bruce was dating a girl named Honey. The one time we doubled, he and I both contracted diabetes. Candy actually got my sense of humor and catered to it. More importantly, as my first true girlfriend in high school, she was a great partner who always had my back . . . in the nicest sense. Back in the late '60s, there was nowhere to take my girlfriend to do what was commonly and cryptically called "submarine watching." My house was too risky. My grandmother had the superpower to be everywhere at once without even an old wooden step creaking. Candy's house was off-limits, as there were not one but two brothers lurking about who were very cool but definitely capable of blackmailing their sister and me along with her. Also, I had no doubt that if her father caught wind of it, he would tar and feather me as merely the warmup.

The only two choices were the drive-in movies, Eatontown Drive-In and Shore Drive-In, or going parking. Both require explanations. Drive-ins were outdoor movies your parents took you to when you were a kid. Mom and Dad often took me and Paul. He and I would have to get in our pajamas before we left home in our '56 Packard. Little pillows and blankets were de rigueur as were plastic bins filled with fresh fruit and pretzels to hold us over until intermission when Dad would take us to the concession stand for popcorn and sodas. Dad explained to us that the concession he was making there was half his paycheck. On the giant movie screen outside, dancing hot dogs and somersaulting french fries would sing "Come on out to the lobby," enticing us on the one hand yet sternly pressuring us on the other with the strict announcer's continual official and serious-sounding audio warnings, "Six minutes till showtime!" "Five minutes till showtime!" "Four minutes till showtime!" The only two movies Paul and I managed ever to stay up and watch to the end at a drive-in were *Voyage to the Bottom of the Sea* and *Some Like It Hot*. I'm so glad I remained awake, because when my parents heard Joe E. Brown's last line in *Some Like It Hot*, I'd never ever heard them laugh so hard and so long. It was such a moment of family joy with my mom and dad and my brother and me savoring a good, funny movie together in the snuggly warmth of our favorite family car and laughing out loud together in a moment that for me will always be frozen in time. In the back seat of our Packard that night, I just knew that this was what Heaven was going to be like someday. I wasn't quite so frightened of the future after that.

But when a boy turned seventeen and got his driver's license in New Jersey, the family drive-in suddenly became not an outdoor movie theater but a hothouse of hormones percolating in the comfort of your own car. The car was old, but it had class. It was one of the first autos with power windows and seats, and those seats had real power. The front bench seat slid back and rotated so that it damn well nearly formed a bed! How excited was I about my prospects? *The Green Berets* with John Wayne and David Janssen was playing at Eatontown Drive-In early in my senior year, and I went to see it three times in one week—with three different girls. How did I ever exist as a teenaged boy without a driver's license? Life back then was even stranger 750 miles away at Cinema West outside Bloomington, Indiana. That drive-in showed porno movies! The good news and the bad news were that the giant movie screen faced the highway. Everyone driving by at 60 miles per hour got a cheap thrill . . . and an expensive accident. That spot, year after year, was the number-one site in the state of Indiana for car crashes.

So where was I? Oh yeah! Candy!

She and I went parking. That was the other Jersey Shore choice if you had insufficient funds for a movie or if it was wintertime when the drive-ins were closed for the season. We had our nighttime spot on Madison Avenue in Wanamassa by a job construction site on a dirt road that was almost assuredly devoid of cars, foot traffic, nosy neighbors peeking through curtains, or cops. For the sake of accuracy and posterity, these were innocent times. Nothing happened but kissing. Good kissing, but kissing. Just kissing. We used to call it "necking." I don't know why. My "neck" was about the only body part not affected by the process. I remember it was a Wednesday night. How do I know this? Because I had in my car a stack of new comic books I had just bought at Deal Pharmacy and new comic books only come out on Wednesdays. Now, pay attention—if there's nothing else you learn from this book, acknowledge that you should *not* go parking in Deal, New Jersey! The Deal cops had magic radar when it came to teenagers parking. So as Candy and I were doing what we did best, I suddenly became aware of a swirling red light behind us illuminating the interior of my Chevy, decorated with a small statue of Atom Ant replacing the little dashboard statue of Jesus that some former owner had once perched there. I was Jewish and didn't believe in Jesus. But I was a comic book and cartoon superhero fan and did believe in Atom Ant. Experience told me that Candy and I had approximately twenty seconds from the time that red light flashed until the cop could get out of his car, walk over to the driver's side window, shine his elongated flashlight in, and rap on the glass in that dreadful salutation only cops can deliver so well. I immediately went into crisis mode as we made ourselves look something akin to presentable. Like a bolt of lightning, Candy quickly grabbed a comic book and tossed one to me as she whispered loudly, "Quick! Pretend you're reading this!" I only wish we had paid more attention to the titles of those comic books. Obviously, the cop noticed their titles while Candy and I were too naïve for the whole thing to register and I was preoccupied with the worry of being arrested for parking with a girl (this, however, in a long-ago era when there was *no* law mandating that all activity inside a car be "hands-free"). As he shone his light directly onto the comic books, he saw I was reading the first issue of a new Archie comic titled (cross my heart and hope to die!) "Jughead's Eat-Out," while Candy was reading a new Marvel comic titled (cross my heart again and hope to die again) "Giant-Sized Man-Thing." I honestly don't know if he was really pissed off or was just about to crack up when he told us, "You two get out of here and quit using Deal streets for your playground!" But like I said, Candy was innocent... what we used to call a "good girl" as opposed to a "nice girl." "Nice" girls weren't. Candy, on the other hand, was the kind of girl you brought home to meet your mother without any cringing. She was the absolute cutest junior at Ocean Township High School when I was a senior. But far more importantly, when the chips were down, she had my back and was a supportive partner... even in parking crime.

When the day came in early April 1979 when DC Comics welcomed my proposal to buy the rights to Batman in order to make dark and serious Batman movies, I knew as a kid in my twenties that I needed someone who knew how to raise money, secure global distribution, and mount a production. Benjamin Melniker would become my partner, my friend, my mentor, my idol, and my second father. Like my dad and Nancy's dad, he stressed the importance of always acting honorably with integrity, as it's really a small business and all you have is your good name. Ben also taught me something keenly important if I wished to survive in the movie industry. What do you do on those occasions where a director or producer pal or a studio exec invites you to a state-of-the-art little screening room for a special showing of his upcoming film and that film is not an Oscar contender and, in fact, may be a bomb as opposed to "da bomb," and as it ends, there's only one exit . . . but that director or producer or exec is standing at that one door, embracing all viewers on their way out as if it was his Bar Mitzvah receiving line? I mean, the first lesson in the movie industry addresses the uncomfortable question, "What do you say or not say to him?" Ben knew. Ben knew everything. You shake his hand; look him in the eye; smile; say, "That was *some* movie!" and quickly move on.

When I was contemplating making Ben my partner on all things Batman, I did some investigative homework. I knew that among his many actions, he was involved in one of the most infamous firings in the history of the movie business. Dory Schary had been MGM's head of production and was quite beloved. You probably remember him best as the head of MGM whom Ricky Ricardo was always so worried about impressing while Lucy was up to her antics in Hollywood on *I Love Lucy*. I read Schary's account of that firing, and he described it as being led into a den of vipers with MGM execs making all sorts of promises if he resigned voluntarily. He said he turned to Ben and asked him if what was being said was true, because to Schary, only Ben had the integrity he could trust. That's when I knew I had found my Batman partner.

Ben would wind up being the last of his generation not merely standing but still sharp, walking unassisted, and actively working in the business just shy of his 105th birthday, nearly five years after they forced him to give up his beloved game of golf. He was the only person in the history of movies to have actively worked in nine different decades! When it comes to the most important singular issue in the motion picture and television industry, I will reiterate that when you dig your foxhole for the siege, make certain you know who you are inviting in with you to watch your back. Three times in my four-plus decades in

Me and Ben Melniker on the set of *Swamp Thing*. Photo by Russell Jeffcoat.

the Biz, I made a bad choice, and each time it nearly killed me, or at least, nearly sent me off the battlefield preparing to wave a white flag. Do your own due diligence, don't always assume everyone is telling the truth, and then don't give everyone and anyone the benefit of the doubt. Cynical, I know. But that's the scars you accumulate in Hollywood, the land of bilk and money.

I was with Ben at the Universal executive dining room the final time he met with one of the true kings of Hollywood, Lew Wasserman. "Ben," Lew asked, "do you remember that weekend in 1964 we spent at the White House with LBJ and formed the Motion Picture Association of America?" Ben replied he still had the pictures from that weekend and quickly ticked off the names of all the other major studio toppers who were there with them... Arthur Krim and Bob Benjamin from United Artists, Barney Balaban from Paramount, Leo Jaffe from Columbia... the list went on. Ben reported to Lew that he still used to see Adolph Zucker, the founder of Paramount Pictures, taking his daily constitutional in New York City right up till 1976 when he was well over one hundred and challenged Lew that they both needed to shoot to break Zucker's record. Ben did. He and Lew then started chatting in detail about that weekend at the White House and the startling secrets that had unfolded. Ben made me promise not to tell what I heard until 2025 when he figured all the parties involved would be gone.

I loved hearing and encountering movie history at Ben's feet. He had been one of the architects of the original Canadian tax shelters that propelled the financing of movies in the '70s and beyond. He had made movie history when Bob Rehme, then the head of Avco-Embassy Pictures, summoned him for help when a big movie they were shooting, *Winterkills,* lost its financing while in the midst of shooting. "Lost its financing" maybe doesn't quite sum it up. It was being independently financed by two men, one of whom was murdered during production and the other was sent to prison for a long time in connection with a drug operation. The picture starred Jeff Bridges, John Huston, and Elizabeth Taylor. Omigod! I haven't told you the Elizabeth Taylor I-hate-Ben-Melniker story! Put a pin in *Winterkills.* I'll get right back to it. I swear! But first...

Ben at MGM had signed Elizabeth Taylor to a three-picture deal, paying her $50,000 for her acting services on each film. After completing two, she asked to be let out to do *Cleopatra* for 20th Century Fox, which had made her an offer to become the first actor ever to receive $1 million for a role. MGM agreed, provided when she was done, she'd do the third picture under their deal. After *Cleopatra,* representatives for the star informed Ben her price was now $1 million if they wanted her services. Ben didn't exactly see it that way. The MGM Lion held his ground and his contract and made it clear no one was working anywhere until this picture was made at the agreed-upon price. She wasn't a happy camper but ultimately had no legal choice. MGM board members rained fire on Ben for holding firm, claiming she wouldn't do a good job and the picture would be a flop. Ben maintained that she was the consummate professional and would do the best job she could no matter the contractual circumstances. So she did it. It was *Butterfield 8,* the movie that won her a Best Actress Oscar. I later confirmed this story with Liz Taylor's grandson.

But where were we? Oh, yeah! *Winterkills*! So Ben was called in to deal with a terrible crisis. He not only had to come up with a plan that would refinance the film but he would also have to get all the actors and the crew back together after a lengthy shutdown to complete it. As he investigated the situation, it got worse and worse . . . much worse. Withholdings had not been turned over to the government, so there was an IRS tax lien on the thing, as well as state tax liens, and a list of creditors a mile long. So Ben formed a creditors' committee and realized that there was no way he could bring in fresh financing if the new investors didn't get their money first after the picture was released and started generating gross receipts. But that was impossible with IRS and state tax liens taking first recoupment position, never mind what the guilds were owed on top of all the individuals and companies. So for the first time in the history of movies, one picture was put into Chapter 11. Then Ben went to meet with the IRS; if it wasn't willing to take second position, no new financing would appear, and no one would get anything. Ben succeeded in getting the IRS to agree to take second position and then everyone else backed off a notch too. He found new money, closed the deals, brought the cast and crew back together, got the film finished and released, and then paid off the priority creditors in order. Again, it was history . . . movie history.

All Ben's stories didn't have to be behind-the-curtain stuff. Sometimes it was just listening to his recollections of the night his wife, Shirley, and he attended the premiere of *The Seven Year Itch* and sat behind Marilyn Monroe, whom Shirley refers to looking like a fragile, beautiful "powder-puff." Or about the tough-guy tales of MGM's colorful head of physical production, Eddie Mannix, a man tied to some of the stories of the suicide-or-was-it-murder of George Reeves, TV's Superman. I was devastated when I was eight and I heard Superman was dead.

My dad tried hard to make sure I wouldn't ever see the headline that day from the *New York Daily News*, which he knew would traumatize me. So my big brother, Paul, made sure I saw it. And Ben told the tale as to how Howard Strickling protected MGM's stars from bad press or scandal . . . even one of its actors who, when he got drunk, liked to dress up in women's clothes and was taken into LAPD custody but kept in a very private area until Strickling could have him picked up without the press getting wind of it. Or selecting Charlton Heston to play Ben-Hur over cheesecake after a lunch on the third floor of the Thalberg Building on the Culver City lot with all the MGM producers from Pandro Berman to Richard Brooks being called in for lunch and their opinions. Ben remained proud of the groundbreaking deal he made whereby Heston received only $250,000 up front and back-ended the rest to take the gamble with MGM that the film would be a blockbuster. Oh! And Ben the raconteur told of the excitement of giving Stanley Kubrick the freedom to perfect his breakthrough special FX while shooting *2001*, and then insulating the great filmmaker when the $5 million budgeted picture came in at $10 million. It was Ben who would join in on the corporate jet taking them to the Moscow Film Festival where *2001* won the big prize, and then each day taking the film to the capital city of a different Iron Curtain country to show this amazing movie.

But one of my favorite Ben stories dealt with *Dr. Zhivago*. This was to be another MGM masterpiece with a script by Robert Bolt and with the immortal David Lean as director. Ben ran into a full-blown board insurrection as to MGM's going forward with this hugely expensive undertaking. Led by board member, Random House president, and, most importantly, panelist on the TV game show *What's My Line?* every Sunday night, Bennett Cerf, the disgruntled contingent did not want *Dr. Zhivago* made. Cerf contended that the mass audience would think it was a medical story and claimed that even he as a book publisher had a hard time getting through Boris Pasternak's novel. Ben's best ally on the board was General Omar Bradley, who was part of the board arguing to allow the film to be made. When the opposition saw their chances dwindling of stopping the film, they fired back with a new reason to kill it. The contract MGM had with Pasternak stated that the screenplay had to "adhere to the spirit of the book." Cerf and company claimed that MGM could spend millions on this movie and then be told that it didn't adhere and MGM would be stopped from releasing the picture. The anti–*Dr. Zhivago* forces were surging toward winning the day. That's when Ben did what Ben does—come up with creative solutions to dead-ends and loggerheads and immovable objects. Ben got on a plane to London armed with two copies of the book and two copies of Bolt's screenplay. He found the leading Cambridge scholar of Russian literature and the leading scholar of Russian history at Oxford. Paying them a nominal honorarium so as not to taint the results, he asked them to compare the two and then swear out an affidavit attesting as to whether the screenplay adhered to the book. They both answered unequivocally in the affirmative. At the next board meeting, with David Lean stating he would shoot the screenplay as written, Ben was able to get the board to approve the expenditure, and *Dr. Zhivago* became part of motion picture history, a huge financial success, as well as a winner of ten Academy Award nominations and five Oscars, an extraordinary feat surpassed, I might add, in 2019's *Joker*, with eleven Oscar nominations. The one smiling more broadly that *Joker* night must have been Ben . . . wherever he was, watching over me I like to think.

P is for Partners, and in the world of comic book superheroes, they are not simply "sidekicks." Ben was not my Robin. He was my Superman, a statement that must be set in the context of my time growing up with a DC comic book called *World's Finest*. Each issue was a Superman/Batman team-up with the accent on *team*. Superman always first and Batman always second was indeed the billing until 1989, thank you very much, when the billing changed to Batman/Superman! In those days, Batman and Superman didn't fight. The Justice League always got along because they were teammates, again with the accent on *team*. Since the *Batman v Superman* movie premiered, the picture became cloudier and darker, and I began getting Q&A theoreticals at Comic-Con after Comic-Con, "Who would win in a fight, Batman or Superman?" My answer is always, "No contest! Batman! Because brains will always defeat brawn." And even in business . . . especially in business . . . if you seek partners who feel less like corporate administrators and more like family, you will find the same extended family success as did The Incredibles or Batman and Superman, together, in mine.

CHAPTER SIX

The PITCH

When I walk into the spacious office of high-level major Hollywood studio execs and pitch my latest project to them and their attendant entourage of vice presidents and assistants, I never see them as high-level anything. I see them all as the four- and five-year-old campers I led as a camp counselor when I was a teenager in the Garden State of New Jersey. Why? Because there are only two elements mandatory to a successful movie pitch: passion and storytelling. And so, I imagine them all as my little campers as I tell them a story around a campfire. Whether I want to give them chills by crafting a ghost story or want to excite them by communicating a superhero tale, the object is to draw them in, captivate them, own their attention, and tell them an amazing story with colorful characters. If you fail to have the enthusiasm or fail to project and share that passion with the people in the room, the pitch loses its energy and dies en route.

I wear a mask. And that mask, it's not to hide who I am, but to create what I am.

—BATMAN: BROKEN CITY

It was 2013. My son, David, was on the advisory boards to both the Stan Lee Foundation and the Los Angeles Unified School District. He helped arrange a special day for kids in schools in Compton and Watts. First, I went to the schools and talked to the students about my journey with Batman as a blue-collar kid who didn't come from money but was still able to make my dreams come true by bringing the world the first dark and serious movies of the Batman. From there, we all piled on to buses and drove to Dodger Stadium as the guests of the team. Everyone was invited onto the playing field to watch batting practice. Stan Lee was set to throw out the first ball of the game while plugging that weekend's opening of one of Marvel's *Thor* movies. David and I were having a blast watching all the excited kids as game time neared and the field needed to be cleared. That was when it happened. Out of the blue! Unexpected!

A tied and jacketed Dodger exec approached me with a panicky look on his face.

"Mr. Uslan," he said in a sort of begging voice, "we have a problem maybe you can help us with."

Always the problem solver, I offered any assistance I could provide.

"We just got a call from Stan Lee, and he is stuck in a massive traffic jam and simply won't make it here on time to throw out the first pitch today."

I still didn't see it coming. David did, and his eyes got very wide.

"Uhh . . . we know who you are. Batman. Would you throw out the first ball for tonight's game?"

I was stunned but kept calm. My reply was reasonable and firm. "I haven't touched a baseball since my thirty-something son here was in Little League. Give me like a half hour on the side to throw and see if I can do it."

The Dodger exec's reply was far less reasonable and far firmer than mine. "Mr. Uslan, this is happening in two minutes. There's no time to practice throwing."

Semi-relieved, I smiled and said, "Well, then, I'm sorry, but I can't do it. I've been a huge baseball fan since birth. If I got out there and bounced the ball to the catcher, that would be the biggest humiliation of my life and so I can't."

Few are quicker on their feet than David in a pinch. My son quickly interceded, got in my face, and ordered, "Dad! Look at me! I want you to look at that pitcher's mound over there! Dad . . . Sandy Koufax stood on that pitcher's mound. And now they want you to take the ball and stand out there, too!"

Having no idea where it came from, I suddenly heard myself say, "I'll do it!"

The exec told his assistant, "The fool's gonna do it!" Or maybe he said something different. All I know is the next instant I found myself standing along the first base line with all the Dodgers as "The Star-Spangled Banner" was playing, TV cameramen were lining up in front of me, and someone put a baseball in my right hand. I spied my wife in the front row next to Rob Reiner, who was eating the biggest sub sandwich I'd ever seen. Nancy looked ready to throw up, and I knew the culprit was me and my sudden situation and not Rob Reiner's dripping sandwich.

Suddenly, that tied and jacketed exec nudged me and walked me toward the pitcher's mound . . . the Holy Land of baseball . . . as I saw myself on Diamondvision across the scoreboard and heard an echoey Mount Sinai–type voice proclaiming, "Ladies and gentlemen! To throw out the first pitch of tonight's game, let's all welcome the originator and executive producer of the *Batman/Dark Knight* movie franchise, MICHAEL-EL-EL-EL USLAN-LAN-LAN-LAN!"

There was a scattered string of applause and, surprisingly, no boos from what I imagined might have been a stacked Marvel crowd. I then realized that the figure I saw about a mile and a quarter away was the Dodgers catcher. *Time out*! Seriously, you have *no* idea how far away that pitcher's mound is from home plate! It's ridiculous! It looks so close on TV! The catcher crouched down. I realized that if I bounced it, I would never live it down. Never! So I just thought I had to throw the damn ball as hard as I possibly could and release it more on the up portion of the pitch and not on the downside. Honestly, I didn't care if this sucker wound up in Row E, I was *not* going to bounce it. And I knew absolutely that I didn't care if my right arm became dislocated, broken, or fell off; I was going to put every bit of adrenalized strength into this that I could humanly muster. And I let it fly. The catcher had to jump up and catch it at his left shoulder! "I love the smell of Dodger Dogs in the evening. It smells like . . . Victory!" As the beaming catcher rushed to hand me the ball and marvel at my feat, the first person out of the dugout to congratulate me was my Yankee idol, Don Mattingly. As I slowly walked off the field, realizing that people in the stands were still clapping that I hadn't bounced it in, my son proudly rushed up and gave me a hug. I handed David the ball as we walked off the field of Dodger Stadium, simultaneously noticing the slumped, passed-out figure of my wife, as Rob Reiner struggled to untangle her from his no-longer-impressive sub sandwich.

If someone puts the ball in your hand, oftentimes you only have one shot to make the perfect pitch. Whether baseball or movie producing, the story and the results are the same. Do *not*, under any circumstances, just "bounce it in"!

I have had successful pitch meetings that went on in excess of two hours. *Constantine* was one of them, as was my pitch for our live-action feature film version of the smash computer game of its day *Where in the World Is Carmen Sandiego?* But more about those later. For now, let's focus on that unforgettable day and once-in-a-career pitch during which I sold a studio my movie . . . and I did it in three words.

On the heels of the success of *Batman*, I wanted to translate another crown jewel property from one medium into another. If Batman was the lifeblood of DC Comics, the board game Monopoly was the lifeblood of its manufacturer, Parker Brothers. When I told Ben I wanted to make a movie with characters and a real story out of a board game, he did *not* think I was crazy, but once again we hunkered down and prepared for the rest of the world to tell us I was.

Every winter in New York City is Toy Fair. It's the closest thing you'll ever find to Comic-Con for professional people. As a father, each year I became a man on a mission, spying the hottest upcoming secret action figures for Batman, Star Wars, GI Joe, He-Man, and Transformers, all of which defined my son, David's, childhood in the '80s and early '90s, although his mother will contend it's still ongoing. For my daughter, Sarah, I had to report on the newest Barbies, Cabbage Patch Kids, Rainbow Brite, My Little Pony, and Strawberry Shortcake, in that precise order. It was at Toy Fair that Ben and I had our first meeting with the Parker Brothers execs. Rather than call me nuts, *they* went nuts! They thought my take on Monopoly was totally unique and loved it. So off we marched to Beverly, Massachusetts, to negotiate a long, tough deal. As always, Ben was brilliant and, eventually, Monopoly was ours. My take would turn it into a modern-day *Wizard of Oz* meets *Jumanji* as our characters entered a Tim Burtonesque Atlantic City world inspired by the properties on the board as well as the Chance and Opportunity cards and the tokens.

Brandon Tartikoff was one of the most brilliant, and nicest, guys in the Biz. At this particular moment in time, he was the president of NBC, and Paramount had just tried to lure him to head up its motion picture and television operations. To entice him to stay, NBC allowed him to set up a small feature film division. One of his first films there was *Uncle Buck*, starring comedian/actor John Candy, who was also, by the way, one of the nicest guys in Hollywood.

It was around the time of *Batman Returns*, and Ben and I went to NBC to see Brandon and his right hand / head of business affairs, John Agoglia, another brilliant industry veteran. Every pitch meeting begins with "the schmooze." This is the five or ten initial minutes when you're offered water or coffee and everyone hobnobs, either getting to know each other or reconnecting. The schmooze is an essential part of the pitch. Every producer is looking for a way to relate to or find a connection with the studio executives in the room. It's an attempt to get on the same wavelength prior to the pitch beginning.

At the conclusion of our warm and fuzzy, reconnecting schmooze, Brandon turned to me and said, "Michael, I absolutely loved your *Batman* movie. I hope you have something else like that up your sleeve. So, what did you bring me today?"

I had spent the last six months perfecting my pitch, beat for beat, in three acts. I knew it was going to be tough to pitch this IP without a complete story and character arcs, so I made sure I had every single detail and arc worked out in my head. I had practiced and practiced this pitch and was more than prepared for whatever questions or concerns Brandon would hit me with. I took a deep breath!

"Monopoly—The Movie," I announced.

Brandon lit up like the proverbial Christmas tree. "I love it! This is great! Let's do it!" he proclaimed with a passion equal to mine. His reaction stunned me.

"Wait a minute! You haven't even heard my pitch yet!" I responded.

"No need to!" Brandon said as he stood up at his desk. "It's terrific! You and Ben go with John now and work out the deal terms, and let's get cracking on this right away!"

"Yeah, but you really need to hear my pitch. I can lay out all the details of the story and characters. I've been working on this for six months," I mildly protested.

"I'm sure it's fabulous! So go make the deal, and we'll get into all that after!" He smiled with excitement. "Thanks for coming in! It'll be fun working together!"

I have a blurry recollection of simply stammering, "But . . . but . . . I have this great pitch . . ."

I never got to pitch it. As the movie gods would have it, the project originally set up with NBC would move to another company. The issue was that it was going to be a blockbuster with a blockbuster budget. The films being made at NBC were much smaller in scope and budget size. Down but never out, Ben and I took it to one of the great showmen in Hollywood of that era, Mario Kassar at Carolco. He was in, provided we found the right writer, and we did with Jim Hart.

Jim had written *Hook*, and I loved his script significantly more than the film itself. He went on to write Francis Ford Coppola's *Dracula*. But Jim needed one-of-a-kind research to be able to complete his script. He informed me and Ben he needed to see the internal workings of a security operation in an Atlantic City casino. And that would prove to be as hard to get into as the outer doors of Oz were for Dorothy and her friends. But, as luck would have it, I was by then a member of the New Jersey Motion Picture and Television Commission (becoming its chairman in 2016), a commission that goes to the ends of the earth—or at least New Jersey—to accommodate whatever filmmakers need to film in the Garden State, including one of the best tax incentive plans in the world, featuring a bonus if a producer's crew and cast meet New Jersey's diversity requirements.

Miraculously, executive director Joseph Friedman and his noble henchmen, Steve Gorelick and David Shoner, came through for us! Joe was an old-time industry exec and had spent decades with Paramount and Joseph E. Levine, Otto Preminger, and Jerry Lewis; he knew how to get things done. Through the good offices of the commission, we were allowed to see the internal workings of security at one of the major casinos. And it proved to be as eye-opening an experience as it sounds!

Ben, Jim, and I had to sign in, provide ID, and give our fingerprints before they'd give us badges. Our badges started with the letter *D*. A casino official who had a badge with an *A* on it escorted us through some doors to a more imposing door where someone with a *B* on his badge took over the lead, as the first person's *A* badge did not allow him access to where we now found ourselves. The *B* badge guy soon turned us over to a *C* security guy, who ushered us into the security command center for the casino, though he, himself, was not permitted inside. I was expecting two-way glass and lots of catwalks. Instead, I saw a rather small room with lots of video screens, some on automatic pilot and the rest being manned by three trained professionals whose "eyes" seemed to be everywhere at once.

Now I understood what all those dark, smoky glass "lights" were all over the ceilings . . . not lights, but cameras. They had cameras trained on players, cameras trained on dealers, cameras trained on pit-bosses watching the dealers, cameras trained on floorwalkers watching the pit-bosses, and cameras trained on stairwells and any place else they thought people might actually have or stage accidents.

It was a producer's "Wow!" moment for me, once again being somewhere people just don't get to go, yet here I was doing research for a movie. The security pros didn't like us being there. They were nervous having onlookers they didn't know. We were at first very quiet, just taking it all in, but gradually we started asking questions, slowly winning their comfort level if not their confidence.

"How often do you catch people cheating?" I asked.

"Every day," one of them replied.

I was surprised. "How often do you come across some new scam you've never seen before?" asked Jim.

"More often than you'd believe!" was the response.

"What's the most unusual way of cheating you've seen?" Ben inquired.

"Well, last month, we had a man come in and sit down at one of the blackjack tables. After a while, he started to win. And then he started winning a bit too consistently. The pit-boss called up here and asked us to take a look at what was going on. He believed cheating was taking place but couldn't tell how or if the dealer was in on it. So we turned some of our cameras around and focused on this guy. We quickly knew he was counting cards, which is illegal here. But we didn't recognize him as one of the known card-counters. So we kept watching . . . and watching . . . and watching, knowing he was cheating somehow. We came in tight with a camera and saw he was getting computer readouts on the face of his watch. With that, we sent in a couple of our security boys to bring him in. What he had done was build a computer in his cowboy boots and was operating it with his toes and using it to count cards."

After a long while, the three people in the booth really opened up and we learned three tips for the next time we walk into a casino, which I'd like to pass along: Ladies, don't wear a low-cut dress if you plan on bending over a craps table to roll the dice. Those cameras can zoom right down if someone in "high" places is acting irresponsibly. Second, as those cameras are capable of the equivalent of Minnesota Fats's best-positioned bank shots, ladies, if you are wearing a micro miniskirt while seated on a swiveling blackjack stool, unless you enjoy being The Flash, you might want to be careful. Third, do not cheat. You *will* get caught.

Jim was terrific to collaborate with, and we set up *Monopoly: The Movie* for financing and distribution through Carolco. We were nearing production. Ben and I spent a few days in Atlantic City location scouting. It was at a time in those early years of the new Atlantic City that provided a stunning visual contrast between the gold and marble high-rolling hotels/casinos and the dilapidated slums and adjacent neighborhoods, nothing at all like today's city by the sea. Our mission was to locate stretches of the Atlantic City boardwalk to use for our locations, as well as choice areas of town. We had to find a deal for sound-stage space and production offices, and a place to house our cast and crew at the best rate. Ben and I wound up meeting with Donald Trump in the process, which was more than interesting. It would lead to a couple of unusual meetings with him at his Fifth Avenue tower to be revealed in a book yet to come. Thanks to the unrelenting efforts of the New Jersey Film Commission, the mayor, and the governing body in Atlantic City, everyone bent over backward to be accommodating. They offered us a block of the boardwalk 24/7 while we were shooting and the same for various blocks in town. We were lined up with a great deal for rooms, a screening room, editing suites, and production offices at what was then the Playboy Hotel/Casino. Even better, once Miss America cleared out, we'd be able to use legendary Convention Hall as a studio. Knowing our budget would not be busted shooting on location in Atlantic City, Carolco went ahead and exercised the option on the rights to the board game Monopoly, paid Parker Brothers the big bucks, and got us in position to be green-lit for filming. And we were for about three days, before Carolco went bankrupt and everything ended.

Hooray for Hollywood.

But before you think *Monopoly* was the biggest singular frustration of my career, know that it . . . *gulp*! . . . wasn't "singular." While we were (we thought) bringing *Monopoly* to fruition, I came up with another wacky idea for Parker Brothers. Long before *Toy Story* was developed, I figured out how to bring Mr. Potato Head to television. When I told them how I would do it, they agreed I was crazy. But they loved my creative take so much, they were willing to give me a brief period of time to see if I could get anyone in Hollywood to go for it. Many of the toy execs started taking bets as to whether I would be physically thrown out of someone's television network office due to the ridiculous, out-of-the-box, insane nature of my pitch. As reliable as the sun rising in the east, Ben never said I was nuts and, instead, happily buckled his seat belt for yet another roller coaster ride with me. And I sold *Mr. Potato Head*! But not without some drama and some comedy.

My pitch was to be made to our old friends at USA Network with whom we had done *Swamp Thing*. When word spread that Uslan was coming in to do some sort of crazy pitch, there was literally a room full of people to hear this. I, of course, never saw them. The only people I ever saw in that huge, imposing office were my little campers from Oakhurst Day Camp, the four- and five-year-old boys who actually taught me how to pitch by forcing me on the spot to deliver energetic, interactive storytelling sufficient to keep them seated for half an hour at a time.

In 1966, I began my five-summers reign as "Coach" Mike, junior camp counselor at Oakhurst Country Day Camp. On this one special day, I was about to get a dramatic life lesson. Remember when our parents used to refuse to let us go swimming for a half an hour after we ate? That was no old wives' tale. Far, far from it . . .

One particular Wednesday was Barbecue Day at camp. My senior counselor and boss man told me I had to try to keep the campers seated for half an hour after lunch before going swimming on the hottest, most humid day of the summer. I was warned that if I couldn't contain them for that long, I was to just give it up and take them swimming. The only way I could think of to keep them in place was by telling some kind of story that would hook them and hold their attention despite their post-toddler attention deficits. The *Batman* TV show was then the rage, and all the little kids knew Batman, Robin, and a host of supervillains. Drawing on my decade of *Batman* comic book reading, I begin telling Batman stories. I quickly discovered that the only way to keep the boys seated was to try to communicate great excitement and pull them into the story, making it interactive, leaving it to them to tell what was about to happen next. This was instant on-the-job training. It would take me a few weeks to polish this storytelling technique that would ultimately keep the kids rooted at the barbecue table. But this first day, the best I could do was ten minutes before I threw in the towel. As a result of all that, my classmate and fellow junior counselor assigned to handle the herd of thirty-one little boys, Marc Summerfield, and I led the freshman boys group to the big pool. We thought it was a chancy move but had no viable alternative. What transpired after the swimming lessons went on to become legendary in the annals of Oakhurst Day Camp and a recurring nightmare for me for the rest of my life.

It was such a hot, hot, humid, humid day . . . one of those days in which most of my boys would normally have ignored half their lunches and concentrated on the concentrate that made their delectable fruit juice. But, it was Barbecue Day . . . inspiring the campers to eat like pigs right before their concentrated swimming lessons. Before we could move to the next event on our group's schedule of activities, crab soccer, the boys had to change in the freshman boys' locker room. The locker room was a white and green wooden room near the pool. It had benches around three of the walls and hooks above them for tote bags and clothes, with cubbies below for their little sneakers . . . which only six of the thirty-one knew how to tie. The rest fell to me and Marc. The locker room was a sweltering hotbox by the peak of day, and as we all walked up the two steps and entered, we never suspected the horror show we were stepping into and the terrible thing about to happen . . . a thing so utterly terrifying, I didn't think it had a name, until sometime later, after consulting expert scientists and doctors, I found out there was, indeed, a name for it. It is called . . . a chain vomit. What a title for a horror movie! Clearly better than *Nightmare on Elm Street*! I mean . . . just consider it for a moment: Wes Craven's *Chain Vomit*! Seriously, what kid would *not* rush to see a film called that at midnight on opening weekend?!

It started innocently enough. While thirty-one kids began changing out of their wet bathing suits in the hotbox, cross-eyed and cute Elliot Froehlich let us know just how much extra fruit juice he drank at lunch that day by unexpectedly peeing on the floor of the locker room. With that, four-year-old and very sensitive Joey Beymer started crying. Then crying hard. Then screaming. He screamed so hard that, without warning, he threw up. That made him cry even harder and made Elliot Froehlich cry too. Now others were crying as the smell of freshly blown chunks was merging with the pee to create what writer John Steinbeck might have called "the summer of our discontent." Elliot cried just too damn hard and would have shit his pants . . . had he been wearing pants. But no such luck. He was in the middle of changing out of his wet bathing suit and just shit right there on the floor. This made Joey Beymer go crazy. Literally! In abject panic, he started running to me, slipped in Elliot's shit and pee, and slid in it all the way to the door as if he was the Silver Surfer and coasted right out the locker room. Joey was the lucky one, because by this time the growing number of crying kids amid the heat and the stench coaxed the vomit right out of George Little (who, needless to say, was the tallest kid in the group, by far . . . in fact, the tallest five-year-old I had ever seen; he was my height, and I was fifteen). Five-year-old Shadrack Prizemore watched him and then puked himself. Concurrently, little Mark Kessler, the smallest four-year-old in the group, let rip a projectile vomit from the left side of the locker room to the wall of the right side of the locker room, and, with that, we lost the only mirror in the place. What followed were thirty-one boys vomiting one after another, triggering reprises, with two more frostings of diarrhea.

The extent of this raunchy pandemic of reverse-peristalsis, this colonic holocaust, cannot be fully appreciated without reviewing what all thirty-one of these human bombs had eaten for lunch: a hot dog (traumatically, thirteen of these campers who were each in the process of spewing a diarrhea/vomit combo had sauerkraut on their dogs), a caked wad of baked beans, a clump of potato salad, and a glop of coleslaw. Converted into vomit, at *best* this all meshed together as some nightmarish, colorful, giant bowl of Trix. At *worst*, it was the worst thing you could ever smell or imagine! So, being a responsible fifteen-year-old junior counselor, I did the only thing I could do amid the panic—I ran. As I leaped out of the locker room and raced for cover, I was wondering if this was what our soldiers in the jungles of Vietnam were then experiencing. Within moments, both word and scent spread around the camp. As the camp director, Mrs. Devlin, got on the intercom and cried out to the now unable-to-be-located janitorial staff, "Cleanup in freshman boys' locker room" (in retrospect, she should have said something like "Code Blue" so as not to create further panic), other counselors were rushing to aid in the search-and-rescue operation, helping tend to the muck-encrusted walking wounded. But the emergency disaster process quickly turned its focus on recovery, realizing that all the permanent wounds were mental. Thoughts of that day still haunt me, as even today, I know in my heart, and with some degree of shame, that on that one summer afternoon long ago, I had one moment to rise to the occasion for the kids and be Batman. Instead, I turned into The Flash.

Now, a producer and an adult in Hollywood, it was time again for Coach Mike to fire some imaginations with a new story. As I entered the office, in the doorway I dropped a large throw pillow I had carried there with me. When the programming chief pointed out to me I had dropped something, I told her, "I know. I dropped that pillow on purpose."

"And why on earth would you do that?" she asked, already with a smile.

My response set her up for the pitch, "Because what I'm about to pitch you is so utterly ridiculous . . . so patently absurd . . . I think there's a chance you're going to kick me out of your office, and if you do, I'll have a soft place to land." Everyone cracked up, and I launched into my *Mr. Potato Head* pitch.

"I have the rights to the enormously popular toy Mr. Potato Head," I stated.

"It's a great, classic branded property, Michael, but—" (she was already trying to apologize and pass) "we're not focusing on children's Saturday morning animation."

"I know," I answered without pause. "My show will be a prime-time half-hour weekly series . . . in live action."

There was stunned silence in the room. Before anyone could ask if I was kidding, I began my spiel.

Two scientists are working exclusively for a multinational conglomerate, using recombinant DNA to solve the world's food shortage by growing human-sized fruits and vegetables. In a breakthrough attempt to grow a potato the size of a tree, they mistakenly combine a potato and a human's DNA. Picture the slab in Frankenstein's lab. On it is a five-foot-round potato wrapped up in aluminum foil. With a lightning storm raging above, the scientists crank up the slab to the ceiling. Of course, this is today in America and it doesn't go up there to be hit by lightning but to be placed in a giant-sized microwave oven mounted under the ceiling. The scientists press the buttons: 2 minutes, High power, Start. Two minutes later, they slowly lower the slab. The aluminum foil ball starts to vibrate and shake. Suddenly, a little white-gloved hand pokes out from within. Then another. Struggling, it tears open the aluminum foil as, amid all the onrushing steam, out stumbles Mr. Potato Head. The scientists can't believe what they've accidentally created! It's *alive*! The scientists begin to teach it and learn that it is very, very smart, learning our language and ways quickly. It also learns that this evil corporation wants it to become the spokesthing for its line of products, all of which Mr. Potato Head learns are the exact opposite of "green." He won't do it. They lock him up in a subbasement cell. Poor Mr. Potato Head is so sad and lonesome. The two scientists feel terrible and decide to help him out by going back to the lab and creating a Mrs. Potato Head for him. They succeed, but the power mongers running the evil corporation are now angry. The two scientists place their own lives in jeopardy to give Mr. and Mrs. Potato Head a chance to flee for their lives. The scientists get them into the hands of their friend who's an FBI agent. The FBI then places Mr. and Mrs. Potato Head into the federal Witness Protection Program and relocates them to a small town in Idaho. Neighbors are led to believe they're a lovely new couple who suffer from a nasty skin disease. Thanks to the two scientists, Mr. and Mrs. Potato Head sprout three children. The first is their teenage daughter, Julienne, who wonders what's wrong with her when no boy will ask her to the prom and so he tries changing her nose and switching to a different set of lips. The middle spawn is Bud Jr., your typical ten-year-old boy. The baby is Chip. And the adventure begins here . . .

So they bought it as a modern-day *Munsters, Addams Family,* or *Bewitched.* It was going to be the most expensive prime-time show USA Network had done to that time. The writers came out of some greatly strange and funny old shows like *Mork & Mindy* where they wrote for the young Robin Williams. We had the best animatronics and SFX makeup pros who would be handling everything from then state-of-the-art servo motors to appliance makeup. We were to get the "go" for thirteen episodes, but at the last second on the last day, the head programmer's boss (a lovely guy but not, in the end, a risk-taker) got cold feet worrying about how totally different this show was from everything else on TV and the expense; he pulled the plug. Had *Mr. Potato Head* been produced, Ben and I would have shared in a piece of those spiking toy sales. Instead, our time ran out and Disney swooped down and grabbed Mr. Potato Head as a character to be used in its excellent feature film *Toy Story,* with Don Rickles voicing our hero.

What's that expression . . . "Hollywood—Boulevard of Broken Dreams"?

As I often say, the one and only thing I can promise everyone is that at some point in life (or too ridiculously often, as you can now tell) doors will slam in your face. And when they do, you have only two choices: go home and cry about it, or pick yourself up, dust yourself off, and start knocking again. It was time to start knocking on doors once more.

Between *Batman* and *The Dark Knight* great projects were produced, yet half the time, there were painful ones that got away and never came to pass. When people in the Biz hear that, they smile and pat me on the back and say how amazing it is to bat five hundred in this crazy industry. That's nice, but it doesn't lessen the pain when you lose your dream project or when you spend years in the trenches striving hard to make people and companies understand why it's so important to respect not only the integrity of comic book characters but also to respect the integrity of the fans.

There were two movies that Ben and I were tied to that we did everything we could to convince the powers that be *not* to go forward with . . . at least not in the direction they were immovably insisting on going. It was against our own financial interest to try to stop them from progressing the way they were heading, but if I could have just magically wished them to go away, I would have. Those two films for me were the apex of pain to this comic book geek-at-heart. But as I've learned the hard way, it can all be much more complex than simply a case of pleas falling on deaf ears. Generally, in the industry, what used to be just movie studios are often now worldwide media conglomerates that own many businesses and have had their fingers in many pies, from theme parks and video companies to toy companies and T-shirt companies. Many corporate wheels need to be greased. Sometimes, generally speaking, the tail starts to wag the dog, and priority is given to merchandising, toys, and Happy Meals over great scripts and great filmmaking. If filmmakers are told that a movie must have multiple heroes and multiple villains with two costumes and two vehicles each, then the danger becomes making two-hour infomercials for toys rather than great films. But if an inspired filmmaker has a respectful vision for a particular comic book character and knows how to execute that vision, then there is the chance for something special... something amazing... to occur. Too often, for reasons which may be limited to ego, people want to put their own stamp on a comic book movie and make wholesale changes in the character and premise just for the sake of change. To ignore ten years or twenty-five years or fifty years of history and mythology to create something out of a whole new cloth can be akin to peeing on the heads of every fan who ever was. In this day and age, it's not the way to make these translations from one visual medium to another work successfully and be embraced by the fans and public alike on a global basis. As a producer, I've probably spent more time over the decades trying to stop certain movies from being made in a certain way than trying to just make them and make them the right way.

When I started in this business in 1976, studio production execs all seemed to have extensive backgrounds in literature and English and mythology and the literary classics and the craft involved in screenwriting. Today, more and more, I'm stumbling across very young execs whose qualifications for the jobs appear to be that either they have watched tons of movies and TV or they are some important Hollywood person's dentist's son. The trouble then becomes exacerbated when they spend all their time looking over their shoulders, afraid of who might be coming up behind them to take their jobs, rather than looking forward and being daring or different or innovative in backing new projects from creative filmmakers. After so many decades in the business, I've found that small group of forward lookers and thinkers at the major studios who are so great to work with, and I desperately try to avoid the others.

In the early 1990s, after having produced a movie based on my favorite comic book of all time, *Batman,* I wanted to make a film based on my favorite syndicated newspaper comic strip ever, *Terry and the Pirates,* created by the immortal Milton Caniff, the dean of comic artists who brought cinematic storytelling techniques to the comic strips like no one had before. His work in comics is the equivalent to Orson Welles's work in movies. *Terry and the Pirates* would go on to inspire such creations (either "heavily influenced" by *Terry* or "ripping off" *Terry,* as such varied from time to time) as the Luke Skywalker / Han Solo relationship in *Star Wars,* the *Indiana Jones* films, *Tin Tin,* and *Jonny Quest.* But I knew if we brought back *Terry* as originally done by Caniff, today's audiences would erroneously believe we were ripping off all those other later projects rather than vice versa. I needed to find a way to make it contemporary. Modern-day piracy was beginning to make new headlines. No longer was it exclusively high-seas piracy but also high-tech piracy. I convinced the owners of *Terry,* Tribune Media Services of Chicago, to bring the comic strip back to newspapers in America and around the world. For a period of a year, I would write it seven days a week and reintroduce the characters in a modern-day setting. There would be four story arcs in that year, which would rebuild Terry's great rogues' gallery of supervillains, headed by the most famous supervillainess in the history of comics and who influenced the creation of Catwoman, the Dragon Lady.

But reviving a dramatic comic strip in an era of shrinking panels squeezed and squished onto the comic strip pages of today's shrinking newspapers posed a nearly insurmountable challenge. If we were going to convince newspapers to pick us up, we had to deliver artwork equivalent to the old masters of Caniff and Alex Raymond of *Flash Gordon* fame. At that time, the most famous fantasy painters of all were the Brothers Hildebrandt. Not only did twin brothers Greg and Tim paint the original *Star Wars* movie poster for George Lucas but they also drew nearly all the great Tolkien *Lord of the Rings* art seen since the '70s, which subsequently would influence the look of the popular trilogy of movies based on the Tolkien works. More recently, they had painted an entire set of definitive upscale Marvel trading cards, and here I was asking them to lay down their paint brushes and do pencil, ink, and hand coloring of what would turn out to be fifty-three weeks of comic strips. The agent who deftly handled their careers was Jean Scrocco, whose reputation in the publishing industry was renowned as a smart and savvy businessperson who maximized every deal and opportunity for her clients. Jean also proved to be a creative force in her own right. She said that because this was nothing less than *Terry and the Pirates*, she would ask the boys if it was a massive undertaking they wanted to leap into. As humongous *Terry and the Pirates* fans and collectors and devotees of Caniff, they couldn't say no. As two boys growing up in the Midwest during the 1940s, they would often be found with red towels tied to their necks while jumping off the roof of their, thankfully, one-story house, while playing "Superman." In the '90s, for those fifty-three weeks, I would be lucky enough on a daily basis to witness Greg and Tim's creative process from conception to finished art as we explored the world of *Terry and the Pirates*. Even now when I look back at each panel of art, somewhere in there I see two little boys draped in red towels, holding a comic strip in each hand and leaping off the roof of their home . . . and into comic art history.

Ben and I then plotted and planned on converting this new work into a weekly syndicated television series with a commitment from a TV stations group to kick us off. We made a whirlwind trip to Europe to make deals with foreign television networks for co-financing of the series. The following will give you a picture of the so-called glamorous life of a producer (keep in mind that I don't sleep on airplanes and always use my time on flights to write or just work):

Day 1—Fly JFK to London. Arrive 6:00 a.m. Shower and have breakfast at the British Airways airport club. Head to a meeting with the head of the BBC at 9:00 a.m. Meetings all day. Business dinner that night. Hotel by midnight. Day 2—6:30 a.m. flight to Paris. Morning meeting with the heads of French network, M6, followed by lunch with them. Afternoon meeting with the head of TF-1, followed by dinner that night with him and his wife. Midnight flight to Munich, Germany. Day 3—Up at 6:30 a.m. Breakfast meeting with one TV group. Lunch and afternoon meeting with big German network RTL's execs. Dinner meeting with the head of RTL and his wife. Check into hotel at midnight. Day 4—Wake up at 3:30 a.m. to make an early morning flight to Rome. Lunch meeting with execs from Italian network RAI. Dinner with our closest ally at RAI. Hotel at midnight. Day 5—Up at 5 a.m. to make flight from Rome back to New York. Exhausted and sleep-deprived, while checking in, am informed that the airline overbooked first class and all it had left was a middle seat in coach. Not a happy camper, I raised quite a ruckus. The airline's highest-ranking person apologized and offered me what would be a useless coupon, but he told me if I accepted, the captain on board would make a special accommodation for me, but he could not say what. Having no real choice since I was desperate to go home, I accepted.

Uncomfortably squeezed into my middle seat, once we were at cruising level, the flight attendant came to me and said the captain would like to see me. This was also before September 11 and would be impossible to duplicate today. She ushered me into the cockpit of this quite massive 747 where the heavily accented pilot said to me, "Monsieur Michael, I understand our airline has caused you some problems today, no?" "Yes," I replied courteously. The captain pointed to a jump seat behind him and a copilot. "Why not sit there and ride with us for a while and enjoy the view from here?" I thanked him profusely and then spent the next two hours experiencing the cockpit of a 747. It was exciting, fun, and all my exhaustion evaporated amid yet another experience of a lifetime! To top it off, our meetings throughout Europe had borne fruit and would be enough financial commitment to sufficiently supplement the US/Canada domestic deal we had been offered by the US TV group. But by the time Ben and I returned home triumphantly, at the very last second, the US TV exec from whom we had a deal commitment suddenly and without explanation threw his efforts into another show for reasons that remain fuzzy if not suspect to this day, depriving *Terry* of its slot and dooming our television series.

"Oh, Hollywood, where is thy sting?" Once more, in my butt.

We needed a quick domestic replacement partner. Time was of the essence. I had a great pitch for *Terry and the Pirates* and felt confident when I went in to pitch my new, modern-day version of the classic comic strip to a cable network. I had dealt with these execs before, but now there had been a complete housecleaning, and everyone I knew there was gone with the wind. All the new people had just come in, and I was slated to meet with the woman who would be overseeing development for prime-time TV series. It was like going to my family home and finding that my parents and brother had moved out and strange new people were now living there. You adapt. No choice. I sat down in the waiting room, and soon a young person in a white T-shirt and jeans came out and asked, "Are you Michael?" I said I was, and she led me back to the office of the woman I was to meet. She showed me in, but no one else was in the room. She then went around behind the desk, sat down, and asked me what I was pitching her that day. Averting panic, not because of her gender but because of her young age, I reasoned that this young lady was not much older than my daughter and that my daughter was someone I could pitch to. So I launched into it with enthusiasm and passion, eventually getting to the backstory of the greatest villainess in the history of comic strips, the Dragon Lady.

I set the scene: It's the end of the Vietnam War and the fall of Saigon. As the Viet Cong descend into the city, the people flee in panic to the fence surrounding the American embassy. Flames dance everywhere. Smoke billows as the soldiers keep the people at bay and US personnel are evacuated by helicopters on the roof. A Vietnamese couple is being crushed to death at the fence by the crazed and fearful crowd. The man holds his baby girl up over his head, trying to hand her to the hardened soldier stationed above him with a gun pointed at the mass of people. At the last moment, the soldier takes the baby in his arms as the parents are crushed, and he and the child are evacuated in the last chopper lifting off from the burning embassy roof.

When I finished telling that story, the exec in the T-shirt and jeans looked at me with eyes wide open. "Wow!" she said. "That was awesome! Did you make all that up?" she inquired. I explained that I had made up the part about the baby girl and her parents, but the rest was exactly as the fall of Saigon had unfolded. She stared at me wide-eyed with a friendly but frozen smile on her face. Something had not registered.

"Have you ever seen the footage or the stills of the fall of Saigon and the choppers taking off from the roof of the US embassy?" I asked her. She shook her head gently so as not to disrupt that smile. "Are you familiar with the fall of Saigon?" I responded with a smile all my own. Again, she shook her head no, smile intact. In desperation, I went with the million-dollar question, "Have you ever heard of the Vietnam War?"

Without missing a beat, she shook her head no and told me proudly, "I don't read newspapers."

I was devastated. I concluded that I had become too old for this business. I was distraught that this is the pit into which the industry had descended. As someone who in high school and college had demonstrated and protested for women's rights, I was furious that someone had installed this young lady into this position clearly without qualifications under circumstances that I felt were a slap in the face to women in this profession and to women generally. It took weeks for me to bounce back from this incident and convince myself that it was an aberration and not the rule. But it also opened my eyes to the rampant ageism flourishing in such a liberal industry. Seemingly beginning the day I turned fifty, at any and every meeting I've been to in Hollywood, I've been either the oldest or second oldest person in the room. Most of the people I knew who started out in this industry with me in the 1970s are across-the-board long gone—drummed out. And when the head of a major studio recently informed me that age twenty-five represented the older portion of the audience they were trying to reach in movie theaters, it all crystallized and made Hollywood sense—and dollars. But I digress...

It's time to take out my scorecard and look at some other career wins and losses...

WIN: I couldn't wait for Parents' Back-to-School night at Montclair Kimberly Academy so I could congratulate my son, David's, fifth-grade computer teacher on a job well done. I loved how into her computer game David was. He was so entertained playing it that he didn't even realize how well it was teaching him geography and research skills. She explained to me that it wasn't her creation, but that *Where in the World Is Carmen Sandiego?* was the most popular computer game for kids. I begged her for information. Who makes this game? Where are they located? Two days later, Ben and I were en route to San Francisco to meet with Broderbund to acquire the rights. With an agreed-to carve-out for the PBS quiz show, for two years, we were shunned by TV networks and cable companies when they heard we were pitching a kid's show that in animation would be educational. It didn't matter when I tried explaining that the kids would be so entertained, they wouldn't even realize they were being educated. They did everything just short of holding crucifixes out in front of us when we walked into their offices. We felt like unwanted vampires . . . until the Feds started tightening the screws on them all regarding educational value in their children's programming requirements. Suddenly, those slamming doors started to open. Not only did we get great ratings and have a sensational five-year run with *Carmen Sandiego* on television but we also won the Emmy Award.

It was an amazing night. My mom had passed away, but my dad took root at the house with David and Sarah and their friends to watch the Emmy Awards on TV that evening. With good luck hugs and kisses from the family before the limo whisked Nancy and me off to New York, I computed our chances. Not only were we up against Disney shows and Nickelodeon shows, but ironically, we were also up against the Batman cartoon show, a previous winner in its own right, and deservedly so. The brilliant animation work of Bruce Timm, Eric Radomski, writers Paul Dini and Alan Burnett, and so many other talented people, crowned by the voice casting and direction of the queen of animation, Andrea Romano, and the now-legendary voices of Kevin Conroy as Bruce Wayne and Mark Hamill as The Joker, created some of the best Batman stories and character arcs ever.

The moment they announced we won is frozen in time in my brain and heart. Ben and I walked up on stage with Andy Heyward, Mike Maliani, and Robby London from DIC animation studio and received our golden naked ladies. The Emmy Award is heavy enough to hold up an entire line of books on my bookshelf. I now must try to win one more to complete the world's finest bookends. My dad and my kids went nuts at home, reportedly falling off of the couch in the process. I couldn't wait to get offstage and call them. While still onstage, I lifted the statue and looked up and showed it to my mom, assuming that wherever she was, she was not missing this moment. We've won some great and cool awards over the years: an Annie Award, the top of the heap for animation; the Peoples' Choice Award; the Independent Spirit Award; two Oscars for acting; and some Golden Globes . . . but this one meant the most. We actually achieved recognition from the television industry for a network kid's show that was educational! Apparently, *nothing* is impossible!

WIN! WIN! LOSE: There was a second pitch I needed to do regarding *Where in the World Is Carmen Sandiego?* I had envisioned making a live-action big blockbuster movie out of the IP. As I had previously done with *Monopoly,* I worked for months planning the story; the act breaks; the characters and their arcs; the tone; the humor; and a corresponding writers list, directors list, and actors list. At that time, one of Hollywood's top actresses was Demi Moore. She and her development execs jumped on it and with that package, I pitched it to Chris Meledandri at 20th Century Fox. The world at large knows Chris best as one of the kings of Hollywood animation, producing *Despicable Me, Minions, Ice Age, The Secret Life of Pets,* and *Sing* (which starred my favorite singer/songwriter, Tori Kelly—what a voice!). But back then, I knew Chris as perhaps the smartest, savviest production vice president of all the major studios. I had no doubt Chris would be prepared for my pitch, and I prepared as if I was going in to defend my thesis at my doctoral orals. Good thing I did. This pitch was the polar opposite of my *Monopoly* pitch. Chris allowed me to tell my story but at appropriate moments pummeled me with piercing questions testing the details of the story, the actions and reactions of the characters, and it was relentless. Parry-thrust-parry-thrust! I felt as if I was in one of those cerebral duels . . . the kind Sherlock Holmes and Professor Moriarty used to have. I was on the edge of my chair, leaning into this challenge, absorbing every literary probe and nuanced question Chris led with. By the time this . . . not a pitch . . . this match . . . ended some two hours later, I had pretty well soaked through my shirt, and I think Chris may well have done the same. It was a Hollywood producer's version of going fifteen rounds with Muhammed Ali in his prime. It was the most exhilarating . . . the best pitch experience of my career! The pitch worked! Chris and 20th Century Fox were in, and then a funny thing happened. Not "funny" in the true sense of the word, but "Hollywood" type of funny business. In the process of development, Demi Moore dropped out and Sandra Bullock came in. On the heels of her hit *Miss Congeniality,* she seemed like a good box-office choice. And then the day came when she dropped out, Fox dropped out, Disney came in through the Hollywood abandonment process, and Jennifer Lopez came in. Our rights in the IP and our attachment to the project moved with it and we started almost from scratch. I met J-Lo once, as I took a number of meetings with her business partner and her staff. And then Disney faded and the project sat in that limbo we who love comic books know as the "Phantom Zone." Shakespeare's Hamlet merely thought, "Something's rotten in the state of Denmark." I knew better. Once more, something was rotten in the state of mind called "Hollywood." *Fade out.*

WIN. LOSE: When you talk about Hollywood producers with talent, brains, vision, plus honor and integrity, one of the people dominating that conversation is Alan Riche. When he was a studio exec, he went to bat for us and was a pillar of support. When he was a producer, he summoned me to his new chamber and explained that he was accessing a few comic book properties and wanted my input. One was *Magnus, Robot Fighter,* a favorite of mine as a kid due primarily to the incredible artwork by creator Russ Manning, who would go on to fame for his work on *Tarzan.* I was interested, but when he mentioned the other, *Green Lantern,* I was captivated. Alan appreciated my ten-year struggle to bring a dark and serious Batman to life in the movies and asked if I saw another "out-of-the-box" approach to Green Lantern. But first, he wanted to make sure I was a true Green Lantern fanboy. When I was done reciting Green Lantern's oath, and even the oath of the original 1940s Green Lantern, he was convinced. Could I come up with a pitch like I had done for Batman . . . more grounded than the old comic book fare? My Bat-partner Ben smiled and sat back in his chair, looked at Alan, and simply said, "Watch this . . ."

I had an idea . . . a different vision for what Green Lantern could be on film. First, I explained to Alan that the original GL was Alan Scott, whose magic lamp gave him great powers and a vulnerability to anything made of wood. I revealed that when initially conceived by Batman's cocreator, Bill Finger, and artist Mart Nodell, his name was to be Alan Ladd, because Green Lantern in the 1940s was to be a modern-day version of Aladdin and

THE GREEN LANTERN
OUT IN THE GREAT WEST, A TRAIN MAKES A TEST CROSSING OVER A NEWLY CONSTRUCTED TRESTLE BRIDGE...
BY MART DELLON AND BILL FINGER
IN THE CAB IS ALAN SCOTT, YOUNG ENGINEER IN CHARGE OF CONSTRUCTION...
I TELL YOU SCOTT, I'M WORRIED. DEKKER ISN'T ONE TO TAKE IT LYING DOWN. HE'LL TRY SOMETHING... HE'S DANGEROUS!
NONSENSE! JUST BECAUSE MY COMPANY'S BID TO BUILD THIS BRIDGE WAS CHOSEN BY THE GOVERNMENT INSTEAD OF DEKKER'S IS NO REASON FOR REVENGE! HE WON'T TRY ANYTHING!
SUDDENLY... A DEAFENING BLAST, AND THE TRAIN HURTLES TO CERTAIN DE-STRUCTION BELOW!
FROM THE WRECK RISES A STAGGERING FIGURE... ALAN SCOTT!
DEAD!..ALL DEAD!...YET BY SOME STRANGE SORT OF MIRACLE I'M STILL ALIVE!
THIS LANTERN...I'M STILL HOLDING ONTO IT!... WHAT A QUEER LIGHT! FUNNY, I SUDDENLY FEEL DIZZY ..GOING TO FAINT...
THE EERIE GREEN LIGHT SEEMS TO SWELL IN RADIANCE ... TO FLAME WITH INCREASED INTENSITY!
FROM WITHIN THE AURA OF THE GREEN FLAME COMES A VOICE... AN AGELESS, TONELESS VOICE, THAT PENETRATES INTO SCOTT'S SUB-CONSCIOUSNESS....
"I AM THE GREEN FLAME OF LIFE! LISTEN, CHOSEN ONE, AND HEAR THE TALE OF THE GREEN LANTERN!"

his magic lamp. But they decided last minute to change the name, because in one of those classic cosmic coincidences, there was a fast-rising actor in Hollywood whose name was actually "Alan Ladd." (Let's take this cosmic coincidence one step further! In 1949, DC Comics, publisher of *Green Lantern*, would premiere a comic book, *The Adventures of Alan Ladd*, upon entering into a contract with the star. What goes around, comes around!)

That version of Green Lantern eventually faded away along with most superheroes in the years after World War II. He was pushed out of his own comic books by Johnny Thunder, a western hero, and Rex the Wonder Dog. Oh, the ignominy! But that meant as the new Silver Age of Comics began, DC was able to introduce an all-new version of Green Lantern, grounded in science fiction rather than magic. And that guy was test pilot Hal Jordan. This version of Green Lantern, whose weakness was anything colored yellow, was even more successful than the original. But the day finally came in 1994 when DC went with a younger version of Green Lantern as Kyle Rayner took on the mantle.

So with that as background, I started spewing a new idea. A different approach to a superhero movie would be to make it a family saga. In the Scott family, we would focus on three generations: Alan Scott, who received his Power Ring when he was in his prime in the 1940s; his son, Hal Jordan Scott, to whom Alan passes the Power Ring as he becomes the GL of the 1960s and '70s; and the grandson, rebellious Kyle Rayner Scott, who marches to the beat of his own drum to the consternation of his father and grandfather. Alan was intrigued. He egged me on. "In brightest day . . ."

I said we'd open the movie in 1947 with the infamous Roswell incident in which a supposed flying saucer crashed in Arizona, killing the alien inside. Alan Scott is the pilot who witnesses this and is the first one on the scene. At this moment, we use the origin of the Silver Age GL and make that alien Abin Sur, who bequeaths his incredible Power Ring to this heroic military man who desperately tries to save him. In Act I, we see the debut of the original Green Lantern whose career is devoted to understanding and learning about what this Power Ring is and what it can and can't do. It is all very difficult trial and error, resulting in as many failures as successes in his mission to be the kind of force of good Abin Sur, apparently a galactic policeman of some sort, charged him with before his demise. At the end of Act 1, circa 1967, Alan passes the Power Ring to his son, Hal. Hal's version of Green Lantern has him driving across America in the 1960's Age of Aquarius with Carol Ferris, his former boss and the woman who becomes his love interest, as he devotes his power not against global bad guys but in service of his fellow man, one individual or community at a time. One of those people is an African American man named John Stewart, who joins the journey and helps Hal finally discover the secret of the Power Ring.

The secret of the Power Ring is all so simple. It's not about "ordering" it to perform a task. It is instead intrinsically tied to the very psyche of the one who wears it. It is a physical manifestation of the ring bearer's willpower and, more specifically, his belief in him-

LEFT: From "Aladdin" to "Alan Ladd" to "Alan Scott" to "Green Lantern."

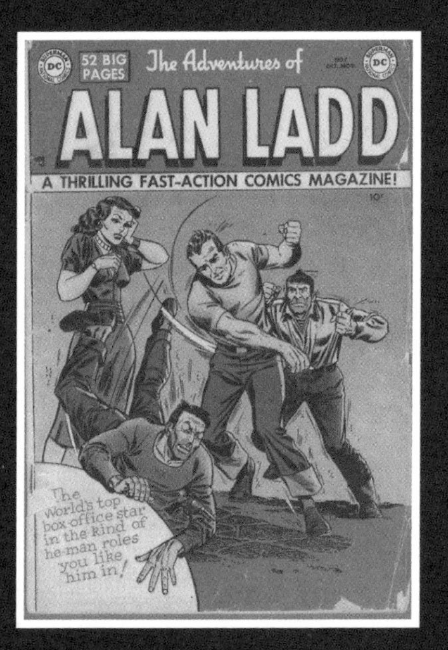
52 BIG PAGES
The Adventures of
ALAN LADD
A THRILLING FAST-ACTION COMICS MAGAZINE!
10¢
The World's top box-office star in the kind of he-man roles you like him in!

self. If he fully believes in himself and what he can accomplish or achieve, he is all powerful and there is nothing he can't do. But . . . the very moment the ring bearer begins to have the slightest self-doubt, he begins to fail; ultimately, as that self-doubt grows, the ring shuts down completely. In other words, in my iteration of Green Lantern, his weakness . . . his vulnerability . . . is not wood or the color yellow. His one great weakness is himself!

Alan and Ben loved that! That's when I added the kicker. "No superhero costumes or masks. Not necessary. Counter to what they are trying to do. They are superheroes in plain clothes."

There was hesitation in the room. So . . . "Let me add that at the end of Act III, Hal and Carol have a baby they name Kyle, and we show an after-credits sequence twenty years later as Hal passes on the ring to a rebellious Kyle with his own new ideas and the first thing he does as the ring bearer is to make the famed Green Lantern costume appear on his body. Smash cut to closing credits."

Alan asked me to write up a treatment, which I gladly did. Any chance to work in partnership with Alan would en-Riche my life in Hollywood.

With no need for details, Hollywood struck Alan like it struck me often enough . . . and every producer often enough . . . and instead of the Green Lantern movie we were exploring to make, the world eventually got someone else's Green Lantern movie. "In blackest night . . ."

WIN-LOSE: I set up *Doc Savage* with Original Films and Sony. Attached was the true Doc fan and writer/director extraordinaire, Shane Black, and the best actor for Doc, Dwayne "The Rock" Johnson. Couldn't miss! It missed. Word from on high was that the guys could never get their schedules in synch. Time ran out. Will Doc resurface on TV instead? Who knows?

The Shadow knows! I had the project set up at a major studio in partnership with Sam Raimi, one of the leading Shadow fans as a kid growing up near Ann Arbor, Michigan. With me being one of the writers of *The Shadow* over the last forty years, from DC Comics's mid-1970s run to the Dynamite Comics era of the 2000s, I felt our chances were great to actually make this movie, the film story being more closely aligned with the pulp magazine Shadow tales of the 1930s and '40s in a hybrid with the DC Comics versions. We also all agreed that the Shadow's chief adversary, Shiwan Khan, would not be the villain of the first movie. We found richness, however, in another Shadow villain perhaps more in tune with modern-day sensibilities: Benedict Stark, alias Mr. Remorse, alias the Prince of Evil. As revealed in the prior chapter of this book, that's when we heard from the studio that "period pieces don't sell." So you see, the silent rule in Hollywood is that certain genres and types of films don't work. Period. End of story. Until one works. Then Hollywood does what it may be best at, saturating the marketplace and ultimately killing the goose that laid the golden egg.

LEFT: Actor Alan Ladd gets his own DC comic book title without having to become Green Lantern.

LOSE: The pitch was scheduled for David Stern, commissioner of the National Basketball Association (NBA), and a host of his vice presidents. Thanks to an intro by one of basketball's all-time greats, Ernie Grunfeld, and his wife, Nancy, I was proposing something different . . . a cartoon series I created to be produced in association with the NBA as a brand-new universe of basketball-powered superheroes who would band together to defend the world as "the National Battalion of All-Stars." David summoned his litany of vice presidents into his large office and had me pitch them the show. Declaring it to be a high priority to be presented to one of the networks at an NBA pitch meeting in LA on November 13, David asked everyone in the jam-packed room if that date was clear. Everyone nodded . . . except I raised my hand. I spotted Ben across the room holding his hand over his eyes. He knew me well. He knew what was coming.

"Uh, David," I apologized, "that won't work for me. November 13 is my wife, Nancy's, fortieth birthday, and if I want to be welcomed at her forty-first birthday, also, I better be here at home for her fortieth."

There was absolute silence in that room. Except from the one lady present, who inadvertently let loose with a huge sigh. The silence seemed to last an awfully long time.

Finally, David asked, "Well . . . what about the afternoon of November 14?"

I quickly assured him I could be in LA by lunchtime that day. Everyone seemed happy, and Ben seemed like he had just dodged a major bullet.

Some months later, David invited Ben and me to be his guests at the NBA All-Star Weekend in Salt Lake City, Utah. Amid nonstop parties and one fun basketball event after another, we arrived at the All-Star Game and found our seats in the luxury box with the heads of Nickelodeon and the USA Network. Before halftime, David Stern popped in to greet us all. I introduced him to Nancy, and he smiled and said to her, "I've been wanting to meet the woman who was able to stop a big meeting in LA from happening!" I couldn't believe he remembered that moment! Unfortunately, when my animated project's best advocate within the NBA, Vice President Jon Miller, left to become head of Nickelodeon Europe (before becoming chairman of AOL), the animation initiative lost steam and petered out. But as it turned out, *two* of the veeps at the NBA I had been working closely with wound up becoming the president of Marvel Comics—the deft marketing maven, David Schreff, and the king of the NBA trading cards programs, Bill Jemas. (Told ya ours is a small business.)

WIN: If my son, David, was responsible for me and Ben rushing out to secure the rights to the computer game *Where in the World Is Carmen Sandiego?*, then it was Nancy who was responsible for me and Ben pursuing the rights to the best seller by author Robin Cook, *Harmful Intent.* Nancy insisted I read it after she bought it and couldn't put it down. It was his best medical thriller since *Coma.* I knew all the studios had passed on it because at that moment in time, medical thrillers weren't "hot" and they were all looking for the next *Batman* or the next *Lethal Weapon.* But I felt in my gut that the timing was perfect for another great medical thriller. If the studios weren't a potential buyer, I was sure a television network would be. But our first challenge was to convince Robin Cook we were the guys who could get this made. We had a great meeting with him in which I put all my cards on the table creatively. I had heard he did not have particularly positive experiences with the studios on some of their translations to the big screen of his previous best sellers, so I laid out exactly what parts of his novel I would cut and why in adapting it to a two-hour movie. He agreed with all my creative choices and indicated he was prepared to make the rights deal with us. That's when Ben worked his magic. Ben made it clear that we were not a studio, but rather just two independent producers. We couldn't pay anything like what a studio could pay. In the end, we had our deal.

I prepared a detailed pitch designed to knock the socks off our first choice, CBS. To the head of M.O.W.'s (movies of the week) and miniseries, I began with my opening salvo: "The best seller *Harmful Intent* is Robin Cook's best medical thriller since *Coma*, and it's been far too long since there's been a great medical thriller movie."

The high-level CBS exec cut me off enthusiastically. "You're so right!" he said. "Let's do this! I'll have our business affairs person call you later today to get the deal done and let's just do it!" he declared.

In a flashback to my pitch meeting with Brandon Tartikoff on *Monopoly*, the masochist inside me again reared its head. I felt cheated. The meeting was over, and I never got to do my whole elaborate pitch! Ben said, "Don't press your luck!" and took me down the street to buy me a corned beef sandwich and a chocolate malt at Cantor's Deli, supposedly to celebrate, but more likely in an attempt to keep me from going back and demanding a full pitch.

Meanwhile, back at *Harmful Intent*, we needed a deficit financier to coproduce this film with us. A deficit financier would put up any additional production funding we'd need above and beyond what we got from CBS. Ben called up one of his buddies from his MGM days, Norman Rosemont, who used to be the president of Lerner and Lowe when MGM was making its superb, classic musicals. Norman and Ben negotiated many a deal together and had a fantastic rapport and mutual respect for each other. Norman was now in business with his son, David. David and I bonded as we listened to some great, historic Hollywood stories traded between our elders. *Harmful Intent* would turn out to be a great financial success for CBS and us and be an enjoyable experience working with the Rosemonts from start to finish. Grandpa Sam would call them "mensches." And he would be right.

The art of the Pitch is one of the most crucial *P*s to producing. It means being able to target an IP that in many cases can potentially play the globe and be commercial and marketable. Then comes the passion and enthusiasm linked to a producer's ability for storytelling. Packaging, often optional, becomes the cherry on top of the project.

CHAPTER SEVEN

The PACKAGING

A producer must have relationships and genuine friendships with agents, for they are the gateway to the talent pool. This is why a producer makes up lists of potential talent to consider attaching to a project. There are writers lists, directors lists, and actors lists as producers and their staffs seek out everyone's litany of credits and box-office results domestically and globally, picture by picture, securing input from their studios or other financing sources as well as from the talent agencies themselves. In recent times, we consider their social media status, such as number of followers or hits or likes.

Teamwork makes the dream work.

—BATMAN AND THE OUTSIDERS

Packaging often is the key to getting your movie made in Hollywood. Regarding streaming/TV, there is so much clutter in the global marketplace that the chances for breakout success increasingly depend on basing a project on a recognizable brand or having a significant star actor or actress attached. Over the decades, I've attached amazing talent and failed to attract amazing talent. In Major League Baseball, if you hit one out of every three chances at bat, you're considered a superstar. In my career, I've done slightly better than that vis-à-vis talent acquisitions. Here is my BATting average (pun definitely intended!):

Let's start with Nickelodeon. I was friendly with a bunch of the top Nick execs in the 1980s and '90s. We were working with their feature-film division on a live-action film based on Jim Krueger's comic book *Foot Soldiers*, which became the first movie Nickelodeon agreed to allow a PG-13 rating instead of PG. That was a huge accomplishment. But as *Foot Soldiers* began wallowing in development hell, I had lunch with some Nick TV execs. They informed me they were looking for kid/family game shows. The first one I proposed they loved—*My Dad Can Beat Your Dad*! This was a fun competition among fathers and sons. Half physical and half cerebral, the game show I invented was right on target for their needs. But over the course of the couple of years we attempted to move it out of development and into production, things began to cloud the picture. Someone at Nick TV said that some kids don't have fathers and the title needed to be changed to reflect that. Then, another exec said we couldn't be sexist and exclude girls. Someone else quickly added, "And their moms!" Another exec felt badly for kids whose moms may have lost their husbands or been divorced; as single moms, they may have significant others who were like fathers to their kids. Someone else said something about some kids of gay marriages have two mothers and no fathers or have two fathers, and the show's title must be inclusive and state that. In principle, I understood and agreed with their vision. Everyone then became baffled about a title for the show. In theory, the title went from *My Dad Can Beat Your Dad* to *My Dad, Mom, Mom's or Dad's Significant Others, Both My Dads, and Both My Moms Can Beat Your Dad, Mom, Mom's or Dad's Significant Others, Both Your Dads, and Both Your Moms*! They turned it down because it didn't take into consideration kids without dads at all. At least that's the way I recall it so many years later. Maybe I exaggerate, but in the end, the project died. I probably killed it before they did. I saw my weakness in that situation as being devoid of a star to carry the show. I learned that lesson the hard way and vowed not to make the same mistake on my next game show adventure. And that came about quickly!

My kids were in the thick of prepping for their SATs or PSATs, and I saw other parents panicking and enrolling their young'uns in this review class or that review class, all guaranteeing success (that too often didn't come). I realized that students all over North America were taking these tests, and it was a big deal to most of them and their families. It was a bit of a mania. So I went directly to the source. In a feat that hadn't ever been done and maybe never will again, I met with the head honchos of the SATs in New York. I laid out my vision to them of training a generation of students to understand the types of questions used on SATs, what each was designed to extract from each test taker, with an opportunity to improve scores. They loved the concept of the show and believed it was time for them to do something bold and out of the box. The last thing they needed at this meeting before they rendered a decision was the name of this quiz show for teens. I hadn't given it much thought, concentrating instead on the concept and format. Where it came from so spontaneously, I'm not sure. But I knew it was dead accurate as I replied, "SATeasers"! They were more excited by the title than me. Deal done! Halfway to paradise! Now, I had to sell a network or cable company. The key? Packaging! I called my comrade Chip Cronkite, who was one of my editors on the miniseries I produced for PBS, *Three Sovereigns for Sarah*, and was my roommate for close to six months during prep and production when we shared a stately old house in Salem. Turned out that Chip had a dad who was merely the long-running journalist and anchorman for CBS News and was voted "the most trusted man in America." Walter Cronkite was an icon and on a level that is unreachable by anyone on television news in the most recent generation or two. He stood for integrity, truth, facts, and honor. Chip loved *SATeasers* and brought it to his dad. Walter was in! Combining the brands of the College Board/SATs with Walter Cronkite quickly attracted the money we needed to shoot a pilot. As a parent and former taker of the SATs and the PSATs, I knew that this show would be embraced by teens, preteens, and their parents. We made learning and SAT prep fun and effective. The pilot turned out fabulously, and so we set up appointments with all the biggest TV outlets from the networks to the most appropriate cable companies and syndicators . . . just at the moment that the management of the SATs changed. The new execs were not the bold envelope-pushers we had been dealing with and ended our rights to the brand. This time, it was not another "Hooray for Hollywood!" It was "Hooray for New York, New York, a development hell of a town." If the Bronx was up and the Battery down, I was as down as the Battery.

Another New York–based producer's calamity was worth every bit of time and effort we poured into a project, because it allowed me and my pal Robin Steele, of Wildbrain Animation, to spend the better part of an afternoon in the Big Apple with David Bowie. Our goal? We wanted to turn his incredible album *Ziggy Stardust and the Spiders from Mars* into an animated feature. We spent hours with David, who was there with his business/legal team. It was hours of nirvana. We had in-depth conversations about his philosophies, which turned out to be so in line with our own thinking concerning the meaning and themes of his work. The back and forth we shared was energizing as we explained how we wanted to approach that work in animation. The barrier was that David had an offer on the table to turn *Ziggy Stardust* into a Broadway musical. Robin and I played devil's advocate, talking about how long a Broadway musical remains in development; how so few shows ultimately are actually produced; and then, if produced, the high percentage that fail and close early. Ah, but a computer-animated, 3D movie would be lasting, and David would creatively oversee it with us and be an integral part of the process. His entourage kept pushing the Broadway offer. It was real and on the table. We could make a substantial offer but not like the upfront money our competitors were offering. We hung our hat on being in creative synch with David and our heartfelt position that animation was the best way to go. We believed that a feature film would stand the test of time and not just shrivel and die. Robin and I walked out of there that day as if we just had an audience with the pope. We were so excited by what had just occurred and the possibilities looming ahead. We felt great that in our pitch, we had an answer for everything David brought up or threw at us. The rest of the day—no, the rest of the week—I was on an extraordinary natural high. One week later, David thanked us profusely and said he'd loved our time together and our creative vision, but the businesspeople wanted him to go with the Broadway play. We were crushed. As you already know so many years later, there is no *Ziggy Stardust* 3D-animated feature. And there is and never was a Broadway play. In the words of Queen, "Another one bites the dust"!

I did some research. No one had ever done a true TV series based on the Secret Service, and I quickly saw there was a treasure trove of stories to be mined if they would open up their files and cooperate in the making of a quality show. In addition, it would be a packaging coup to have an official series backed by the Secret Service. I approached them and had the opportunity of working with one of the Secret Service's finest in developing enough material to pitch and sell the series. For a while, I commuted every week to Washington, DC, on the fantabulous Acela train from New York, which puts first-class airline service to shame. I *love* trains . . . always have since my dad bought Paul and me one of the most extensive Lionel train sets ever. Each year around Chanukkah/Christmastime, we'd pull them out of the basement and rebuild an entire city for the train to run through. It was fascinating and as exciting as could be for two young boys. Make that three, including my dad. Paul still has them. The culmination of my lifelong love of trains came after *Batman Begins*, when I took Nancy, David, and Sarah, and we set out from London on the Orient Express to Paris, then across Germany and Slovakia to Vienna, Prague, and Budapest. I became the first one in my family to return to Hungary, ninety-nine years after my grandparents left. It was overwhelmingly emotional as we entered the Jewish ghetto and the still-standing synagogue and graveyard the Nazis failed to destroy. I walked the very same market my Grandma Miriam did as she bought the family's meats and fruits and vegetables each day when she was a cook and servant girl. Back on the Orient Express, David and Sarah enjoyed, as much as Nancy and I did, walking into the bar car before dinner—a pianist sitting at the grand piano, everyone in tuxedos and evening gowns, no people talking the same language from cocktail table to table. From there, we'd enter the dining car for lobster, steak, and champagne as if we were all in some 1930s black-and-white Turner Classic Movies Essentials movie. We slept with the window open, feeling the wind and listening to the clatter of the train on the tracks, our car lit by the moonlight of a European countryside. It was perfect.

Oh! Where was I? Oh yeah . . . the Secret Service!

Working with them was a real learning experience, as I finally grasped how much beyond just guarding the president their duties and responsibilities extend. I have the greatest admiration and respect for the men and women of this superb organization. They took me to lunch with them one day at the Press Club to hear Oliver Stone talk. They weren't fans. They introduced me to Boris Yeltsin in front of the White House. And they invited me and my family on a VIP tour of the White House and the Executive Office Building, in the pre–September 11 days when such was still possible. The kids got to slide on the White House bowling alley, sit in the president's screening room, visit the White House florist and kitchen, and see the old Executive Building offices of Teddy Roosevelt, FDR, and then–vice president Dan Quayle. (The kids were allowed to roam his office while Nancy and I waited outside with the secretary. Sarah reported his desk was completely empty except for a puzzle on it. "A jigsaw puzzle?" I asked her. "No, Daddy," she said. "It only had seven pieces." Hmmm . . .)

The Secret Service then asked if we'd like to see the Command Security shack for the White House. Remember, this was all prior to September 11. Not only would an opportunity like this never again happen but also I'm sure the shack has been significantly updated since then. The kids were excited to see a man in there who looked and sounded like Barney Fife from *The Andy Griffith Show*. He was so happy to have visitors. He reminded me of Mel Blanc when he played the part of the sentry to Jack Benny's vault of money and had been standing guard there since the Revolutionary War, hoping for visitors with news of the outside world. The man told the kids how the radiation detection system worked and all sorts of other things that seemed right out of Indiana Jones and James Bond. I mean, just picture Barney Fife excitedly telling my children, "Over here is the radiation detection center! If anyone comes to the White House for a party on a Saturday night and had a dental X-ray the Tuesday morning before, I'll pick him up on this here *de*-vice!" The kids were enthralled, and so were we. Again, here I was in a place and time I never could have experienced but for being a producer and having such unusual opportunities . . . *if* I took advantage of them. To me, this was the big bonus, not going to fancy parties and meeting celebrities. It keeps coming back to the history major in me and the spectacular rush I get whenever I have the chance to touch history. It's called "passion." And these experiences were a hundred times richer whenever I got to share them with my children.

Just when I completed all the research and writing up of the Bible for the TV series and the preparation of all the pitch material, one of the networks announced it was doing an unauthorized Secret Service show inspired by some real stories but mostly fictionalized stuff on a low-budget basis. And to my dismay and to the chagrin of the Secret Service guys I had been working so hard with, we were beaten to the punch by something they knew was not at all the great series we had planned. We were now competitively foreclosed from pitching our official series.

Remaining in New Jersey to raise my family around my parents, cousins, aunts, and uncles certainly had its career disadvantages, but it also gave me some great opportunities to give back to my state and have some creatively wild fun in the process. As a commissioner on the New Jersey Film Commission, I learned that the then-governor had done some across-the-board budget cutting, erroneously assuming our commission was under the aegis of "the arts" when it was rather all about "economic development" and had already brought in so much motion picture and television and new media production as to give New Jersey back a 20,000 percent return on its yearly investment in the already-lean budget of the commission. Talk about both a direct financial boost to the local economy and a jobs provider! But now, the commission needed to raise funds to carry on. We needed a big event to wow and lure people to purchase high-price tickets as a contribution. I had an idea. Everyone's first reaction was that I was crazy. (Do you detect a pattern here weaving throughout my life? Maybe they're all right. If so . . . I can live with that.)

Casablanca is my favorite movie of all time. One of my biggest moviegoing thrills was seeing it on the big screen when I was in college. After having already seen it a dozen times on TV, it was like seeing it for the first time. Every actor is perfect, and nearly every line of dialogue is wonderful. In college, I started reading every book I could find about Humphrey Bogart. I cherished Woody Allen's *Play It Again, Sam*. While working at United Artists, I pestered our production guy, Lee Katz, for every detail and every story about the making of *Casablanca*, as he was the 1st AD on the set (excuse me . . . for the layman, he was the first assistant director). And then I finally read the marvelous book *Round Up the Usual Suspects* by Aljean Harmetz on the making of *Casablanca*. The final element that made my crazy idea click in my head was the local lore of Montclair, New Jersey. Over by Montclair State University (Bruce Willis's college . . . where Montclair resident Yogi Berra once gave the commencement address and advised all the graduates that in life, when they come to a fork in the road, they should take it . . .) was the Robin Hood Inn, a historic restaurant and catering hall owned by the well-known Knowles family who also owned four of the best and most critically hailed restaurants in the state—The Manor, Highlawn Pavilion, Rams Head Inn, and Pleasantdale Chateau, which, collectively, have served as the locations for more movies and TV shows (including lots of *Sopranos* episodes) than probably any other place in New Jersey. Harry Knowles entered the restaurant business after having been a pilot in World War II. Not only was he a daring flier during D-Day but he also wound up in the courtroom during the judgments at Nuremberg. With his two sons, Wade and Kurt, Harry owned the Robin Hood Inn, knowing its place in movie history. One of its nightly patrons back in the good old days was the often-imbibing songwriter from Montclair, Herman Hupfeld. It was on that very piano still in the bar area that Herman composed his most notable song, which he titled, "As Time Goes By."

That was it for me! I then wrote an entire stage play on exactly this subject that, although accurate historically, was pretty damn funny in the process. The successor to Montclair's noted Whole Theatre Company, run by resident Olympia Dukakis, was Jacqueline Knox, a founder and artistic director of 12 Miles West Theatre Company. We knew the only way we could pull this off was by packaging the right people with *Casablanca*.

Jackie pulled together a cast of forty top Broadway and Off-Broadway actors who agreed to contribute their time and talents to our fundraising efforts that would bring more movie and TV work to the state. Headlining the play would be New Jersey's own wild man, comedian, actor, and prosocial benefactor, the incomparable Joe Piscopo, who ruled *Saturday Night Live* with Eddie Murphy and was now doing Vegas and Atlantic City shows amid his regular acting stints. Joe would play the fiery Hungarian director, Michael Curtiz. The coup was my getting Robert Sacchi to fly in, not simply to play Humphrey Bogart but to *be* Humphrey Bogart! Seriously, even Woody used him in his play. Robert is an *exact* photo-double of Humphrey Bogart. It's absolutely astounding! He even sounds like him! When he arrived at the Robin Hood Inn, I did what I was dying to do. I took him over to the bar next to Hupfeld's piano, and the two of us had bourbon and sodas. Now, I *never* drink whiskey. I had never tasted bourbon before. But, by God! I was about to drink bourbon with Humphrey Bogart! That moment is frozen in time for me and is one of those memories that still gives me the chills. I was in Bogie heaven! *Casablanca* nirvana! And the good stuff hadn't even started yet! Christie's Auction House in New York loaned us for that night's festivities the actual car used in the end of the movie to drive the stars to the Nazi-held airport.

The following was the premise of the evening's big event:

The moment the guests arrived at the Robin Hood Inn, shining under the glow of huge Hollywood searchlights crisscrossing the night sky of Montclair, they would be stepping into the soundstage at Warner Bros. in 1942 and would be greeted and treated as if they were extras in the movie *Casablanca*, which was in the middle of principal photography. Every actor from Jackie's group would be in period costumes and would never break character. As couples entered, a prop person might give a woman in an evening gown a long cigarette holder while a makeup and hair person might do them over. A costumer might give the gentleman a fez to wear or change his dark suit jacket to a white dinner jacket. And the guests were not simply local Montclair folks or people from high-society New Jersey. Academy Award–winning actress and dear friend Celeste Holm attended along with her husband, noted actor Wesley Addy, and the immortal movie star, Eddie Bracken, was in attendance too. We not only invited book author Aljean Harmetz but also Murray Burnett, the coauthor of the original play *Everyone Comes to Rick's*, upon which the film *Casablanca* was based. They all regaled us with one amazing Golden Age of Hollywood movie story after another! We also invited all the sons and daughters of the stars of the movie and were honored by the presence of Ingrid Bergman's daughter, Pia Lindstrom; Claude Raines's daughter, Jessica; and others.

That night was a fanboy's blur, but one story I heard, and which I have no idea if it was true or not, was particularly memorable. One of the cast's kids heard that back in the '70s, Peter Lorre's daughter was driving home very late one night on an LA freeway when she suddenly saw a red light flashing on what was clearly an unmarked police car behind her. There were two cops in the car. They pulled her over by a deserted, dark, grassy hill. One of them got out of his car and walked over to her, requesting her driver's license and registration and telling her to step out of the car. She handed him her wallet with her license exposed, but the cop had a difficult time seeing it. He walked around to the hill side of the car to get a little light from a nearby pole and ordered her to follow him around. As he looked at her ID, the cop noticed the photo.

"Why do you have a picture of Peter Lorre in your wallet?" he wondered.

She explained that she was Peter Lorre's daughter.

"Really?" asked the cop. He stared at her for a bit, then handed her back the wallet and said, "Peter Lorre was my favorite actor." After a long pause, he commanded, "Get out of here."

She got back in her car and drove off with a wave and with no speeding ticket. As it later turned out, these two cop impersonators were collectively the notorious "Hillside Strangler" of LA, and she became one of the only people able to identify him when he was captured. True or not, ever since I heard that story, I've kept a picture of Peter Lorre in my wallet just in case!

I learned never to leave home without a photo of actor Peter Lorre in my wallet.

The festivities that night included an authentic Moroccan dinner provided by The Manor amid sets designed and built to duplicate Rick's Café Americain from the movie, as designed by Michael Anania, the award-winning production designer from the much-heralded Papermill Playhouse regional theater in Millburn, New Jersey. The culmination of the evening took place when a group of Nazis drinking beers around the Hupfeld piano (and you don't want to know how difficult it is nor the intense stares you receive when you try to buy or rent Nazi uniforms) started singing "Deutschland Uber Alles," as our spot-on actor playing Victor Lazlo in his pure white suit told our 1940s swing band to play "La Marseillaise." Play it! Robert Sacchi, as Rick, nodded his head and the band launched into the patriotic number. All three hundred paid guests slowly rose and with phonetic lyrics printed in their program books, started joining in to sing the national anthem of France and drown out the Nazis, with everyone shouting, "Viva la France!" at the end and applauding! I'm telling you . . . it was *exactly* as if we were all back in the 1940s actually filming *Casablanca*. The *Star-Ledger*, New Jersey's leading newspaper, had sent its famed theater critic, Peter Filichia, to cover the happening. In his review the next day, he called it "the theatre event of the year," which included his coverage of New York productions as well. Everybody who was there still talks about that magical night. As a *Casablanca* fan, it was fun, enriching, unique, and simply unfor-

Me heading upstairs to my Bat-Cave office, stopping next to the poster for *Doomsday*, the animated prime-time Howard Stern TV series we were all set to do until it was halted in the aftermath of September 11.

gettable. For me, it was yet another passion/fantasy come true, as if I was in possession of my very own time machine. Wow!

Mel Torme's son, Tracy, came up with a cool idea, "Doomsday," that he pitched to me as an animated prime-time TV show. It dealt with the misadventures of a totally dysfunctional family who, following some nuclear holocaust caused by some event we never learn about, set out in their RV to rediscover postapocalyptic America and find out who or what may still be alive and well in this increasingly alien landscape. I felt the best way to separate us from the thirty other shows competing for a rare prime-time slot was through the magic of packaging. My idea was to attach shock-jock Howard Stern, then at the very peak of his illustrious career as king of all media. The first time I met Howard, we quickly got into a discussion of comics, particularly DC Comics. I had heard that my old friend, former longtime DC production manager Jack Adler, was Howard's cousin. He was, indeed! Howard loved the project and signed on. We immediately got an on-air commitment for thirteen episodes via Film Roman and UPN with what at that time was a titanic budget. I was even going to get to write an episode I outlined about the family's trip to see what was left of Las Vegas. Each hotel/casino had devolved into a city-state with its own government and army utilizing the theme of each casino. Thus, Caesar's Palace had legionnaires on chariots while Excalibur had knights on armored horses. The Luxor hotel pyramid had been half-destroyed in the nuclear blast and now all its Jewish guests were being rounded up and ordered to help rebuild it. Luckily for them, just at the time of the disaster, famed *The Ten Commandments* and *Ben-Hur* actor, Charlton Heston, who was also then-president of the National Rifle Association, was in Vegas for an NRA convention and was trapped there. Now sporting a long gray beard and a tattered red-and-white shawl made from an American flag, Heston heads to The Luxor and, using his AK-47 rifle as a staff, leads the weary Jewish guests away from the pyramid and into the desert and freedom once they pass over the waters of the Hoover Dam. In the final scene, we see them pass the iconic sign "You are now leaving fabulous Las Vegas." It was sick stuff, and I loved it! Everything was a go. And then September 11 occurred and the aftermath of a nuclear disaster was no longer deemed funny or appropriate material to deal with; the series was killed at the last minute. Remember what I said—if you are to survive in this business, you need a high tolerance level for frustration. A *high* tolerance level.

P is for Packaging as an important component of a producer being able to attract to his or her project the financing and distribution needed to make it happen. But packaging alone is not a guarantee of success, as the hot director this weekend may be yesterday's news. There are no guarantees in Hollywood. There are only people with passion and prayers, prep, good partners, perseverance in the face of the process of development, and a hell of a pitch!

CHAPTER EIGHT

The PROPERTY

When I first entered the motion picture industry in 1976, I was told a good producer must make movies that "can play Peoria." What this meant was that it wasn't enough to make movies that would only appeal to the sophisticated citizens of New York and Los Angeles. To be successful, a movie at that time had to also be able to play the Midwest and South . . . America's heartland. But today, a good producer must make movies that "can play Peoria, Paris, Prague, Peru, and Peking."

Changing is always harder than staying the same.
It takes courage to face yourself in the mirror
and look beyond the reflection.

—BATMAN: BATTLE FOR THE COWL

In addition, a good producer is not simply focused on what type of movie would play today but what type of movie will play two, three, or four years from today. What's around the next few corners? That takes reading . . . massive reading: numerous daily news sources, books, screenplays, posts, and sites that will keep a producer plugged into a fast-changing national culture and quickly evolving international cultures. A good producer must maintain connectivity to youth and keep abreast of the changes in language, style, music, and tech. Is it that important to communicate with global audiences across the generations? Just ask the baby boomer who said to his best pal and drinking buddy, "Let's hook up at this bar next week" as younger family members overhearing them cringed and suggested they no longer use the term hook up *in that context. Or ask the millennials who are told by their baby boomer grandparents to put their valises on the hassock or ottoman and then stare as if they were stranded in some remote part of Latvia. Look at the rolled-up eyes of baby boomers as they show their baffled grandchildren a rotary telephone and watch the kids try in vain to figure out how to make a dial work . . . or even to understand what the dial is for. Meanwhile, look at the rolled-up eyes of millennials as they try for the twenty-sixth time to explain to their grandparents how to turn on their TVs using four different remote controls . . . if they are even still called "remote controls." How would I know? I'm a baby boomer. You can see the challenge of reaching across demographics and cultures. Of course, not every property needs to appeal to everyone. But there is so much "clutter" out there! Globally, if you add up all the TV channels and platforms, streaming and digital platforms, theatrical and assorted nontheatrical distribution, what is clear is that the worldwide consumption of content is 24/7 and never-ending, never more so than during our pandemic year. So what property has a great enough story with colorfully delineated characters that is capable of attracting name actors to help a project rise from the clutter? What property can be adapted to mobile gaming, merchandising, location-based entertainment, music, and publishing, to build it into a branded franchise? It's the concept of marketability of that content that has to be considered by a producer and by any financier or distributor as much as the very story itself. To acquire these rights in an underlying literary property is the life-blood of any producer.*

So always remember, you need a great intellectual property but also the ability to deliver it with some great storytelling. But part of the mystique of producing occurs when you find yourself in strange and unique situations that would happen to no one in the normal world ever. Sometimes, instead of bizarre and incredible situations or experiences, this means what I call "rubbing elbows with history," as you find yourself in the company of historic or high-profile people or become privy to a secret part of the life of someone famous or infamous. For example . . .

It was the exciting eighties! My producing partner and mentor, MGM's legendary Benjamin Melniker, and I were working on a feature-film project that could bring in revenue while our dark, serious *Batman* project was crawling along at a snail's pace after every studio had not only rejected my pitch but also told me it was the worst idea they had ever heard and that I was crazy. We were inputting on a feature film's marketing campaign, working alongside the senior exec of the studio division that handled advertising and publicity. Ben knew him well from his already forty-plus years in the movie industry and had nothing but respect for him and for his professionalism. One of the exec's staff was a very smart and affable businesswoman who was a breath of fresh air in Hollywood. She always wore a conservative, tailored suit; she had a great command of business; and she knew her marketing facts and figures. The epitome of efficiency, (let's call her . . . "Elaine") instilled confidence in everyone involved in the campaign. So when she told Ben and me that she'd be in New York in two weeks and wanted to talk to us about "something new," we readily agreed. We assumed we were getting together to discuss a new strategic element to our marketing plan. Instead, she turned our lives upside down.

Elaine appeared on time at our Batfilm Productions office, then located at Suite 1104 in the MGM Building at 1350 Avenue of the Americas. (Note to tourists: It's Sixth Avenue. Always was and always will be to native New Yorkers. Never give a New York cab driver an "Avenue of the Americas" address; you could wake up in Hoboken.) Ben walked out from behind his large desk, which was always stacked with what looked like tons of random clutter but were always specific papers, files, and contracts, each of which he could access in mere seconds. He welcomed her to New York and sat in one of our two swivel chairs as Elaine sat opposite him and I settled into the dark leather couch.

Elaine got right to the point. She wanted us to know how much she enjoyed working with us. That's why she wanted to meet. Elaine explained that she wasn't always in the motion picture business. Back in the early 1970s, she was a computer programmer for the Defense Intelligence Agency (DIA), the military branch of the CIA. In 1981, the existence of the DIA was suspected but not yet officially confirmed. Elaine explained that they reported directly to Henry Kissinger and that she had top security clearance, which was necessary to her job. As her story unfolded, Ben and I were mesmerized to hear how one day she was at work and accidentally stumbled across a file marked "Marilyn Monroe." Elaine was flabbergasted. Why on earth would the DIA have a file on Marilyn Monroe? She reminded us that back then it was not common knowledge that John F. Kennedy—*and* his brother, Bobby—had allegedly had affairs with the actress. So, of course, her curiosity was piqued, and so, of course, Elaine decided to take a peek at that file. For the first time ever, she was denied access to a file. But she had security clearance. Puzzled and intrigued, she vowed to find a way into it in her spare time. It was six months before she was able to open it and read the file on the murder of Marilyn Monroe.

Elaine claimed that the story she read began with Joseph Kennedy's outreach to the mob in an effort to help his son, John, win the election for president of the United States. Turning-point help was needed in Illinois, West Virginia, and other states to pull off what might be the closest election in history to that time. She said that among others, Sam Giancana of Chicago, Carlos Marcello of New Orleans, and Jimmy Hoffa of the Teamsters Union agreed to a deal with Joe Kennedy, whose career had its own dark side. The mobsters believed they had a deal and that if they helped Kennedy's kid get elected, they would have an easier time of it during his term of office. These men felt they had lived up to their side of the bargain, so when Kennedy became president and made his brother, Bobby, attorney general, and their operations were among his first targets, they felt betrayed. It would be years before it would come to light that JFK and Giancana shared a mistress via their self-confessed lover, Judith Exner. According to the file Elaine claimed she had read, a plot to terminate JFK's presidency was hatched in order to strike back at the Kennedys.

Knowing of the Kennedy boys' relationships with Marilyn Monroe, the plan was to make it appear as though the Kennedys had her killed because she was about to go public and expose the affairs, which, in pre-Monica 1962, would most likely have toppled the administration. Evidence was planted in her house that night to incriminate the Kennedys, and Marilyn was forced at gunpoint to make a couple of calls linking her to the president (one of which, as I recall, was to the Kennedys' brother-in-law, actor Peter Lawford), and then she was killed with a poison or drug in the form of a suppository that was believed to be untraceable. Elaine went on to explain that the file she read indicated that the mob's mistake was not knowing how closely Bobby Kennedy was connected to a certain person of rank in the LAPD at the time, who tipped him off and gave Bobby and his guys enough time to get in and, between them and his LAPD connection, remove any planted evidence before the authorities officially arrived on the scene. And so, the plot failed and Marilyn Monroe was dead as collateral damage.

Ben and I were stunned! Blown away! The file ended there, said Elaine, but what were the chances that the mob would simply have accepted this failure and let it all go? Would they have tried again to terminate the Kennedy presidency? She then wondered aloud at the connection between Marcello of New Orleans and Lee Harvey Oswald's activities with the Fair Play for Cuba Committee in New Orleans, and about some long-standing boyhood connection between Giancana and Jack Ruby. Then there was the Judith Exner connection. The possibilities were chilling.

Elaine asked us if we would work with her to turn her story into a movie. We agreed to talk it over that night and meet again with her the next afternoon.

So as you can tell, sometimes you are exposed to stories and people you know could be the basis of a literary property of the decade, if not the century. It has all the elements to be a smash from story and branding to commercial appeal worldwide. But despite that, you still don't move forward. There are other considerations a producer has . . . such as the welfare of his or her family. Yet again, for example . . .

Ben grabbed the LIRR back to Long Island that evening as I hopped on the bus to New Jersey. At home with our wives, we each discussed the shocking story we had heard that day at work. Nancy was adamant: we had a year-and-a-half-old son and if I were to produce this project, it could involve some of the most powerful and dangerous forces in the country. And what of Elaine—did I believe her? Knowing her as I did, I believed that she believed she was telling the truth. But were the contents of that DIA file real or accurate? There was no way to tell. Ben had a similar discussion with his wife, Shirley, and we concurred on our course of action. The next day when Elaine came in, we explained that we couldn't develop this as a movie project, but we urged her to go to the *New York Times* or the

Hal Gefsky, my cousin, mentor, and guide through the history of Hollywood's Golden Age, with one of his best friends, Cary Grant, and Cary's wife, Barbara.

Washington Post and find an ally in a top investigative reporter if she wanted to make this project happen. Images of Woodward and Bernstein and *All the President's Men* danced in our head. That sort of investigative skill and veil of both credibility and protection over her could result in an authoritative and controversial book that could then be made into a film. Elaine agreed that this was a good course of action.

It was not long after that the company she had been working for was sold, and everyone lost their jobs. Ben and I never saw or heard from Elaine again. Occasionally over the ensuing years, I've run across people who worked at that studio and I've asked about Elaine, but nobody has any clue where she went or what she did thereafter, and no one has seen her or heard from her. With the advent of Facebook and Internet searches, I tried to find her, as I wondered whatever happened to her quest to make a book and a movie out of her unique IP. I couldn't find a trace.

I assumed that I would never again hear anything weird and strange and bizarre and scary enough to top this chapter in my career. How wrong I was!

It happened twenty years later. Whenever I went to LA (usually for a week each month), I always tried to stay with my cousin Hal Gefsky at his amazing house a block north of

Sunset Boulevard. The house is haunted and has been written up in books and featured in documentaries about "haunted Hollywood." Hal had been an agent in Hollywood since the late 1930s. His friends over the years included Cary Grant, Ring Lardner, Sharon Tate (prompting Hal's appearances on every other documentary about the Manson murders), Arnold Stang, Andy Devine, John Candy, Brian Stokes Mitchell, Jim Morrison's admiral father, Dyan Cannon, Bernadette Peters, and Marni Nixon—the greatest living trivia question in the history of Hollywood!

It was Marni who dubbed the singing voice of Natalie Wood in *West Side Story*, Deborah Kerr in *The King and I*, and Audrey Hepburn in *My Fair Lady*. One evening over an extended family kind of dinner at Hal's, I said to Marni, "Tell me something about your career no one knows." She asked me if I recalled a song from *West Side Story* featuring Maria and Anita musically arguing over "A Boy Like That." Of course I remembered that song. I already knew she had dubbed Natalie Wood's voice.

"In that particular song," Marni said, "I sang *both* parts." She then told me that in *My Fair Lady*, she and Audrey and the director were frustrated because there was too big a discrepancy between Audrey's speaking voice and Marni's singing voice in songs like "I Could Have Danced All Night." Marni and Audrey tried all sorts of tricks to make it work but nothing succeeded. Finally, they decided to back up four lines of dialogue so that before each song started, Audrey would say a line, then Marni would voice a line of dialogue, then Audrey would, and then it would be Marni speaking the final bit of dialogue before launching into the song. The voice transition worked perfectly. A Hollywood secret revealed! You heard it here first! I can't verify it's accurate but can verify it's what I was told.

Everyone had a Hal story, and Hal had a story about everyone in Hollywood. My favorites were about Cary Grant, Margaret Dumont, and Andy Devine. Cary had the second-best box at Dodger Stadium next to Walter O'Malley, the owner. He knew how much Hal loved baseball, so he often took him to the games with him. It was Hal, in fact, who introduced Cary to his wife, Dyan Cannon. When Cary passed away, he provided for payment to renew his Dodger tickets each season, and those tickets were divided up between Hal and two others, to be used by them until they were no longer able. Hal kept his tickets through 2005 when he was eighty-seven and his legs were giving out.

Margaret Dumont, the society fall girl eternally bedeviled by the Marx Brothers, didn't drive, so when Hal got her a job in a movie, he would drive her to the studio each day. He cherished her and revealed to me that in real life she was *exactly* as she appears in all the Marx Brothers movies. She truly never understood their humor and had no idea what was so funny.

When Hal's buddy, the gravelly voiced Andy Devine, came to Hollywood as a young man to make his way as an actor, Andy experienced lots of pavement pounding but no success. He lived in a tiny fleabag apartment while he tried to make it in the movies. He became more and more depressed. Finally despondent, Andy Devine decided to commit suicide. He sealed his windows and door and turned on his gas oven and lay down on his bed to put himself out of his misery. As the fumes filled the apartment, he fell asleep. He awoke the next morning with a king-sized headache but clearly still alive despite his best efforts. The problem was that he hadn't paid his gas bill for months, and public service had finally cut him off, foiling his suicide attempt. That afternoon, Andy received a callback for a significant movie role and wound up getting the part that jump-started his amazing and long career, including an appearance on the *Batman* TV show in 1966.

Hal had thousands of these stories. He had palled around with Chaplin and Garbo. He was an attaché to General Eisenhower in World War II and drove Ike's paramour, Kay Summersby; he later made sure she was happy with the job at CBS that Bill Paley secured for her. Hal was one of the first American soldiers to enter Hitler's office at the end of World War II, bringing home such souvenirs as a tile from the wall of Hitler's bathroom and a packet of Der Fuehrer's personal stationery lifted right out of the demon's desk drawer.

Now Hal lived in a haunted house. It had been designed and built on this prime cul-de-sac location in the early 1950s as a wedding gift to Academy Award–winning actress Anne Baxter (who just so happened to have also played villainess Zelda the Great on the *Batman* TV show) upon her marriage to actor John Hodiak. The gift came courtesy of the bride's grandfather, world-famous architect Frank Lloyd Wright. Though Wright had conceived the house and its look, he turned the job of building it over to John Lautner (who has become famous in his own right) to execute and build. Hodiak, who starred in many films including *Lifeboat*, died suddenly in that house. In the 1960s, the place housed Bob Marcucci and his singing/acting teen sensations Frankie Avalon, Fabian, and Bobby Rydell. The day the Beatles arrived in America, those three careers were cut short, and the house went up for sale. Hal bought it, and it became the scene of legendary Hollywood pool parties featuring plenty of starlets and not so many bathing suits.

But the biggest event that ever took place there was a party in the late 1960s. One of Hal's favorite clients was Simon Oakland, who always played tough guys, cops, and detectives (think Officer Krupke's plainclothes boss in *West Side Story*). Si and his wife were at this wild bash. Before long, clean glasses became hard to find, so Si's wife rounded up a bunch of used glasses and started washing them in the kitchen sink. As she did so, she saw a man in the backyard come up next to the kitchen window. He was walking back and forth as if searching for a way in. Mrs. Oakland assumed he was one of Hal's guests who had ventured out into the backyard and found himself accidentally locked out. She motioned for him to wait and that she would come around and open the back door. She spotted Hal across the room and told him what happened. "He's doing what? Walking back and forth in front of the kitchen window?" asked a confused Hal. Mrs. Oakland insisted Hal take her around back to let this poor man in. When he brought her around back, her jaw dropped. She hadn't realized that Hal's house was built on a cliff and that the kitchen window was three sheer flights up. Anyone moving back and forth outside the window would have to do so in midair. Momentarily, her shock was replaced by anger at Hal. The only thing her brain could grasp was that somehow, some way, Hal and some of his actor buddies had hoaxed her by suspending the man from the roof or trees by some sort of harness and pulley. Hal tried to convince her that that would have been impossible, but she wouldn't hear of it, and she finally bolted, more in frustration than fear. She was convinced that she was the butt of a bad joke.

Ten days later, shortly after eleven at night, Hal's phone rang. It was Mrs. Oakland.

"Hal Gefsky, you sonofabitch! I *knew* that was a prank you and your actor friends were pulling on me at your party! You almost had me convinced it was a ghost, but I'm watching an old movie on TV and the guy who was moving back and forth in front of the kitchen window is in it! He's an actor! You had him on a rope or something!"

Hal was again baffled and asked her what channel she was watching. He flipped on the station and waited until Mrs. Oakland saw the close-up.

"There!" she shouted. "That's him! That's definitely him! He's one of your actor friends, right?"

They were watching the movie *Lifeboat*, and she was pointing to the late actor John Hodiak, whose honeymoon house this once was and who had died suddenly and tragically in it many years before.

Hal panicked. Mrs. Oakland became unnerved when she realized Hal was telling the truth. Was the ghost of John Hodiak haunting Pinetree Place? Hal and his friends reached out to one of the two major universities at that time that had courses dealing in parapsychology. Famed ghost hunter Hans Holzer was assigned to Hal's case and showed up with infrared and other kinds of high-tech equipment along with a medium by the name of Sybil Leek. Everyone was ordered out of the house for an entire day and night while Holzer and his crew set up and then ran their litany of tests. The verdict? There indeed was a presence in the house, someone whose happiest years were spent there and who simply couldn't let go. John Hodiak's spirit was what Holzer defined as a "stay behind." He assured Hal that this presence was not harmful or threatening and that one day it would be able to move on. There were half a dozen more encounters over the decades with the ghost of Mr. Hodiak.

For the record, no one from New York or New Jersey who stayed in Hal's house ever saw or heard the ghost. Only people from California did. Draw your own conclusions.

It was September, twenty years after the Marilyn Monroe incident, and I was in LA for my usual one-week-a-month, ten-meetings-a-day work trip. It was a Saturday night, and I was out at an upscale Hollywood soiree commemorating a big birthday of a producer friend of mine. She wanted everything at this party to be special and elegant and so was chagrined when invited guest Nicole Kidman showed up with twelve uninvited Aussie friends in tow. I volunteered to greet some of these unexpected guests while she tended to the others. There was one young couple about my son's age who really impressed me, and we wound up talking for hours about their coming to LA, working as actors in the Biz, what this Hollywood jungle is like, and the incredulity of one's journey in life. They introduced themselves to me as simply Heath and Naomi. Who could have possibly foreseen that six years later he'd be playing The Joker in one of my *Batman* films, thanks solely to the genius of director Christopher Nolan, who had a vision and knew how to cast it and execute it. And Naomi would become one of my favorite actresses on the movie scene today, especially in films like *21 Grams*.

Heath and I continued our conversation in July 2008 in Chicago on the set of *The Dark Knight*. When I reminded him about our first meeting, he had just come off some strenuous takes in the hot, humid summer sun with a policeman's garb over his Joker outfit and all the makeup on. I introduced him to my wife, Nancy, whom he had never met, and being the gentleman that he was, he spoke to her for some twenty minutes, giving her his complete attention during his entire break. A consummate actor, a gentle man—but, alas, I digress . . .

The party ended, and it was now 1:30 a.m. I drove up Sunset Plaza, parked my car, and began to walk across the cul-de-sac. As I passed under a lone lamppost, I suddenly heard an echoing voice.

"Are you Michael?"

I froze. Was this at last to be my personal encounter with the ghost of John Hodiak?

"Yes," I said to no one.

"Michael . . . hi. This is [let's call him . . . "George"] George. I'm the head of security at the mansion."

Aha! The mansion next to Hal's was built by one of the richest men in Mexico and sometimes served as a getaway place for the president of that country, or so it was rumored by the help. Besides the grand gates, there were TV cameras, microphones, and sensors planted throughout the tall hedges and trees.

"Uh . . . hi, George," I replied. "Is everything all right?" I asked.

"Yeah," he replied through a speaker somewhere. "Your cousin Hal told me you were staying with him and that you're the executive producer of all the *Batman* movies and, well, you got a minute?"

Should I even respond to this voice that seemed to be coming from every direction? "Sure, George," I said, and I held my breath.

With that, the iron gates slowly opened and out walked big, tall George in a tie and jacket. Thus our encounter began at 1:40 a.m. under a lamppost on a deserted cul-de-sac overlooking LA. Could a screenwriter have written this any better?

We formally introduced ourselves to one another, and after some time, George started spilling his guts. He told me something had happened to him that had been haunting his conscience for a long time and that he wanted to reveal it to the world by making it into a movie.

"*But,*" George emphatically stated, eye to eye with me, "you have to change all the names! You can't use anyone's real names, especially the one member of the president's Cabinet!" He asked me if I'd be interested in producing the movie.

"What's the story, George?" I asked him, now intrigued by his panicky reference to a Cabinet member. He reiterated the need for everyone's anonymity, and the paranoia was pervasive. I agreed that if I was interested in producing whatever this was as a movie, I would change everyone's names. "But what's the story, George?" I asked once more.

"Back in the eighties," George said, "I was in the DIA and we reported directly to this high-ranking government official."

I froze! I could *not* believe that twenty years later, I was once again stumbling across the DIA at 1:45 a.m. under a lamppost on a dead-end street in the hills above Los Angeles. Perhaps this story would be just as chilling and fantastic as the last one! But in 2002, the existence of the DIA was confirmed and known by most Americans. I could understand why he wanted this very high-profile man's name kept out of this. But that's all I understood. "So what's the story, George?" I asked for the last time.

His eyes locked on mine. "Chernobyl wasn't an accident. We caused it."

I got chills. It took at least a few seconds for his words to register; my brain was on overload. This was too much to grasp immediately. "But George . . . didn't that accident kill, like, twenty thousand people?" I asked, trying to remember my facts.

"I told you it's been haunting my conscience," was the only reply he could muster.

"OK, George, what exactly did you do?" I asked, though I was afraid. He told me that he "and others" were called in by the guy whose name needs to be changed and were told that there was a growing belief that the Soviet Union could potentially be toppled from within if there was continuing sufficient civil, social, political, and economic unrest. The DIA had developed a number of missions designed secretly to do just that. George and his small group's mission was to get into the nuclear reactor in Chernobyl and loosen the bolts at the base of a metallic apparatus over the core that was used to move rods in and out for purposes of control. And then they were to get the hell out. And that's precisely what they did. No one told them why they were loosening these bolts or what they were accomplishing by loosening them.

So I asked George why, then, he felt he was responsible for the biggest nuclear "accident" in history. The answer was clear—because years later, a certain unnamed someone called George and the others in to congratulate them on having been one of the causal factors that led to the downfall of the Soviet Union. George wanted to know if I would produce a movie based on his story, and I told him I wanted to think about it; I was off to New Jersey the next day but would see him when I came out to LA again in a few weeks.

"ARE YOU OUT OF YOUR MIND TO EVEN THINK OF GETTING INVOLVED IN THIS?!!" was Nancy's greeting when I brought the subject up. The powerful forces at work here were far more dangerous than the ones that had been at play in the DIA / Marilyn Monroe story. There was no way I should get involved, especially since I didn't know George like I had known Elaine. Was he even telling the truth?

The next morning, I was having breakfast in the Sub Shop in Cedar Grove, my dad's favorite hangout, where he had held court each morning amid his friends and the townspeople who had come to know and love him for his stories, his jokes, and his intellectual curiosity, which he retained even up to age ninety. Throughout his career, my dad always found some luncheonette or diner or coffee shop to function as his own sorta satellite office. Weequahic Diner in Newark, Larry's Luncheonette in Wanamassa, Sunset Landing in Asbury Park, the Chocolate Soda in Deal, and the Plaza Sweet Shop in the Middlebrook Shopping Center were his former Jersey hangouts.

It was at the latter that Paul and Nancy and I planned a surprise for him for his sixty-eighth birthday. Since he was young, Pop had a personal fantasy all his own that he used to joke about. He fantasized about being driven to work in his mason's work clothes with his pail of tools in a stretch limousine. And so, on this March day, at 6:30 a.m. when my dad stepped outside to get in his truck, a new stretch limo was awaiting him. He panicked, and my mom convinced him to just relax and enjoy the experience, courtesy of the three of us. His driver then chauffeured him to the Plaza Sweet Shop, where all his friends and cronies came running outside to see what famous person had just pulled up. When the driver opened the limo door and my dad popped out in his work clothes carrying his trowel, everybody bowed, their arms extended in that "I'm not worthy, sahib" pose. Following all the hubbub at breakfast, the chauffeur drove my dad to his job. The deal was he would take him back to the Plaza Sweet Shop for his 10:00 a.m. coffee break. By that time, word had spread around Ocean Township and there were over two dozen people gathered there to watch him pull up in his limo. By 12:15 p.m. when he returned from lunch, over fifty people were there to applaud his arrival, including the *Asbury Park Press*, which sent a reporter and photographer to cover this unusual breaking story. My dad was big-time. He loved every second of his day. We made his dream come true, the way he and my mom helped make our dreams come true.

My dad had spent that ninetieth birthday winter in Boca Raton, where he rented a fire-engine red Mustang convertible and tooled around Boynton Beach with his seventy-year-old lady friend, my darling aunt Shirley, one of the world's Great Ladies, who was my dad's companion in the years after my mom passed away. We had a king-sized blowout in Boca for his ninetieth birthday, and cousins, nieces, nephews, friends, and grandkids flew in from all over to celebrate with him. He stood up to address his flock at the end of the day's great celebration, and he summed up his journey through life with his very favorite quote to bequeath to all of us:

Yesterday is history.

Tomorrow is a mystery.

Today is a gift. That's why we call it "the present."

Two weeks before he turned ninety, I sat down with my dad at his table in the Sub Shop and said to him, "Pop, you're gonna be ninety. Are you scared?"

He thought for a while and then said, "I'm not afraid of dying. Everyone dies. I'm only afraid of running out of time. There are still people I'd like to meet, places I'd like to see, experiences I'd like to have. I'm just afraid of running out of time."

Like the rest of us, he had his heart torn out piece by piece watching my mom die an inch a day for a year and a half. He always said his wish was that when his time came, he would just go quickly. He did not want to linger and did not want to wind up in a home or some facility. Less than a month after his ninetieth birthday, my dad died, sitting in his favorite chair when the massive stroke hit. He got his wish, my dad did. We engraved that favorite quote of his on his gravestone. I still speak to him and my mom every day as I promised them each I would. As always, they are wonderful listeners, and I do not apologize for this digression.

Into the Sub Shop this particular morning came my dad's friend, whose name must clearly be changed. Let's call him . . . "George II." Everyone in town knows George II is CIA. He disappears at night and resurfaces a week or two or three later depositing satchels of cash into various local banks. He goes to Korea, India, Israel, Germany, and places that weren't places when I was learning geography in grade school. And everyone knows he has something to do with nukes. I called him over to my table and asked him if he knew anything about nuclear reactors. He replied he knew *a lot* about nuclear reactors. I told him that I was working with some screenwriters in Hollywood and they had come up with a great story but that if it was totally improbable, I couldn't produce it. I then asked George II if it was possible that Chernobyl had not been an accident. He shook his head dismissively and told me, "No, that was an accident." So I asked him if there was a metallic structure over a reactor that was bolted down and used to move rods in and out to control the process. He said there was. I then asked him whether loosening the bolts on this structure and allowing it to collapse into the core could have created the same result as the actual disaster.

George II sat down, pulled a napkin from the dispenser on the table and a pen out of his pocket protector, and started sketching. He turned the drawing around to face me and explained, "This is the interior of a nuclear reactor. Now, you're telling me that someone loosened the bolts here, here, and here, causing the structure to eventually collapse . . . which would do this . . . and then that would do this . . . then this would do that . . . and then—" George II suddenly looked at me suspiciously. "Yes . . . this *could* have caused it! *Who* told you this?"

I innocently reiterated that it was just an idea dreamed up by some movie writers. I don't think George II really bought that explanation, but I was now convinced that what the first George told me may have been true.

Two weeks later I was back in LA and George and I agreed to meet out in the street again. I reported that his story checked out and I believed him. That said, I felt there were too many powerful forces at work here to take this on as a movie project and suggested, as Ben and I had counseled Elaine (I can't believe I had to say this twice in one lifetime), to go to the *New York Times* or the *Washington Post* and work with a top investigative reporter who could be his Woodward and Bernstein. George understood the sense this made and thanked me for my guidance. That's *two* great properties we chose not to produce. It made me sad but allowed me to sleep better at night and keep true to the oath I made before I ever stepped foot in Hollywood . . . family first.

My next trip to LA came four weeks later. I pulled into Hal's after dinner, and he and I had a chance to get caught up before I unpacked in my room in my own wing of the house. I asked him how his friend George was doing next door. Hal informed me that George didn't work there anymore. One of the security guys told Hal that George just didn't show up for work one night. He never came back, and they figured he found some new job and quit. No one knew what happened or where he went. Hal never heard from him again, and neither did I.

A spooky business this producing is sometimes. But it can be so much fun! It's the only job I could find where I get to be six for half a day and sixteen for the other half no matter how gray I get. Every day is different. When I wake up in the morning, I truly don't know what I'll be doing or where I'll be doing it. What do I actually do? Simply put, every day, I report to a sandbox and play with my favorite toys. All in all, it's a helluva sandbox.

If you like sand, you'll love what's beneath it! My friend Tom Seligson wrote a fun book based on tons of research. It's called *Kidd,* and it's about the search for Captain Kidd's buried treasure underneath modern-day New York City. My friend Roger Birnbaum beat me to the punch in getting an option back in the days he was working with Henry Winkler and Ron Howard in a deal at Paramount. I waited patiently until the day their option lapsed and Ben and I grabbed the next option. There really is an entire world that exists underneath New York City, and several books have been written on the subject. Below what today is Park Avenue used to be the train tunnels; Franklin D. Roosevelt's private train car still lurks there below the Waldorf Astoria. There are still entrances into steam tunnels dotting the city that can take you down multiple levels. If you go down far enough . . . past abandoned highways started and never completed, past original subway tunnels and sealed-off stations, below the foundation of the World Trade Center where they found the hull of an old merchant ship that had to be moved out before the towers went up, you can still find the original topography of Manhattan Island. At the turn of the twentieth century when they were putting in the subway, they went down so far they found a petrified forest that had to be leveled before construction could get underway. Original streams and landmarks still exist down there. What a backdrop for a movie! This was my chance to produce a modern-day, urban *Raiders of the Lost Ark.*

Captain Kidd was not the malevolent pirate Hollywood has made him appear to be. Tom Seligson's research showed he was a merchant seaman who had a farmhouse in lower Manhattan and was a member in good standing of Trinity Church. He was set up by Lord

Bellomont and other ranking British officials to be accused of piracy against English ships so that they could grab the huge treasure he amassed from his missions for them raiding ships of other countries in and around New York. That treasure could be worth billions today. But history tells us it was never found. Where did Kidd bury it before he was captured by his enemies and hanged? Did he make it north to New England . . . east to Long Island . . . or south to the Jersey shore? Or is it much closer . . . perhaps directly under the feet of people rushing through the streets of Manhattan today? I was hooked and wrote a twenty-five-page treatment for this thriller of a movie involving one of the all-time great historic treasure hunts. Murder, intrigue, scares, and romance fill the story, and no one is ever really whom he or she appears to be. Everywhere we went, studios loved my pitch, and we set *Kidd* up for development and production at Dreamworks. We lined up Jonathan Hensleigh to write it, and I couldn't have been more excited. Then one day came news of another project that was a history-based treasure hunt to be set in Washington, DC, that Jon Turtletaub was putting together. After much discussion and consternation, the two projects merged and the end result was *National Treasure*. Yet the story and character elements of *Kidd* and its peculiar history tied to the good/bad captain remain unique. My goal is to make it happen one of these days. And it's that special story that will drive me every few years to keep pestering the studio, desperately trying to convince the powers that be to let it happen. *Kidd* . . . remember that title . . . the greatest movie never made!

And what about the greatest property that never was? In the 2000s, we began taking globalization very seriously and began our bimonthly trips to China, South Korea, Japan, and Thailand. China was our primary target because of how fast the world around us was changing. We saw the day coming fast when China would become the biggest film market in the world. We understood that no matter how much technology and delivery systems changed, content would always be king in a world with a never-ending appetite, absorbing it twenty-four hours a day, seven days a week. The future as my son, David, and I saw it was that the need would be for global content that would be culturally sensitive and be able to play all over the earth. Unlike Hollywood majors that were still producing lots of content for American boys who played video games, global content could span so many demographics. Generations older than the millennials still love movies and want to go see good ones, but no one forty and older wants to see a studio's *Nutty Professor 5*. Programming like that will only become a self-fulfilling prophesy as to the claim that "no one older than twenty-five today goes to movie theaters."

And with that backdrop, the day came in the past few years when a company claimed it had skazillions of dollars to sink into content, provided the feature films would definitely be able to play the US, China, and everywhere in between. We met at the hotbed hotel bar for pre-COVID-19 meetings, the Montage in Beverly Hills. The head of this company was laser-focused on American-made content that could shoot at least 50 percent in China with a story virtually guaranteed to appeal to the masses there. The upside in China for a theatrical film could be as high as $700 million plus box office, he claimed. Turning to me, he asked quite directly, "Do you own or control a property that fits this bill? If not, we can pleasantly finish our drinks and be on our merry way. But if so, I need to know about it now."

With David playing it cool and looking on, I replied, "We have precisely the property you've been searching for! It's a series of novels that will be hailed as the Harry Potter of China, not yet published. We have the manuscript for the first book and the outlines for the second through fourth novels. It's *Hu Peng and the Secret of the Terra Cotta Warriors*!"

The guy absolutely *loved* the title and was now dying to hear the story. What I laid out for him was this pitch of the property:

Our story opens in China. We meet a highly respected paleontologist at the forefront of the many incredible dinosaur discoveries coming from that country over the past two decades. His son is a Chinese teen with blond hair. We soon see that he is tortured at night by his dreams and nightmares, which are quite terrifying, containing images of red demons and monsters. Meanwhile in San Francisco, in the high-class home of an American woman, we find her teenage daughter being plagued by the same dreams and nightmares as the boy in China. Clearly, there is some sort of psychic connection between the two. An important business trip finds the mother arriving in Xi'an, China, with her daughter in tow. Xi'an is the home of the Terra Cotta Warriors. Only several thousands of these statues have been unearthed so far, but the experts say there could be hundreds of thousands more buried within the overall site. Each one looks unique and the details of their weaponry and conveyances and armor are beyond awesome!

When the boy and girl inadvertently meet, they explore their connection and learn, to their chagrin, that the evil forces of the Red Emperor, a famous tale from Chinese mythology and culture, are coming back to life in today's China. The only counter to their onslaught will be for the two young people to use the powerful artifacts they find to summon the forces of the Green Emperor, yet another famous legend of Chinese mythology. The entire burden of the cosmic battle with life-and-death consequences for the world falls on the shoulders of these two young people. If they fail, the legends tell them that the result will be the beginning of the Epoch of Darkness, in which the sun and moon will reverse themselves and, literally, all hell will break out on earth, with the first two beachheads being Xi'an and San Francisco. Using magical armaments that they discover and train with, the two finally learn that they must overcome their cultural differences and team up in order to oppose the Red Emperor as he brings to life the hundreds of thousands of Terra Cotta Warriors who now begin to climb out of their Chinese graves in a force that seemingly cannot be stopped.

The head of the new company was both mesmerized and excited. He said that this book, the entire series, is exactly the perfect property he's been searching for. He asked to read the materials. I told him yes, as soon as he signed a nondisclosure agreement. He quickly agreed and said he'd sign whatever we sent over. He was already sure this would be the first project made by his new financing company.

As David and I were leaving, David turned to me in his all-knowing way and said, "Dad, I never heard about this property before. Where did you find it or . . . did you just make all that up on the spot?"

My reply didn't throw him. "I just made the story up as I went along. I've already been researching Chinese myths and legends and knew about the Red Emperor, the Green Emperor, and the Epoch of Darkness. I just modernized it by making up a global story."

The next challenge was to buy us some time with that NDA bs. When I got home, I quickly started putting that story down on paper. Knowing time was of the essence, I called on David's and my close friend, an incredible writer of fiction with a number of books and graphic novels to her credit, Erika Lewis. We pulled her into our circle for this. She and I talked it through and in as fast a time as I could imagine, we had a detailed outline for this book, shorter outlines for the next three, and she had written a third of the first book in eleven thrilling chapters!

Here's where we should place a comic book panel's yellow caption box with the lettered word, *Suddenly* . . . because as we started steamrolling ahead, into office came a new US president who didn't get along with the president of China, crushing most business between the two countries. Then came COVID-19. Will *Hu Peng and the Secret of the Terra Cotta Warriors* novels see print? Will the international blockbuster movie come to a theater or streaming service near you? As with everything else in Hollywood, stay tuned; this will take another ridiculous amount of time, and we shall see if the Movie Gods act favorably or wrathfully.

P is for Property . . . the gateway to success and the foundation upon which a picture can be developed. When you see a hot one, pursue it, protect it, and produce it.

CHAPTER NINE

The PRODUCTION

The production phase of moviemaking is all-consuming madness, akin to a lawyer in the midst of litigation or a surgeon performing a marathon operation. The most important moment I ever had on the set of a film as the line producer was the day my office was filled with department heads in crisis. It was a bad day: bad weather, bad logistics, bad completion bond guarantors working against us instead of in support of us, bad clashes of egos, and bad ramifications of a certain actor with a certain drinking problem.

Sometimes it's only madness that makes us what we are.

—BATMAN: ARKHAM ASYLUM

My overwrought coproducer came to me in a panic. "We have so many problems they've absolutely become overwhelming," she warned as she shook. That was when I used something I had actually learned in law school of all places. Calmly, I replied that she was wrong. We had no problems. "Are you nuts?" she deservedly asked/screeched. "We have huge problems!" Undeterred, I explained, "No, we have no problems." There is no such thing as a problem. There are only multiple solutions. Our leadership job was to thoughtfully and responsibly choose the one we best believed would serve our purpose. We had to pick up this thing she called a "problem" and hold it up to the light, staring at it like a faceted diamond as we turned it up and down and side to side, until we came upon the creative solution we would choose to implement. Ergo, there are no problems, only multiple solutions. And that was an epiphany.

Production does not necessarily mean moviemaking exclusively to me. In addition to the heralded *Casablanca* event I wrote and produced, this gem began as an idea as to how we in New Jersey could join in on the celebration of the one hundredth anniversary of Thomas Alva Edison's invention (with a bow to his associate, W. K. L. Dickson) of the motion picture camera and, following that, the first movie studio (known as the Black Maria) and the first projector. "I am experimenting upon an instrument which does for the eye what the phonograph does for the ear, which is the recording and reproduction of things in motion," declared Edison in 1888. His laboratory facility was located in West Orange, New Jersey, a proverbial stone's throw from my home. Every kid growing up in the state was bused in for a grade school class trip. It was also where the phonograph was created, as well as the storage battery and Dictaphone. A national historic site, the lab was also named as one of America's most endangered historic sites.

I had served for quite a few years on the board of the Thomas Alva Edison Media Arts Consortium, which annually ran the internationally respected Black Maria Film Festival for independent filmmakers (the heralded John Sayles, included) as well as the Young Filmmaker's Film Festival, which encouraged students to be creative, daring, and inventive filmmakers from junior high to high school to college level. But now, my pal Wade Knowles, of the well-known Knowles family of five-star restaurants in New Jersey, including The Manor and the Robin Hood Inn of "As Time Goes By" fame, one of the most dedicated 24/7 philanthropists I'd ever met, approached me in his capacity with the Friends of Edison, a group formed to support the national historic site. I knew whatever this was about was going to be both monumental and first class, as he had with him in tow one of my favorite mentors, Joe Friedman, executive director of the New Jersey Motion Picture and Television Commission.

Massive money had to be raised to save and preserve the entire Edison site. Wade and Joe explained the need to come up with a special way not only to celebrate Edison's laboratory and the upcoming hundredth anniversary of the motion picture but also to raise funds and bring global attention to the plight of the site. And thus, they asked me, "What can you come up with, Michael?" Uh-oh. Then they really rubbed it in. "We're totally behind you and whatever wild idea you come up with for this occasion," Wade and Joe harmonized.

The New Jersey Film Commission's "Making of *Casablanca*" event.

To pump me up about the site and spark some ideas, Wade and Joe arranged for me to be taken on a very special private tour of the underground concrete bunker housing the papers and artifacts of Edison. It was down there they handed me the inventor's actual scientific journal detailing—in his own handwriting—his attempt after attempt until he actually succeeded in inventing the light bulb. I was intrigued by a large file box marked "World War I Secret Submarine Plans" and an oil painting of the classic RCA-Victor logo with Nipper the dog looking confused, with his head cocked, into the gramophone, listening to "His Master's Voice." But in one of the great revelations of my life, this old painting portrayed Nipper and his gramophone sitting atop a polished coffin. That was the coffin of his master! I suddenly understood the dog's confusion now listening to "His Master's Voice."

One of my favorite Thomas Edison inventions they told me about was, of all things, the word *hello*. The way I heard it, Alexander Graham Bell invented the telephone, but when it came time to string it up in the first city, he was unable to lick the problem of sufficient amplification. Bell and the businessmen behind him turned to Thomas Edison for help, and he solved the problem. But another problem arose at the last minute. Every form of communication had some code word to acknowledge receipt of a signal. Thus, what should a person say to acknowledge a phone call when the phone rings and he picks up the receiver? Bell was quite sure that the proper word to say at that moment was *Ahoy*! The businessmen wanted something more formal and suggested, "Are you there?" as the proper response when one's telephone rang. But Edison thought this new invention should have its own unique language. From an old English hunting call, "halloo," he coined the word *hello.* Since it was Edison's job to package these first commercial telephones with instruction booklets, he plunged ahead and wrote that *hello* should be said when one answers a call. *Hello* became the new catchword of the 1870s and, supposedly, at the first convention for people in the new telephone business, everyone was given an identifying badge to wear that stated, "Hello! My name is . . ." And, I guess, on the seventh day, Edison rested.

Lastly, the kind rangers at the national historic site showed me a host of early Edison films from the 1890s through the early 1900s, including *The Sneeze* (the first copyrighted film); *The Kiss* (the first on-screen kiss); *The Barbershop* and *Smashing a Jersey Mosquito* (early use of special effects and stunts); *Alice in Wonderland, The Wizard of Oz,* and *Frankenstein* (all three from 1910); and *The Great Train Robbery* (a 1903 seminal work in the advancement of films). And that's when it hit me. We would have a black-tie dinner event in which we would not only show these original early Edison films to live piano musical accompaniment but also I would pull together a great professional cast and take them inside Edison's Black Maria studio on the grounds of the laboratory site where we would remake them and premiere them at the fundraising dinner.

And so, I had the golden opportunity to produce and direct stars from the Golden Age of Hollywood moviemaking including such luminaries as Eddie Bracken in our new version of *The Sneeze* and Celeste Holm and Wesley Addy in *The Kiss.* For our remake of *The Great Train Robbery* we had Dan Lauria, the dad from *The Wonder Years*; Ray Wise, the man who killed Laura Palmer in *Twin Peaks*; Ron McClarty from TV's *Spencer for Hire*; Robin Lange, star with James Gandolfini of Leo Penn's *Remembrance*; June Lockhart of *Lost in Space* and *Lassie* fame (whose parents worked for and met at Mr. Edison's company); and Ruth Warrick, the last-surviving principal cast member of *Citizen Kane.* It all made for a magical night of entertainment and gave Celeste Holm, one of the most elegant of stars in Hollywood history, a forum to regale us with some of the greatest and bawdiest stories from that Golden Age. My favorite was a tale from the days that she, Betty Garrett, and Marilyn Monroe were each working on a project at one of the major movie studios. On most days, these three great actresses would have lunch together in the studio commissary. But every day, Marilyn would sit down with them and gobble down her lunch at a speedy pace and then say, "Gotta go!" Celeste said she and Betty weren't stupid or naïve. They knew what fancy office Marilyn was expected to appear in each day during her lunch break. Finally, Celeste and Betty had gotten so upset and angry about the situation that they agreed to do what today we would call an intervention. "Marilyn! Sit back down! You do *not* have to do this!" the two women said. Marilyn reacted with a wave of her hand and replied, "Oh, it's no big deal, Celeste. It only takes a minute!" And off she went.

This fun gala evening brought significant national and international attention to the Edison national historic site, which eventually led to my teaming up with the legendary Douglas Fairbanks Jr. to unveil at the Thomas A. Edison National Historic Site a *Great Train Robbery* US postage stamp commemorating the one-hundredth anniversary of movies. It also eventually led to Hillary Clinton taking an on-air tour of the place live on the *Today* show with Jack Welch from General Electric (formerly known as Edison-General Electric, by the way) who handed Mrs. Clinton a check for $11 million toward the saving of the site. That was a turning point. The place ultimately closed for many years for desperately needed reconstruction and reopened to great fanfare.

The Production Setup: My big brother, Paul, tricked me into watching *The Day the Earth Stood Still* when I was six, scarring me for years in fear that the robot, Gort, with the death ray coming out of his eyes, would come into my bedroom at night and open his visor so his disintegrating vision would zap us all!

The Production Payoff: Decades later as a movie producer, I spent an evening with actress and grande dame Patricia Neal in New York City. The female lead in *The Day the Earth Stood Still*, Patricia was forced to hear my confession as to how scared I was of that robot. I asked her if she was as scared while working with Gort on that film. She cracked up. Bob Wise, the director, was sooo mad at her! When she had her chilling confrontation scene with terrifying and intimidating Gort, she quite simply could not stop laughing. She thought it was all so stupid and hokey and that the tall guy in the silly suit looked funny and preposterous. And so, when it came time for her to look terrified, she just started laughing. Take 2. She burst into guffaws. Take 3. She laughed so hard she was crying. Take 4. She did a veritable spit-take trying to hold back the laughter. The director was really getting irritated, as time was slipping away and the number of takes was adding up. He reminded her she was a professional and now that she'd gotten it out of her system, he needed her to nail this. Take 5. She laughed. Take 6. After hearing Patricia's tale of hysterically funny woe, I would never again find it essential each night before I fell asleep to say the magical movie words that would make Gort lower his visor, "Klaatu Berada Nikto." I was cured at last.

And speaking of weird production tales, *Swamp Thing* made my heart sing!

The financier behind *Swamp Thing 2* wanted the property set up for exploitation ultimately for kids. It would spark a Swamp Thing network animated series, a Kenner toy line, and mountains of merchandising. And it did. Production would commence in Savannah, Georgia. We set up our production office there, then flew in Heather Locklear and the cast in the final week of prepping for production. As we were nearing our start date, my able and talented production designer, Robb Wilson King, who had served hard time with us in the raw and untamed swamps of Charleston, South Carolina, on the first *Swamp Thing* movie, was deeply concerned that we had not yet found a location for the mansion of the villain, Arcane. We did not have the money in our budget to build that set; we had to find it in town. The next evening, Robb knocked on my door, looking a combination of excited and downright scared. He informed me he had found the perfect mansion in town for our needs and that the owner had been contacted and was open to possibly letting us use his magnificent abode as a set, but he insisted on meeting Robb this very night. Robb said he wouldn't go unless I went too. Figuring something was up for him to not want to go alone, I questioned him. When he replied that the guy was allegedly a murderer in the most infamous murder case in the history of Savannah, my producer instincts kicked into overdrive. There was to be no panic, just extra special prep for this meeting set to begin at 10:00 p.m. at the house, a.k.a. the scene of the murder. That's when Robb also mentioned that some wealthy old-money people in town also claimed that the owner, Jim Williams, was a Nazi. Little did I dream that the man we were about to meet and his house we were hoping to film in would soon become the subject of a best-selling book and movie, *Midnight in the Garden of Good and Evil.*

I must admit feeling nervous as I knocked on the door of the most famous residence in Savannah, the Mercer House, named after the famous songwriter who once lived there, Johnny Mercer. Far from resembling *Batman*'s Joker, Two-Face, or Penguin, Jim Williams looked like a southern gentleman and warmly invited us in. Ushered into his home, I saw spectacular and clearly incredibly valuable paintings, art objects, and historical artifacts dotting each room. Before I knew it, I had a gin and tonic in my hand and Jim had his obviously not first bourbon or whatever southern gentlemen drink. If he was going to allow a film crew into his house, he felt he needed to get to know the boss first in the belief that a fish stinks from the head. And so, we talked, shared anecdotes, and before long, my fears and his suspicions receded and we bonded. I was convinced this man was no threat to us, and he was convinced I would treat his property with respect and undue care.

I gave strict orders to my crew that there would be no smoking in the house and that padding would have to be put down to protect the shiny floors. Jim offered to allow all his priceless works of art to stay where they were to increase the production value of the film . . . including such things as a Fabergé egg. Needless to say, this became an issue among our insurance company, the production, and Jim. To get the insurance company to sign off, the deal was for Jim to be on the set at all times while filming was being done in his house. He enthusiastically agreed, both because he was by nature a night owl and because of his love for movies and the excitement of being part of the actual filming . . . as if the circus had come to town. Too many filmmakers and crews don't realize that insurance is one of the most important and essential elements involved in production. Once the issue was adequately resolved, shooting began. Over the next few weeks, we had plenty of night shooting. I had the crew make up a "director's chair" for Jim positioned next to mine. It soon became clear that as part of the deal, unofficially, I needed to socially drink with Jim during the late-night hours of shooting. Jim was pleased we lived up to what I had promised him and had taken extremely good care of the house and his special possessions.

About halfway into shooting, Jim turned to me, drink in hand, and said, "In all this time, you never once asked me about the murder, Michael. Why is that?"

I replied, gin in hand, "Because that's none of my business, Jim. We have this great working relationship, and that's sufficient for me. You have my respect, and I have no need to ask questions."

With that, Jim stood up and said, "You're my friend. I would like you to know the truth. Do you want to hear what happened that night?"

"Sure," I said with trepidation.

"Follow me," Jim said, more than suggesting but less than demanding.

He walked me over to the grand old winding staircase and began to tell his story. He acted out both parts, then reenacted the fatal gunshot and asked if that clarified for me the fact that while Jim did kill the man, it was done solely and completely in self-defense. When I told him it absolutely did and how much I appreciated his sharing the true story with me, it was as if the weight of the world had lifted off his shoulders. He said it was important to him that as a friend I knew the truth.

As we turned away from the scene of the shooting, Jim asked if there was anything else I'd like to know. So, feeling secure, I came right out with it.

"There are people in this town who have claimed you're a Nazi. I don't believe that, but I imagine there's yet another story to be told."

"Come with me," Jim motioned. We headed into his more-than-magnificent study; inside was a sizable vault. He opened it and removed three objects. "I told you I collect historical artifacts. These are three prizes in my collection." He then placed in my hand a very old dagger and revealed that it belonged to Rasputin, the Mad Monk of Russian history. Next came one of Hitler's formal place settings. Lastly, he unfurled a huge Nazi flag that had once flown over the Reichstag. Jim was careful to explain his interest in history, not in the politics or philosophies of people like Rasputin or Hitler. Then came his tale of why his "jealous, old money, society people" spread false rumors about him and made sure he was tried three times for the murder.

Jim said that a big television production came into town to shoot a historical miniseries. Like me, they wanted to make a deal to use his house as a location. After a protracted negotiation, Jim got the price he wanted and agreed to the deal. The production company went all out, covering the surrounding streets in dirt to fit in with the Civil War period. Unlike me, they didn't pay Jim the agreed-to compensation and began shooting around the exterior of the house, the first of many key scenes. Jim said he stepped outside amid the crew and equipment around his house and found the producer and the location manager he'd made his deal with. When he reminded them they owed him the agreed-to location fee by the start of shooting, the producer told him they figured out a way in which they wouldn't have to film inside the house, just film it from the outside. When Jim again asked for his fee, he was told they unilaterally decided they didn't have to pay it for just photographing the exterior. Jim disagreed and expected them to live up to the deal. They saw it differently and would not do so. So Jim smiled, went inside, pulled out the giant Nazi flag from his collection of historical artifacts, and draped it off his balcony, facing the cameras at work. This was in an era before CGI and computer effects. The production company paid Jim his location fee, and he rolled the flag back up. But those who in town were not Jim Williams fans, he said, used that incident to claim he was a Nazi.

I gave Jim on-screen credit as a consultant on the film and heard he was thrilled to see his name up there in the credits of a movie. The point of this production story? Honor thy father and mother and location deals.

While on location line producing in Savannah, Heather Locklear took me out for my birthday lunch. My wife, Nancy, was visiting the set that week. She and Heather planned this surprise birthday lunch party. Heather had just finished up her TV series *Dynasty*, in which she played Sammy Jo, a mean and cunning bad girl. The ladies took me to a fine old Savannah institution that was located in an old brownstone. Thrilled to host us, the owner made sure we were seated at his best table—front and center, so everyone might see Heather Locklear eating at his place. Heather was sitting between Nancy and me. Midway into my delightful birthday party, a group of women came in. They were led by a woman about sixty years old and burly—and big. Bulky. With thick grandma arms cocked at an angle to support the weight of the huge purse that anchored her right arm. As she walked by our table, she stopped short, eyeing Heather. She bent down and looked right at her, uncomfortably eye to eye, making sure her cataract-glazed eyeballs were seeing what she thought they were seeing. She had a five-word question for Heather. "Sammy Jo—is that *you*?"

Sweetly, Heather smiled and said, "Yes, I'm Heather Locklear and I play Sammy Jo on—" She got no further. The woman launched into a tirade. "I saw what you did to your husband, Jeff, last week on TV! He's such a nice man, and *you* are doing all these horrible things to him behind his back! I think you're the worst person on earth, you *bitch*!" As she said the word *bitch*, she made a fist and punched Heather in her arm as hard as she could. Heather, of diminutive stature, started falling backward in her chair as Nancy and I reached out to stop her from crashing onto the floor. The woman marched off in a huff (or was it a minute and a huff?). (See the Marx Brothers in *Animal Crackers*.) As Heather rubbed her upper-right arm, I got up to call the cops and make the proverbial federal case out of this assault and battery of my friend and my star.

Heather made me sit down and explained, "This happens from time to time. Some people can't discern the difference between what they see every week in their living room on TV from what they see or experience in real life. It's OK."

I gave silent thanks to the Lord that I remain protected behind the camera and can venture out in public without experiencing the curse fame can bring when you are highly visible. But I didn't learn my lesson. On the last day of shooting—it was a Saturday—I offered to take Heather to the best restaurant in Savannah, Elizabeth's, in another old brownstone. Filming went long, and we got there a bit late. The dinner was incredible, but it was after 11:00 p.m. when we finished. We walked out the door and down the old steps leading to the hedge-lined walkway that led to the street. It was dark there. Just as we got to the bottom step, a man jumped out of the bushes, lunging forward toward us. In that split instant, without noticing whether he was holding a gun or what, I remember thinking simply, *I'm going to die*. Heather and I stood in shock and fear as the tie-and-jacket-clad man started talking a hundred miles a minute:

"Don'tbescared.I'mnotgonnahurtyou.MywifeandIwereinsideaandsawyoucomeinand we'reyourbiggestfansHeathersowe'vebeenwaitinghereforovertwohoursforyoutocomeou tjusttogetyourautograph.Pleasedon'tbescared.Look!There'smywifeinourcarparkedright infrontthere!See?"

With my heart pounding in my ears, my ears ringing, and my stomach twisting, I gave a dazed glance to the curb, where a gum-chewing woman with the most pronounced southern accent I'd ever heard was waving frantically, hanging out of her car window yelling, "Hi there, Heather!" While I wavered between a stroke and a coronary, Heather recovered, smiled, and signed an autograph for what she saw as fans and I saw as felons. So yeah, hanging out with famous people can be cool, but doing it in public can be a nightmare.

Ahhh! The joys and ease of that looming *P* for Production! *Not*!

CHAPTER TEN

The POST

When it's Post time in the movie business, horses do not run. Instead, principal photography of the film has been completed, and, under the direction of the director, the process moves to postproduction, including continuing editing, visual FX, music, sound work, color correction, and a thousand other things that make the product a finished product. The point here as it applies to life is that after what you have principally been doing ends and the hubbub dies down and the spotlight moves off you, you are not finished . . . not by a long shot.

I'm still here.

—BATMAN, ARC 14–20

A man's success is not measured by his accomplishments, but rather by how hard he tried.

—JOSEPH USLAN, MY DAD

There is still much to do, much to accomplish, and new goals and objectives to achieve. This is life's "post." So stay tethered to young people, embrace the uncertainty of changing times and the unknown, escape from your comfort zone, and then do not go gently into the night. Without post, a movie is incomplete and remains a work in progress. Life echoes film.

You have to finish what you start. Persevere. See it to the end. Even if it means a stream of endless overnights sitting in a windowless editing room consuming coffee, caffeine, Cokes, and chocolate to stay not merely awake but creatively vital. In the transcendent words of my Yankee baseball hero and onetime New Jersey neighbor, Yogi Berra, "It ain't over till it's over!" The singular biggest mistake people make in Hollywood is that they overpromise and underdeliver. In actuality, nothing counts until you deliver your finished project per your contractual requirements, with a gold star if on time and on or under budget.

With the stunning worldwide success of *Batman*, did I then take a vacation . . . a trip around the world . . . even a week down the shore in Asbury Park? Far from it. The insecure question always is, "Will I ever work again?" As a Hollywood producer, I was totally motivated to roll up my sleeves and get back into the fray.

Let us refer to the aftermath of the incredible success of our first *Batman* movie in 1989 as "post time." Some opportunities came to my door, but I stayed centered on making things happen for myself. And for a while, I tried to find a path to do something with my friends over at Marvel. Bizarrely, that path to Marvel began with the two actors who played Lois Lane and Jimmy Olsen on the 1950s television series *The Adventures of Superman*. No kidding!

The nifty fifties was not only overflowing with boomed babies but also with the booming magical entertainment provider, news informer, sports presenter, and babysitter known as "television." Marshall McLuhan, a famed philosopher of media, called it all a "vast wasteland." Maybe it was . . . except . . . amid that wasteland was a sprinkle of comic book superheroes (Superman, Sheena Queen of the Jungle, Captain Midnight or Jet Jackson as he was called in overdubbed syndicated reruns), a dash of comic strip heroes (Jungle Jim, Flash Gordon, Terry and the Pirates, Steve Canyon, Dick Tracy), and a cowboy who had all the required elements of being a superhero without quite being a superhero (the Lone Ranger). But indisputably, the top of this TV food chain was . . . who else? Superman!

Superman was there on TV in glorious black and white since my earliest memories. I said my prayers every night just the way my parents taught them to me . . . except secretly in my head, when I was hailing down God for one request or another, I was picturing Superman or, more accurately, George Reeves. To me, God and Superman were kinda sorta one and the same.

As I moved into my teen years, my folks bought our first color TV and I learned two important things about this sacred TV series: first, in the opening of each show, the words the narrator was saying were *not* "Ben Steel with his bear, Hans" but rather "bend steel with his bare hands"; and second, a whole bunch of later episodes of *The Adventures of Superman* were filmed in color! Over the years as I began to reminisce about these hundred-plus episodes, the one I always remembered most strongly was the black-and-white episode that had the most spectacular special effects of any TV show of the 1950s. I think it was called "Money to Burn"; it was about a food truck called the Fireman's Friend. I recollected watching as there was a titanic warehouse fire. Lois Lane, Jimmy Olsen, and Perry White were all there covering the story for the great metropolitan newspaper *The Daily Planet*. They watched as Superman flew down from the clouds, crashed through the roof of the burning building, and put out the fire with his incredible superpowers, invulnerable to the flames! Can you imagine such spectacular special effects in a TV program from the 1950s? Well, as it turns out, *imagine* was the operative word.

We now jump ahead to the 1980s. I always derive a masochistic pleasure out of trying to be at the head of change and whatever may be coming around the next three corners. And there is a price to be paid for trying to be a pioneer or trying to be ahead of the curve. That exact situation came about circa 1983 where my cousin Brucie Solomon and I focused on this new term known as *interactive*. We wanted to start making interactive programming, and at that time, the most promising technology came through the advent of what were called interactive videodiscs. They resembled LPs . . . classic vinyl . . . but were high-tech silver, not black. There were only two and a half companies at that time taking the lead in this new field: RCA, which had a system played by a stylus just like the old record albums; Pioneer, which featured the more futuristic laser disc technology; and a company that had not yet put out any product, VHD, a joint venture between Thorn-EMI, JVC, and General Electric. I quickly formed Interactive Productions, Inc. and pitched a project to VHD's Barr Potter, a former member of our United Artists legal team before he moved on up to become president of one of the mini-major studios of the era, Largo.

"The First National Trivia Quiz Disc" covered my favorite pop culture categories: Rock 'n' Roll hosted by 1950s teen idol Fabian; Comic Books hosted by Captain America and Spider-Woman courtesy of Marvel; and Television and Movies hosted by Lois Lane and Jimmy Olsen from *The Adventures of Superman*, Noel Neill and Jack Larson.

Working and just hanging out with Noel and Jack was a fanboy's childhood dream come true in the absence of the late George Reeves himself. Two of the nicest people on earth, they answered every one of the hundreds of questions my cousin Brucie and I threw at them over meals, drinks, and breaks in filming. I thirsted for every story . . . every anecdote they could recall. I literally interrogated them on the murder of George Reeves. Correct. I said *murder*, not *suicide*. I heard all their private insights that when coupled with the stories I heard from my *Batman* partner, Benjamin Melniker, who was the executive vice president of MGM in the days when legendary tough guy Eddie Mannix was the head of physical production for the studio . . . a character Ben purposefully stayed far away from. For a fuller discourse on the lethal connection between George Reeves and Eddie Mannix, go watch the chilling Ben Affleck movie *Hollywoodland*.

But the most staggering revelation that came with working with Noel and Jack was centered on my asking about my favorite episode. Jack listened to me recount the details of that show as my eyes opened as wide as those of a mesmerized six-year-old magically transported back in time. Then Jack quizzed me.

"Michael, you remember seeing Superman fly down and crash through the roof?"

"How could I ever forget it, Jack?" I replied.

He continued the grilling. "And which was more spectacular to you, watching Superman doing that or him putting out the inferno without the enveloping flames killing him?"

I was torn. But I had to go with the crashing through the burning roof at near superspeed. The next day, Jack came to the set with either a VHS or Betamax videotape containing my cherished "Money to Burn." We watched it together. I was far beyond stunned. I was blown away by what Jack and Noel shared with me. Jack prepared me, but to no avail. He posited the rhetorical question, "Michael, how could our show have such amazing special effects when we had a budget for them of maybe $250 per episode?" He fast-forwarded the tape to the immortal scene in question. Feeling as if I was trapped in a cruel episode of *The Twilight Zone,* I watched in shocked disbelief the scene of Superman flying down at superspeed and crashing through the flaming roof of the warehouse. The reason? There was no inferno. There was no warehouse. There was no Superman flying down at superspeed. There was no Superman crashing through the roof. What there was, was Perry White, Lois Lane, Jimmy Olsen, and a couple of the firemen's friends looking up (flickering lights on them substituting for visible flames), some pointing skyward, and such comments as "Look! Here comes Superman," "He's crashing through the roof of the building," and "He's putting out the fire!" Time lapsed: approximately nineteen seconds. Special effects budget: clearly under $250. Ah, but what a miracle of life is the fervid imagination and sense of wonder of a little boy! An important lesson learned by me thanks to *my* never-to-be-forgotten Jimmy Olsen and Lois Lane, Jack Larson and Noel Neill.

Having completed my first state-of-the-art interactive videodisc, I began to imagine just how I could create interactive adventures of America's favorite superheroes in the form of a live-action version of those tech stone-age "Choose Your Own Adventure" books. The technology existed. It could be done. And so, I headed over to the offices of Marvel Comics on Park Avenue in New York. I had a long session with Marvel's president, the forward-looking Jim Galton, and his right-hand exec, the visionary Joe Calamari. I showed them what we had just done and laid out my vision for the Marvel Universe we could bring to life on interactive videodiscs, which also represented the birth of a brand-new revenue stream for Marvel's intellectual properties. But I cautioned them that there were only three companies in this particular business who could finance this massive undertaking and distribute the finished videodiscs. They were both willing to bet on the future and came aboard. When the smoke cleared, I was acquiring all interactive rights to the entire Marvel library of characters for an upfront payment of $5,000. No, not $500 million, not $5 million, not $500,000, not $50,000. $5,000. Looking back, that was potentially not the deal of a lifetime. It was the deal of a millennium.

If my life was, indeed, a comic book, this is where a yellow rectangular caption box would appear over my head and in black hand-lettered print would appear, "Suddenly . . ."

VHD faltered and closed up shop before it ever launched in the United States, relegating our "First National Trivia Quiz Disc" into the eternal drop of amber known as a film laboratory. I quickly raced to RCA Video Productions, also in New York, which at that precise moment blinked while staring into the eye of Pioneer and shut down its stylus system under the glare of Pioneer's laser beams. I was down to one and only one source for financing and headed to the executive offices of Pioneer in north Jersey. And when I presented my silver platter of all interactive rights to the Marvel Universe for $5,000, they responded, "Yeah, well, we really don't have a lot of faith in real interactive programming. We see it more as a great opportunity to present music whereby you can cut to anyplace in a concert you want, and maybe using the two audio channels to have two different languages to narrate documentaries." In desperation, I offered to split the $5,000 with them. They responded courteously, "No, thanks." If my life was, indeed, a comic book, this is where you would see one of those round word balloons with a pointy thingy emitting this lettering from my mouth, all in caps:

"GAAAAAAAAAAAHHHH!!!"

Post-*Batman* 1989, I tried to open an inroad at Marvel again, this time via my idol, mentor, and friend Stan "The Man" Lee. Stan and I were having lunch one day at his primary restaurant in LA, Nate 'n' Al's. He told me that Marvel Animation was going out with a syndicated block of cartoons under the banner of the "Marvel Universe." There were four slots to program with superheroes. Marvel decided on three of them from its library but were leaving the final slot open in order to try something new and develop and produce an original IP. Of course, seeing an opportunity, I grabbed it and pitched Stan on the spot. He loved it and brought me in to see the now-legendary Margaret Loesch, who was heading up the company. I had known Margaret since her days at Hanna-Barbera, the animation house that brought us *The Flintstones* and *The Jetsons.* (Ten years after this project, Margaret would be the one heading Fox Kids as together we brought *Swamp Thing* to animation.)

I was pitching a brand-new and very state-of-the-art high-tech version of the old TV series my generation adored as kids, *Captain Video.* Margaret added her enthusiasm to Stan's, and we quickly made the deal. At the last minute, Stan decided we needed to make it clearer that our character was not the same one as from TV in the early fifties. With my begrudging assent, he dubbed our hero "Commander Video." We quickly made up a sales kit and some ad sheets and prepared to sell the Marvel Universe show into syndication as a Marvel block of programming. Excelsior? Hardly. I don't even recall the order of events, but Marvel was bought yet again, new people came in, Margaret left, and Captain Video and the Marvel Universe show vanished horizontally and vertically into a cloud of static. Who would do such a painful thing? Hollywould!

I reiterated my mantra . . . "Have a high threshold for frustration" . . . and then tried Marvel attempt number three:

Now steering clear of animation, I zeroed in on some live-action projects. First, I acquired the rights to *Luke Cage, Hero for Hire,* which included *Heroes for Hire* and *Iron Fist.* Because Luke Cage was the first African American character to have his own comic book, I felt that this would be best to develop hand in hand with Motown Productions. It agreed and had a deal with Universal for financing and distribution. Everyone loved the concept of a street-smart, urban, serious picture. As work was just beginning on a screenplay, my partner, Ben, informed me of a call he received from one of the truly important behind-the-scenes people in music over the years, Clarence Avant. Clarence was now on the board of Motown and wanted to have lunch with us at the Friars Club in New York, not far from our office at the MGM Building. Clarence heard about the Luke Cage project and was excited to see Motown dip its toe into that genre following the success of our *Batman* movie. He was very much in tune with my work of building or, better yet, rebuilding global branded franchises. He then spoke of all the musical assets it had, generally gathering dust in the Motown library. Clarence wondered if I saw any way to blow off the dust. Instantaneously, an idea hit me. It would be geared for what today we call streaming but back then was limited to syndicated television. As I was formulating the pitch in my head, the words started churning out:

"World building! We create the Detroit version of Gotham City and call it 'Motown.' Within that world, we create groups of urban superheroes. For music, we adapt classic Motown songs into more contemporary music styles sung by new groups. The first superhero group is called 'The Supremes,' and the three powerful women comprising it have Supreme Power, Supreme Grace, and Supreme Beauty. The male group of superheroes is known as 'The Miracles,' and each of the three men are able to make miracles happen. Armed with magical powers, the next three-member female group is called 'The Marvelettes,' possibly the only trademark Marvel doesn't control! And the prince of magic in Motown is a blind boy who channels his sense of wonder into real magic. His name? Stevie Wonder!"

Clarence absolutely, positively loved what he was hearing, but had a crucial question: "Michael, who would they all fight? Who's the supervillain?"

I responded that this villain was eternal and had been the undoing of man since man first appeared on earth. "It's a group of four males known only as 'The Temptations'!"

Clarence almost fell out of his chair. Then, we started together to bring up old Motown hit song titles, and we realized they could be episode titles such as "Turn to Stone" or "Stop! In the Name of Love."

The deal of the century? Hardly. I don't even recall the order of events, but Universal was bought yet again, new people came in, Clarence left, and ultimately both *Luke Cage, Hero for Hire* and *The Motown Superheroes* projects vanished into the night. Why? Continual corporate changes in the industry and bad ol' development hell. Who would do such a painful thing? Hollywould!

There was a time . . . it felt like a minute and a half . . . that New World owned Marvel. The head of it was the great Hollywood producer and exec Bob Rehme. We made our *Swamp Thing* movie deal with Bob when he was the president of Avco-Embassy. He wasn't president of Marvel long before he summoned me to his office.

"Mike, you and Wes Craven worked really well together on *Swamp Thing*, right?" Bob inquired.

"Absolutely!" I emphatically replied. "He's a friend . . . and I have the greatest respect for him and his talent. What's up?"

"I want to start mining the Marvel Comics library, and I know you are the comic book guy in Hollywood. Are you familiar with a comic book character called 'Dr. Strange'?"

"Next to Spider-Man, he's my favorite Marvel superhero! I have a complete collection of the comic books. I'm a total fan of Steve Ditko!" I announced like the fanboy I still am.

"We've hired Wes to write and direct a Dr. Strange TV series. But he doesn't know the character. Can I put you guys together? You'll be an executive producer," decreed Bob.

I jumped in with both feet! I filled Wes in on everything Dr. Strange and then faxed (remember fax machines?) him the entire early Ditko run of "The Hunter and the Hunted" as Doc was being tracked down by the malevolent Baron Mordo. I suggested to Wes that this could become Season One, ending with the initial appearance of the dreaded Dormamu. We could plant teasers throughout Season One of an even greater threat skulking invisibly in the shadows, then introduce Nightmare at the end of Season Two. Season Three would end with Dr. Strange encountering Eternity. As Wes was inhaling the comics I sent him and processing all of it in his usual grandly creative way, something else, worthy of a great supervillain, was lurking around the next corner.

I don't even recall the order of events, but New World and Marvel were bought yet again, new people came in, Bob left, and ultimately the Dr. Strange project vanished into another dimension. Why? Continual corporate changes in the industry and bad ol' development hell. Who would do such a painful thing? Hollywould!

On the heels of that disappointment yet still wanting to do something with Marvel, I wrote a lengthy treatment for a Captain Marvel live-action feature film. But by then, Marvel started to consolidate the rights to all its characters that had been scattered to the Santa Anna winds throughout La La Land.

Frustrated but refusing to give up, I turned my attention back to the roots of comic book filmmaking: the comic books. I submitted two long treatments to Marvel to write as miniseries / graphic novels. Long before anyone thought to make an *Avengers* movie, I wanted to write a miniseries called *The Cosmic Cube* and had a very cool story mapped out as to how its possession adversely affected any hero or villain who tried to access it. I was told that it tied into too many characters whose storylines were already set for the next year or two. My final attempt was to revive the comic book title *Marvel Mystery Comics* as a six-issue miniseries that would create a 1939 to '45 Marvel Golden Age of characters who would be the forerunners of the Silver Age's Spider-Man, Iron Man, Thor, Hulk, Ant-Man, Daredevil, certain members of the Fantastic Four, and X-Men. It won wide praise but fell to the fact that they were not interested in period pieces at that time. Would that be the last time I attempted to do something big with Marvel post-*Batman*? Nope. One more big opportunity came around the corner in the 1990s. Did I say "big" opportunity? I meant to say "BIG" opportunity! Fasten your seat belts!

Marvel had gone bankrupt again. Through a good friend of mine and major domo on Wall Street, I was introduced to bigwigs at a huge investment banking firm. I presented my business plan to them for buying Marvel. I broke it down into the parts of the entertainment industry in which I had experience: comic books and publishing, merchandising, animation, feature films, television, video gaming, and what today we would call "location-based entertainment" but back then were simply referred to as "theme parks." The investment bankers were now excited at the possibilities. They put together a small team of lawyers and accountants to journey with me to Newark, New Jersey, where we spent three days and three nights at the offices of the bankruptcy trustee. I read every contract and saw all the numbers. When finished, we all reconvened at the Wall Street headquarters. That was when they dropped their analysis on me. They saw a company financially hemorrhaging in almost every department and felt Marvel would go bankrupt a third time. So rather than buy the company for $95 million, they told me their strategy would be to wait until the company went bankrupt a third time, and then they'd just quickly move in to cherry-pick the IP rather than buy the whole company. I remember the exact words of my response: "Nonononono." It sounded like I was stuttering madly over the word *no* and couldn't stop. I pleaded my case, going back to my business plan and repeating how I knew what to do to remake each department and showing a list of the creative and administrative top people I would bring in. I ended my plea with, "Pay the $95 million. I want the pencils and the desks and chairs. I want all the IP. I even want Jack Kirby's cigar butts if any are left." They responded calmly, acknowledging that I was an expert in my fields and they were the experts in investment banking and corporate takeovers. Here's a direct quote, circa 1990s: "Michael, relax. Take a chill pill. It will go bankrupt a third time, and we will acquire the IP you want."

It didn't go bankrupt a third time. Another buyer snatched the company and later flipped it to Disney for a reported $4 billion. Current estimated market value of Marvel: $5 billion. And that brings me back to circa 1984, the year I tried to buy DC Comics.

Back then, I was developing the first animated TV series I created, *Dinosaucers*. Mentoring me through the world of television cartoons and merchandising was the great

Stan Weston, one of the architects of the original *Star Wars* merchandising, the man who eventually sold G.I. Joe to Hasbro for reportedly $50,000 after the popularity of the toy dolls died down, and the man behind ThunderCats and SilverHawks. One day in his amazing penthouse suite on Central Park South, Stan mentioned to me that he was going to be having lunch that week with Steve Ross, then head of Warner Communications, owner of Warner Bros., *MAD Magazine*, and DC Comics. I informed Stan that in my various dealings with Warner, there were some execs from an earlier generation who, back in the 1950s, heard the continual attacks on comic books branded as the primary cause of the post–World War II rise of juvenile delinquency in America. I told him I thought some of them might actually be embarrassed at owning a comic book company. This brought to mind a story Stan Lee told me. He said back in the 1950s and early '60s, he hated going to society's cocktail parties in New York. Invariably, Stan said, people would come up to him and ask what he did for a living. Insecure, Stan would reply, "I'm a writer," then would quickly walk away. Often, those people would follow him, intrigued, then ask, "What is it you write?" Stan's patented answer was always, "I write children's literature," and then he would hurriedly head across the room. Sure enough, they would follow him again to ask, "How interesting! What type of children's literature do you write?" Surrendering, Stan would smile and say, "I write comic books." And then, Stan stated, they would walk away. That, indeed, was the context of comic books in society at the time. I felt that some Warner people kind of reacted the same way. I suggested to Stan Weston that if he had an opening, he should ask Steve if he would have any interest in selling DC. Stan agreed it was worth an inquiry.

The day of the Stan and Steve lunch, I was busy writing more *Dinosaucers* material to ready my pitch. Around two o'clock, Stan called me and asked how fast I could make it to his office. I said half an hour and sped out the door. He broke the news to me that I had called it correctly. Steve was willing to sell DC but keep all the rights in Superman except comic book publishing. The good news was the company wanted only $11 million, believing at that time that the one and only valuable comic book property was Superman. Period. The bad news was that we would only have sixty days to get the money and close the deal. On your mark! Get ready! Get set! Go!

We were laughed out of Wall Street offices. "Eleven million for a 'funny book' company?! You guys are crazy!" That was the general response we received from everyone we talked to or met with. Who would give all that money to two obvious nut cases? We couldn't raise the money in time. Stan told me that Steve's plan was to offer DC to Marvel next. And history tells us . . . they did exactly that. Stan Lee wanted the DC characters, but his boss's enthusiasm was quickly quelled by lawyers who warned him of a potential long and expensive legal mess over monopolizing the marketplace. I could only dream of what DC's characters would look like re-created in the Marvel style by Stan Lee. And then . . . I made my dream come true!

The June 1989 world premiere of *Batman* in two movie theaters simultaneously in Westwood was a magical experience. All of the limousine routes to the red carpet were lined by rows and rows and rows of fans and Bat-Maniacs. All of Westwood was jammed with spectators and partygoers celebrating the true dark and serious Batman's debut. With all the top stars there, I remained the true comic book geek I was. I was most excited to hang out that evening with Bob Kane and Stan Lee. As fans came up asking all of us for our autographs, Bob grabbed the pen from my hand.

"What are you doing?" he asked.

Puzzled, I said I was signing a poster for a kid.

Bob said, "Don't cheat them. Give 'em their money's worth with your autograph."

Right there on the spot, he taught me how to draw Batman's symbol so I could place my autograph inside the picture of a bat. I've done it ever since. How cool! Together, the three of us got into conversations with Burgess Meredith and Cesar Romero, respectively The Penguin and The Joker from the *Batman* TV series, but actors I've admired since I was a kid. (Burgess Meredith starred in the most terrifying episode of *The Twilight Zone* that a kid like me with 20-800 vision could experience. In it, Meredith's glasses broke and he was the last man alive on earth, with no chance to replace them! Yikes!)

And then, I listened to Stan Lee and Bob Kane kid each other. Stan instigated it. "Bob, if only I was the writer of *Batman* when you were drawing it! Then you *really* could have had a hit character!" Bob retaliated, "Yeah? Well it's too bad, Stan, that I wasn't drawing Spider-Man when you were writing it because I could've really made it something popular!" And I'm standing there listening to this. Hmmm . . . what if Stan Lee had started his career in 1939 at DC Comics rather than Marvel? Just imagine what Stan Lee's creation of Batman, "Marvel style," might have looked and acted like! Or Stan's Superman or Green Lantern or Justice League . . .

Years later, I would resurrect this moment . . . this notion . . . and be the first one to bring Stan Lee over to write for DC Comics in cahoots with the most legendary classic comic book artists and the most cutting-edge new artists. He and I would embark on a thirteen-issue, yearlong project called "Just Imagine." And I would be in his office in LA the day comic artist legend John Buscema (*The Silver Surfer, Thor, The Avengers, Conan,* and so many more) sent in his original art to the very first such issue, "Just Imagine Stan Lee Creating Superman." Buscema's art was astounding and would prove to be his last full work before his passing. But Stan had a big problem with the way one page was drawn. It wasn't the dynamic layout he wanted. Stan quickly taped a piece of tissue paper over the page of art and handed it to me along with a Sharpie. Stan would dictate and show me what he wanted Buscema to draw. I was to draw it on the page so John would get the idea. Next thing I know, Stan's climbing on his couch and end table to show me the pose he wanted. "Draw this, Michael!" he yelled enthusiastically as he acted out the scene, panel by panel, just exactly the way I had heard and read he used to do with his favorite Marvel artist ever,

RIGHT: I brought Marvel's Stan Lee to DC to re-create DC's superheroes in Stan's own Marvel image. His Superman featured the final magnificent artwork of John Buscema.

DC
Just Imagine Stan Lee's
Superman
Just Imagine Stan Lee with John Buscema creating Superman
Chris Chuckry
M. Uslan K. Baker

Jack "King" Kirby! But here . . . now . . . I was Jack Kirby! I was frickin' Jack Kirby working creatively on Superman with Stan Lee! Lord! I had reached the mountaintop!

And then, the "other" Stan . . . Stan Weston . . . came back to see me with two partners in a new venture. I recognized one of them. It was famed Broadway director George Abbott, who already was about one hundred years old. The men had optioned the Broadway stage musical rights for *Star Wars*. Stan came to me and asked me if I'd be interested in helping them crack this. I leaped! I actually wrote two drafts of a Broadway musical treatment for *Star Wars*, but his business associates freaked when they heard what I wanted to do. I wanted to get the biggest possible theater, rip out the seats, and rig them for movement and vibration. I wanted lasers and state-of-the-art special effects and sound systems put in. I broke down how I would imagine the bottom of the gigantic mother ship entering under the ceiling and how we would project the receding prologue onto the stage. And then I said, as of that time, that only Elton John or Paul McCartney could do the music. Stan totally got it, but some of the more traditional and conservative businesspeople thought I was completely nuts. They lectured me that Jimmy Webb should do the music and that silver-haired, upper-middle-class people (and up) from the city and the suburbs come to see Broadway musicals and they wouldn't tolerate such craziness. I explained that this would be revolutionary and would *not* simply attract those theatergoers but would open Broadway up to an entire new audience of youth and fans. Needless to say, it didn't happen. Not that Stan didn't try everything to make everyone "get it." Decades later, Spider-Man attempted Broadway. By then, I thought they should build a three-thousand-seat interactive theater just for *Star Wars* and not try cramming it into a Broadway theater. Spider-Man became the biggest money loser in history on Broadway.

At this painful point, it sounds as if virtually every project I developed met an untimely end. A lot of my pals in the Biz feel that a success rate in Hollywood would be somewhere between 10 and 20 percent. My own ratio of success to failure would make me a prized major league baseball player. I dwelled on many of our successes in my previous tome, *The Boy Who Loved Batman*. But the failures and misadventures are an important part of my story and really anyone's story. Those are truly what wind up defining you. In the immortal words of Thomas Wayne, "Why do we fall? So that we can learn to pick ourselves back up."

You don't have to be in physical production on a movie or streaming series to learn that every project, big or small, animated or live action, is a big production from inception through final exploitation.

As for the *P* that stands for Post, that's when everything coalesces . . . the film, the editing, the sound, the color correction, the music and effects, the looping, the CGI. In my life, *Post* represents the drive to take action on whatever may be the next ten or twenty projects and, when necessary, force myself out of my comfort zone and reinvent myself, always trying to adapt to the revolutionary pace of change in content and tech, the "show" and the "business," which collectively constitute the state of mind called "Hollywood."

CHAPTER ELEVEN

The PUBLICITY & PROMOTION

One of the many, many lessons my mom drubbed into me over her lifetime was dramatically summed up to me while I was still in school at Indiana University and was about to start teaching the world's first ever college accredited course of comic books. She simply said, "Michael, you can have the greatest creative ideas ever, but if you don't market them and market yourself, no one will ever know of your creative wares."

No miracles. . . . Just life. Just us.

—BATMAN: ABSOLUTION

She was as right as always, and in today's era of social media, podcasts, and postings, this is possible to accomplish on a limited budget for anyone willing to put in the hours and make it work. As Marvel's legendary Stan Lee once told me, he spent decades building the Marvel brand and the day came when the corporation was no longer quite so interested in him or his ideas. That was when he realized he had to start building and promoting the Stan Lee brand. It was a game changer for the entire last chapter in his life. He told me to build my own brand and market myself.

My first years at United Artists when it was one of the major studios were fun though challenging days learning every aspect of the movie biz. I was able to use my law school copyright background often. I learned how to do deals and contracts for novelizations, music, records, toys and assorted merchandising, and even brand-new products when they popped up . . . like when some fellow invented a thing called a "photo-novel," which was a paperback book that looked like a comic book but the panels were made up of stills from a movie that had comic book word balloons added, thus telling the story of the movie. The Italians called it "fumetti." The studio considered them, along with novelizations of the movie screenplays, to be a promotion tool rather than specifically a revenue-generating source. I had to do one photo-novel contract for *Rocky 2* and another for our remake of *Invasion of the Body Snatchers*, which starred one of my favorite actors, *Star Trek*'s Leonard Nimoy. One of the great nights of my career was spending the evening at Leonard's house talking science fiction, old-time dramatic radio, and Judaism with him. He was a very intelligent, warm, and pious man. It was cool to be involved in a movie he had made.

Regarding that movie, the publisher of the photo-novel waited until the last minute to send me the galleys to approve before going to press, and that's when the crisis erupted. The lead actress, Brooke Adams, had in her contract a provision barring the release of any nude photos of her from the film. Yet in one of the stills in the photo-novel there they were, being aired in public! I called the publisher and said he couldn't do that. He had a meltdown. He claimed he would lose tons of money if he didn't go to press immediately. Immediately? I told him, not with this picture in it. But he pleaded it was too late to change that picture. I was unmoved. He shouldn't have waited until the last minute to send it to me to approve. Now he called up our head of merchandising, the deft and adept Bill Dennis, who trotted up to my office. Bill was desperately trying to find a solution. He looked at me and said, "Hey, Michael . . . didn't you work in comic books?" I told him I worked for DC. He wanted to know if I ever worked in production there. I assured him I had served some time in that department. So he asked me if this was a comic book rather than a photo-novel, what would I do? I told him I'd take a razor blade to cut and paste up bits to fix the problem, then would clean it up with a touch of ink or Wite-Out. Bill ran out and came back with a razor blade, a pen, ink, and Wite-Out. Like a top surgeon, I razored out Brooke's word balloon from that still, then repositioned it across the offending breasts. That doesn't sound right. They were offending only her contract provision. I touched up the still and off it directly went to the printer. It was already about 8:00 p.m. on the East Coast, so Bill left and brought back some Christmas cheer and we each grabbed two cups before calling it a night ... but a successful night in the wacky movie biz.

Meanwhile, back at UA, every day was different, and my learning curve kept growing. Some days were grinding and tough, some were fun and wacky, and some were spent just dealing with Hollywood being Hollywood.

I had just started working for the studio. I was fresh out of law school. I got off to an inauspicious start when one of my new superiors assigned me my first task as a studio lawyer—the mundane job of negotiating a lease for new warehouse space in Long Island City just over the Fifty-Ninth Street Bridge that, in 1976, was still "Feelin' Groovy" courtesy of the Paul Simon tune that was popularized by Harper's Bizarre. I was directed to the UA warehouse files to see how these leases were drafted and negotiated. In an effort to do a stellar job on my first assignment, I decided to go above and beyond the call of duty. My research turned up the fact that UA had a warehouse in Brooklyn that wasn't being utilized, and I brought this to a superior's attention in an attempt to save the corporation money.

I had my head bit off. I got yelled at. I felt like I was back at Indiana University in the halls of Sigma Alpha Mu getting hazed up and down and sideways by the brothers. I remembered the sting of the paddle on Hell Night as I was left with a red imprinted "Sigma" on my ass for six days. My butt wanted to race for cover instinctively, but I stood my ground and took it like a man. I thought I was being fired my first week on the job. After a tirade that seemed to go on for a number of days, I was told that I still had a job but that it had a new description: *Do Not Question.*

That's when I started asking questions. I made friends around the many departments of the studio and was rewarded with valuable insight into the "real" world, compliments of a lovely mole in advertising and marketing. The company had just had a big hit with a Stephen King movie called *Carrie* that had put Sissy Spacek on the map as a major star. Happily, the studio had another horror-thriller coming up that also was female driven and based on a novel. I was told that the advertising and marketing people believed that in order to best duplicate the success of *Carrie,* they needed to be able to state in trailers and ads that, like *Carrie,* this movie was based on a best-selling book. It was deemed critical to the marketing strategy. And so, magically, copies of the book apparently began selling like what were once hotcakes but today are more like Springsteen concert tickets, at all the secret bookstores that a leading newspaper was using to compile its best-sellers list. Coincidentally, I managed to learn, that the warehouse in Long Island City was quickly filling up—supposedly with pristine, unread copies of the new book ... just enough copies to make it a best seller for one week.

The day I made this discovery, I headed out to lunch in seedy Times Square. Ads for soft drinks, cigarettes, cars, alcohol, TVs, sexy underwear, airlines, and financial services screamed and blinked at me in neon splendor. I thought about how one movie studio could manipulate my taste in books and movies without my knowledge, and I started wondering about what all those other corporations were doing—the bigger ones. To what extent was

I as a consumer being dangled like a marionette by a host of puppeteers I did not know? Is the freedom of choice I've always thought I've enjoyed not as free as I thought? This was my first real job in what everyone told me was now, postcollege, the real world. Unreal!

In my world, the effectiveness and budget for the promotion and publicity of a film is as important as the film itself. The marketing clout and apparatus of the marketing department of a major Hollywood studio can make the difference between the success and failure of a movie. I believe our 1989 *Batman* movie was possibly the best traditionally marketed film ever. It began with posters and billboards devoid of the name of the picture, showing only a gold oval with a black bat inside. Bold! Creative! Daring! Perfect! The very first trailer followed to let the fans and the rest of the world know that there was no longer a pot-bellied, funny, campy Batman but rather a Dark Knight. And I believe *The Dark Knight* was possibly the best picture marketed to date as social media matured. Kudos to Warner Bros. marketeers and publicists. Brilliant!

But there are other ways promotion and publicity can be used in the entertainment industry. I found out that one company's promotional and publicity efforts can make someone's childhood fantasy come true, if you are willing to seize the moment. It happened to me!

Every January, the television industry has a huge convention called NATPE, the National Association of Television Producers and Executives. These days, it's largely a dinosaur, but back in its heyday, it was "It"! It was, along with Emmy Awards night, the big event of the year for the entire TV industry. Sometimes we took over New Orleans, other years we descended en masse on Houston, San Francisco, Miami, or Las Vegas. Every network, studio, and syndicator erected elaborate booths that were less like normal trade show booths and more like major movie sets. They trotted out every star they could muster. Celebs were everywhere, just waiting to give you an autograph and have their picture taken with you.

The fun and craziness of NATPE is legendary. I had told my best-friend-since-third-grade, Barry Milberg, about it, and he offered to meet me in Vegas and take a few days off from being a pension plans consultant and actuary. After hitting every booth, every party, and every celebrity sighting at NATPE, we stumbled upon our childhood heaven: Turner had a big display promoting its newly revived version of *Leave It to Beaver* along with its perpetual reruns of the original series from the 1950s and '60s. *Leave It to Beaver* was one of our favorite TV series while growing up in Wanamassa. Our friendship was largely patterned after that of Beaver and his pal Whitey (with a dash of Gilbert and a pinch of Larry Mondello mixed in). We had led the life of Beaver Cleaver, because that's just what life in the 1950s 'burbs was like where we grew up. We had our own sweet and kind Miss Landers–like teacher in the form of Mrs. Birkenmeier, who looked remarkably like Sleeping Beauty in the Walt Disney cartoon. Our Gus wasn't a fireman but a school janitor who schooled us in the ways of life without ever using the words our bus driver Crossbones used to describe most people, words like *rat bastards* and *pricks*. No one ever ratted him out to our parents, even while they were washing out our mouths with soap and demanding we reveal our source. Our older siblings were our Wallys (though Barry's Wally was Jessie and she was only a girl, but we forgave her), and they had best friends who could easily have passed for dumb ol' Lumpy and mean and sneaky Eddie Haskell.

So imagine the moment Barry and I turned the corner in the Las Vegas Convention Center and faced the set of the Cleaver family kitchen inside the Turner booth! And who did we see up there signing autographs and having their pictures taken with TV station owners from New York, New York, to Gnaw Bone, Indiana? It was none other than Barbara Billingsley (Beaver's mom, June Cleaver), Tony Dow (Wally), Ken Osmond ("It's Eddie Haskell! Let's get outta here!"), and Jerry Mathers as The Beaver. Taking center stage, Barry and I engaged Wally, Eddie, and Beav in conversation. We were all talking and joking for quite a while when Mrs. Cleaver walked over and said, "My, but you boys have so much to talk about! Sit down here at the kitchen table, and I'll bring you some cookies and milk." *No way*! *Really*? *Actually*! Barry and I now found ourselves seated at the table in the Cleaver's kitchen with Wally, Eddie, and Beaver while being served cookies and milk by Beaver's mom! We didn't talk about it, but I know we all just assumed that Ward (Beaver's dad) was at work. This may have been the singular most surrealistic moment in my life. But it became even more bizarre when Barry summoned up the audacity to ask June, "Mrs. Cleaver, did you in any episode ever really say 'Ward, you're being too hard on the Beaver!'?" Without showing a hint of shock, insult, or embarrassment, Barbara Billingsley bent down and whispered something into Barry's ear. If and when he ever snaps out of it and regains his ability to speak, I intend to ask him what she said to him. Forget Neil Armstrong or Mikhail Gorbachev. On a crisp and sunny day in fabulous Las Vegas, I rubbed elbows with Beaver Cleaver and his family! But I digress . . .

Publicity is also an effective tool if used strategically sometimes to open the door to self-promotion for someone attempting to build his or her brand . . . like the time back in the summer of 1992 in the Big Apple. Democrats from all over the US were amassing in New York City for their convention to nominate Bill Clinton as a presidential candidate. My old law school buddy and former mayoral candidate from Indianapolis, John Sullivan, arrived in town as a delegate from my adopted home state of Indiana. (As you know, I had spent seven magical years at Indiana University in Bloomington—the most magical place on earth; don't be fooled by Disney World's claim to the contrary—while earning my history degree, my MS in urban education, and my law degree.) Sully was the classmate at IU Law I always knew would become a power broker in national politics. He was savvy. Probably his biggest liability for someone with a future in politics was that he was one of the most ethical and stalwart people I've ever met in my journey through life. As you'll see, he also had a great sense of adventure. Sully invited me to be his special guest at the Democratic National Convention, and I was thrilled to be there as a tiny part of the American political equivalent of the Ringling Bros. and Barnum & Baily Circus. He introduced me to his buddies, whose campaigns he had run in one election year or another: Walter Mondale, Paul Simon (the bow-tied one with no Garfunkel), Paul Tsongas, Al Gore, Dick Gephardt, Jerry

Brown, Jimmy Carter, and Diane Feinstein (whose father, Dr. Leon Goldman, had been my wife's lifesaving doctor in Cincinnati back in the super seventies). Gary Hart was spotted there too, having a heated political debate with a southern belle delegate. Before it came to blows, I edged away and then bolted for the California delegation and someone much more alluring: Mary Steenburgen, whom I had heard was a delegate from the Golden State. I'd had a movie crush on her since I saw what I still believe ranks as the best exit scene of an actress in any movie ever, in *Melvin & Howard.* (And if you've never seen the movie *Time after Time,* for which Mary truly won my heart, order it on Netflix now or stop reading this and go out and rent the DVD. While you're at it, check out these vastly underrated great movies on "Michael's Greatest Hits list": *Three Days of the Condor,* which starred my pal Cliff Robertson, who asked me to produce with him the sequel to his Oscar-winning film, *Charly*; *What's Up, Doc?,* arguably one of the best comedies ever made; *12 Angry Men,* my favorite drama that entirely takes place in one room; *North by Northwest,* both my favorite Alfred Hitchcock movie and my favorite Cary Grant film; *Casablanca,* my favorite all-time film; and the three movies I have seen at least fifty times and can watch over and over again for some mystical reason: *My Cousin Vinny* (the perfect movie), *Keeping the Faith,* and *Groundhog Day.* I once tried to convince 20th Century Fox to do *Groundhog Day 2* by rereleasing the first *Groundhog Day* and just calling it *Groundhog Day 2.* They said that was absolutely brilliant and then kicked me out of the room.) But I digress . . .

I found Mary Steenburgen sitting quietly in Section 22, Row 2, in Madison Square Garden. She was as bright, articulate, and cute as I had imagined. We had a great conversation spanning Clinton, politics, and Hollywood, and we found a common bond in a mutual publicist friend. (Thank you, Michael Klastorin! I owe ya one!) Yes, I owed Michael one. And soon, President Clinton would owe Sully one. Look at the two most famous film clips or stills of Clinton shaking hands and giving out hugs amid crowds of people with a lady named Monica Lewinsky in the foreground. Look next to her, and each time you'll find my pal Sully. He, like me, enjoyed rubbing elbows with history. But let me be perfectly clear: only elbows. Others apparently have enjoyed rubbing other body parts with history. I am not one of them. Neither is Sully. So, on this particular night before Bill Clinton would be accepting his party's nomination and addressing the convention, one of the Indiana state delegates received a call that his wife had taken ill and he had to return to the Hoosier State tout suite. He pulled off his lanyard of VIP Delegate Priority Access cards that had been strung as if he had just stepped off a plane in Hawaii and placed this political lei around my neck. With one swift "aloha," this New Jersey–based Hollywood producer became a sort-of voting delegate from Indiana. I accepted this highly quasi-legal responsibility with all the seriousness I could muster and then cast my first-round ballot for Mary Steenburgen as the Democratic candidate for president of the United States. I mean, why not? She was a better actor than Ronald Reagan or Fred Thompson and easily could have played the role of "president" for four years. In the second polling of the Indiana delegates, it was made very, very clear that there was a need for a unanimous vote for Bill Clinton. And when I say "very, very" clear, I mean like back home in North Jersey when "No-Kneecaps" Norman made it very, very clear to my dad, the mason down the shore, that he had a wide choice of *one* concrete company to use on all his construction jobs.

Back at the convention, I took the Wisconsin bull by the horns and quickly made friends with some of the Cheeseheads sitting next to us. Just as Bill Clinton started his acceptance speech, I peered around the arena and spotted the network pool of roving TV cameramen who were searching the seats for the ideal candidates for reaction shots to what was being said by Clinton. When one bulky union guy with a camera neared our section, I knew it was time to act. I reached into my black briefcase and pulled out my official Batman hat from our first *Batman* movie. It was from 1989, and it featured the big black bat logo amid the yellow oval. I put it on and looked as if I was intently listening to Clinton's historic speech, and sure enough, Mr. Bulky Camera Guy caught sight of me and trampled people to get to me. Two rows down, he perched himself in a kneeling position with his camera anchored to his left shoulder as he peered through the lens and prepared to get the shot. I remember thinking he looked like Audie Murphy in that World War II film when he paused to fire a bazooka at a Nazi submachine gun nest. This night, I was that submachine gun nest, for as the red light on his camera blinked, yours truly was preserved for history as the number-one reaction shot captured during Clinton's speech, and by the next day, I had phone calls from dozens of business associates and a whole bunch of cousins I never even knew I had, who'd seen me on TV with the president-elect. Talk about instantaneous results by recognizing and seizing a build-your-own-brand opportunity!

The other side of the publicity and promotion coin is when, as a producer or studio exec, you must arrange for the stars to get out and make appearances on TV, radio, podcasts, online marketing efforts, and so on to promote your film. The second *Swamp Thing* movie starred the wonderful Heather Locklear, one of the nicest people I've ever met. Heather was kind when Nancy visited the set and babysat for David and Sarah. Their other babysitter while on the set was "Uncle Swamp Thing." We tried to preempt our daughter, Sarah, being terrified of Swamp Thing when she saw him for the first time, so we just sorta convinced her he was an uncle with a bad skin condition. I think Sarah still carries in her wallet a picture of herself at age four sitting on Uncle Swamp Thing's lap. David, for some other reason, still has a picture in his wallet of Heather Locklear babysitting him. But I did return the favor when Heather came to New York to do PR and had a busy day booked on everything from "Howard Stern" to "Regis." Ben and I sent over a huge bowl of fruit to the suite at the Plaza Hotel where she and her then-husband, Tommy Lee from the rock band Mötley Crüe, were staying. Tommy and I had had several meetings and meals shared and his knowledge of rock 'n' roll was beyond substantial and we talked for hours about music and the history of the genre.

Shortly after check-in, Heather called me. "Michael, thank you and Ben for sending over that fruit, but you really shouldn't have," said the delightful Ms. Locklear.

"Oh, it was our pleasure, Heather," I replied.

David and Sarah's Uncle Swamp Thing getting touched up on the set.

"No," she retorted, "I mean you really *shouldn't* have. Tommy took all the fruit and is leaning out of our window and bombing people with it in the street below!" She sounded like my mom used to sound on Paul's higher energy days. I tried to apologize, but an apology was not what Heather was looking for. She wanted action. It was payback time. "You guys have me on a nonstop schedule today," she stated matter-of-factly. "I can't take Tommy with me to all these interviews, but, obviously, I can't leave him alone here. Can I drop him by your office on my way to Howard?" Heather and I were now even.

P for Publicity and Promotion applies to us all as individuals and not only to stars, events, corporations, and politicians. Used deftly, it's part of a formula for helping us reinvent ourselves periodically as needed in both our professional lives and our personal lives. These days, social media is the best means of getting results, provided you've done your homework and prep.

CHAPTER TWELVE

The PROFITS (?)

You don't have to be a prophet to realize that in Hollywood, generally speaking, there aren't any profits, so we can skip "12."

The world only makes sense if you force it to.

—THE DARK KNIGHT RETURNS

What there is and has been since the dawn of Talkies is gamesmanship—how the books are kept, based on how the long, long, oftentimes single-spaced contracts with their exhibits and riders are interpreted. For all the people below the A-listers who create great works of art and commerce, who work so hard at their individual crafts that together make the mass experience of moviemaking work so successfully so often—writers, nonstar actors, producers, and directors below the A-listers—the promise of sharing in a back-end participation in the profits of their labors is elusive. Far too often this promise evaporates, time after time, year after year. Case in point: the lawsuit over the long-running hit TV series Frasier, *filed when the studio claimed after eleven seasons and a gross of over $1.5 billion that there were not only zero profits to be shared with the talent but also that the series was still $200 million in the red. Lessons? Better to be driven by passion than by money? David v. Goliath? Corporate America v. creative America? Nikola Tesla v. Thomas Edison? Philo Farnsworth v. RCA? There is an expression popularized if not created by the comic book / comic strip industry that I have never ever heard anyone actually speak in a real-life situation. No one really says or asks, "What the—?" Till now...*

WHAT THE—?

Here's the best lesson I can relay regarding net profits in the movie and television industry...

This page purposefully left blank.

Get the picture?

But it isn't only movie accounting that inflicts itself on the talent. I also write books, obviously, and back in the early days, my cousin Brucie and I wrote a trivia book for a publisher (now long out of business) that taught me a lesson as to how some companies in the Biz keep their books. They use the same jugglers from the old *Ed Sullivan Show*. Case in point: I was in an airport somewhere maybe a year after the book came out. We had been paid a nice advance for it, but the royalty statement indicated that not enough copies had been sold to generate back-end royalties. Now, I spied a copy of our book! Like all proud authors, I picked it up to look at my name looking back at me. Then, like all authors, I pretended to read it with great interest, hoping the lady next to me or the man breathing on my neck would take notice. Then, as soon as I placed the book back down, that lady or man would grab it and race to the checkout to purchase it. As I opened the first page or two, I glanced at the publishing info in small print; it said something I had never seen before: "12th printing." Four days later, Bruce and I, with our new lawyer, were at a lovely and intense meeting with the publisher's editor, accounting person, and general counsel, who apologized for the "oversight." I said that was sort of like going to Hiroshima and apologizing for the "disturbance." He tried to explain that the failure to disclose that not only had the first printing sold out but also that it was up to printing number twelve was legal under the contract provision that stated it had the right to hold back enough royalties as a "reasonable" reserve against returns. In this case, the publisher was saying that secretly retaining over 90 percent of our royalties was "reasonable." Then, our lawyer put some real-world perspective on it, and the publisher settled with us before the meeting ended, including giving us a new contract for an immediate sequel book.

So, generally speaking . . .

P is for Profits (?) . . . *F* is for Forensic Auditing . . . *J* is for Juggling . . . and *N* is for Nothing.

CHAPTER THIRTEEN

The PRIORITIES

Producing is an all-consuming profession. I typically work twelve or more hours per day. My Saturdays and Sundays are often just like my Tuesdays and Wednesdays. I deluded myself that after my first big success in 1989 with *Batman*, life would become easier. It did not. I have never had the luxury of letting up.

With the frosty birth of day, this haunter of darkness "dies" . . . leaving only a weary Bruce Wayne.

—DETECTIVE COMICS #439

There are days I envy my brother, Paul, who gets to close the doors of his optometry office at 5:30 p.m. on Friday and not think about his work again until Monday morning at 9:00 a.m. when he reopens. I think about my business all the time. I never don't think about it . . . the creative, the marketing, the financing, the business, the legal, the challenges, the strategies. If I wasn't doing something I so loved and was so passionate about, they'd have given me a long-armed white jacket and placed me in Arkham with Arthur Fleck, Jack Napier, and the Red Hood. The key to sanity is prioritizing. I was taught by my parents, family first. Always. And I live by that.

Life is messy. Life in the movie and related industries is even messier. If you are successful, life becomes even bigger and messier as you attempt to cash in on your hot streak before the momentum wanes, as it always ultimately does. If you are struggling, however, life becomes even bigger and messier as you attempt to overcome your setbacks by working harder and longer hours, attempting to throw more projects onto the walls to see if anything will stick. Most successful people I know in the industry as they finish a project have a concern, if not a belief, that they may never work again. It sounds crazy, but it's true. And that is a reflection of working in an industry just as famous for its lack of security and safety nets as it is for the famed faces of its stars. What, then, is the thin line necessary to walk between chaos and order? It is an important, yet sometimes intangible line defined by your understanding of your own priorities and how you plan to prioritize both your work and, indeed, your life.

Everyone has varying degrees of responsibilities and obligations. Subject to that list, the rest comes down to the very concept my Batman journey began with way back in my first chapter: passion. My very first mission was to figure out how to incorporate one or more of my passions into my work. The initial two were automatic based on how my brother and I were raised and how we have raised our kids: family first, friends next, work follows.

Regarding my work in this day and age, there is a global incessant demand for content. Content is king. Tech will change. Delivery systems will evolve. When it comes to movies, Hollywood one day may no longer be king. But content will always be king.

But that never-ending appetite for content creates clutter in the marketplace. How can the clutter crisis be addressed? Two basic ways: attach a big star name to a project or base a project on a global branded franchise. The latter explains the explosion of comic book–based movies. Strategized and built or rebuilt smartly, a branded franchise can not only throw off multiple revenue streams but can become evergreen . . . and can over and over again be rebuilt—for example, Spider-Man: comic book to animation to TV series to movie to video games to Broadway to massive merchandising. In the brave new world we suddenly have found ourselves living in, perhaps the answer is to make *ourselves* into human franchises with multiple revenue streams coming in . . . provided we continually self-refresh, retrench, and reinvent ourselves. And sometimes by revisiting the past, we can see how our personal prequels in life got us to the breakout blockbuster moments of our careers. Perspective is a beautiful thing, and we have much to learn by remembering the history of our lives so as to help us keep from repeating our own gravest mistakes.

In revisiting my work from my student years, I see that each step was actually forming one yellow brick after another, paving my road toward my ultimate work goals in life.

When I started working summers in the early to mid-1970s at DC Comics in New York, Vice President Sol Harrison put me on the Edugraphics project. It was groundbreaking in its use of specially prepared Superman, Batman, and Wonder Woman comic books to motivate slow readers to read, to effectively teach English-as-a-second-language students, and to help teach reading to what then were referred to as "brain-injured children." Feeling a need to improve my credentials as this program grew and required me to speak at teachers' conventions and work with researchers from Harvard's Graduate School of Education, I took a summer off and obtained my master's degree in education, specializing in urban education. I wrote my master's thesis, entitled "The Comic Book Revolution," about the ways comic books can be effectively used in education. It was published as a book soon after by Indiana University's Independent Study Division and used by me in the teaching of my newly accredited correspondence course called The Comic Book in America. Did the master's degree help me? Let's just say that we made a presentation of Edugraphics to the New York City Board of Education and it bought the course as a supplementary reading program!

The first book IU hired me to write was to fill the one gap in my comic book course. There were really no comprehensive books out that covered comic books from an academic standpoint. In short, there was no adequate textbook for my course, so they paid me to write one. They published *The Comic Book in America* as the first and only textbook on the subject. It sold out in a flash, not only to the students on campus and those enrolled in the home study course but also to teachers I had lectured to around the country who were interested in finding ways to use comic books to motivate and teach their students. It figured my first two books would be about comic books. I had no clue as to how many more would be coming down the pike.

Stop the presses! Wait a minute! Did I say a paragraph or two ago "a comic book *correspondence* course"?!? Yep! As the publicity about my college course was circling the globe, IU's own Independent Study Division approached me about expanding my focus and teaching it through IU's correspondence program. I jumped at the opportunity! Again, my path was becoming clearer and clearer to me! When a door opened . . . even slightly . . . that might further my efforts to make a lifetime career out of my passion for comic books . . . I had to, without hesitation, stick my foot in that door. One foot in front of the other, one open door at a time, might just make it possible to make my dreams come true. But if starting out, I had a goal to bring the real dark and serious Batman I loved to the silver screen, I may as well have declared, "One day, I want to jump across the Grand Canyon!" Impossible! The chasm was too far to leap over. But one step at a time . . . one foot at a time in every door that wasn't slamming in my face . . . patiently, but unwaveringly, and main-

DC SUPER-STARS OF
MAGIC
50¢
NO. 11
JAN.
31660
GIANT
ZATANNA--
MISTRESS OF THE OCCULT--
TRAPPED BY DEMONS
IN A WORLD BEYOND DEATH!
The FLASH BATTLES
ABRA KADABRA

taining a high threshold for mounting frustration . . . maybe . . . just maybe . . . I could attain my dream goal. My parents knew; and my teachers Mrs. Stiller and Mrs. Friedman knew; and my childhood friends Bobby and Barry knew; and my brother, Paul, knew; and my girlfriend, then my wife, Nancy, knew that my dream since I was eight years old was to write Batman comics. He was my one true superhero. It was that "being human" thing. When I was eight, in my heart of hearts, I believed that if I studied real hard, worked out real hard, and if my dad bought me a cool car, I could *be* this guy! Short of that, I would write Batman comics someday. But first things first . . .

My very first specific assignment at DC was to take a humongous pile of fan letters and reply to them as if I was Superman or Batman or whomever the kids wrote to. I felt DC needed a new contemporary reply card and designed one. Sol liked it and printed them up. Next, I was told to be creative and create and design some house ads for DC Comics. What fun that was as my first two were embraced and published! Then Sol said that if I had an idea for a comic book, he would entertain any ideas I came up with. That's when my fanboy instincts kicked into overdrive! I was a huge fan of the beautiful artwork by Gray Morrow. He had done a Zatanna the Magician backup tale in three parts to the lead feature Supergirl in *Adventure Comics*. Gorgeous! But they had never been compiled into one collection. DC was then publishing a comic book titled *DC Super-Star* and had recently begun focusing on *DC Super-Stars of Space*. I figured if they were doing sci-fi, why not magic? I quickly designed *DC Super-Stars of Magic* along with a cover featuring Gray Morrow's complete Zatanna adventure, backed up by reprinting her very first appearance. Sol got an OK for it with one caveat. He and publisher Carmine Infantino were hesitant to publish it without even one DC superhero in the collection. Hedging their bets, they substituted an adventure of The Flash versus his magical foe, Abra Kadabra, for my chosen backup. I could live with that. I still got my full dose of Gray Morrow!

My next DC assignment came about because Sol knew I was a young comic book historian and already had a book published. Based on those credentials, he put me in charge of a series of three book collections to be published by Simon & Schuster's Fireside Books division, under the brilliant editorial domain of Linda Sunshine: one was to be the best of DC War comics, the next was the best of DC Science Fiction comics, and the third was to be the best of DC Romance comics. Sol wanted me to choose all the stories that would be reprinted in each book, edit them with Linda, and write the introductions to all three with a proper historical perspective. I could not have been more excited! After the first two, Linda felt it would be most appropriate to have a woman write the introduction to the romance book. I concurred. I helped Manuela Soares find the best stories and provided some historical context. She did a super job under the nom de plumb of "Naomi Scott." Since the books were selling nicely, both in hardback and trade paperback (and have become very expensive collectibles today), the plan was for Fireside to extend the contract with DC and

LEFT: I designed and put together *DC Super-Stars of Magic* just to preserve artist Gray Morrow's series of Zatanna short stories.

add three more collections. I started work compiling a list of stories I wanted to reprint in the next volume dedicated to the best of DC Westerns when everything came to an end. Linda had moved on to a big job at Little, Brown, and no one left at Fireside had the passion for comic book history.

My next task for Sol was to clean out "The Closet." As I detailed in *The Boy Who Loved Batman*, it was like the last scene in *Raiders of the Lost Ark*. I uncovered a literal treasure trove of documents, artifacts, and previously unknown history of DC. I was in comic book heaven!

Meanwhile, the group of us young'uns, the first time DC hired fanboys as what one day would be referred to as "interns" but back then were referred to as "Junior Woodchucks" courtesy of Donald Duck's nephews, started DC's own in-house fanzine, "The Amazing World of DC Comics." One of our gang, Paul Levitz, would one day rise to become president and publisher of DC. But for each one of us, these were the "good old days"!

Next, I took some initiative and looked at the then-current DC logo, which was boring and plain. I always loved the old concentric circle logo of the company since I grew up with it. Lately, DC was using as a marketing line, "The Line of Super-Stars." So I sat down and designed a new logo for DC and brought my drawing in to Sol. He loved it! It became the official logo for a few years! As a point of information, my logo was eventually replaced by one designed by the king of design at that time, the famed Milton Glaser.

One of the more outrageous moments came when Sol packed me off to the beaches of New Jersey to try selling comic books, ice cream–truck style, on a vehicle he dubbed "The Comicmobile," while the rest of the company dubbed it "Solly's Folly." That legendary escapade also may be found in my prior memoir for comic book posterity.

So where did all these DC Comics prequel events lead? Only to my writing *The Shadow* comic book . . . which led me to writing a comic book of my own creation based loose as a goose on *Beowulf* . . . leading to my dream coming true as I was chosen to write *Batman*! Me? A professional comic book writer? A writer for DC Comics? A writer of *Batman*? It doesn't get better than this. Except it did!

If we now jump from my childhood days in the wilds of Wanamassa, New Jersey, and DC Comics, New York, the next major yellow brick on my road-to-Batman Movie event was post-school, as I entered the "real" world by my going to work as a motion picture production attorney for a major movie studio, United Artists, as I finally got my foot in the door in the motion picture industry. Three of my favorite moments at UA had to do respectively with my three biggest passions in life: rock 'n' roll, comic books, and movies. For one, I got to negotiate and draft Beatles' drummer Ringo Starr's contract (and the contract of Barbara Bach, his soon-to-be-wife, and the sexy, beautiful star of my favorite Roger Moore Bond film, *The Spy Who Loved Me*) for the movie *Caveman*. By then, my bosses were giving me any project that smacked of comic books or the related fantasy, science fiction, and horror genres, "Sheena, Queen of the Jungle" looming large amid massive development hell. The rights were finally and firmly in the hands of Jerry Iger. Jerry deserves an honored place in history as one of the early founding fathers of the comic book industry. His nephew is former Disney-topper Bob Iger, who orchestrated Disney's purchase of Marvel Comics. Wanna talk about the cosmic coincidences of life?

What might constitute a sequel of sorts to my lifetime love of comic books and my idolization of their creators, the vast majority of whom struggled to make ends meet and put food on their families' tables from the Depression through World War II and then had to endure the scorn of a society whipped into a frenzy in the harsh McCarthy days of the national witch hunt against comic books? For me, it was a mission to see them honored with their works being heralded as an original American art form and their stories constituting a modern-day mythology.

Along with a major, record-setting show at the fabulous Montclair Art Museum in New Jersey, director Chip Cronkite, coproducer Jacqueline Knox, and I produced an important documentary to complement the exhibition, "Legends Behind the Comic Books." This film allowed us to preserve on camera the last surviving creators from the Golden Age of Comics to the Silver Age as they recounted their stories firsthand as to how the comic book industry and the superheroes were all created and why. It won first place at the Garden State Film Festival and has been a fan favorite when shown at the biggest comic cons. In conjunction with New York Comic Con at the Javits Center, I moderated a panel of these great creators including Jerry Robinson (cocreator of The Joker, Robin, Alfred, and many other classic Batman villains), Stan Lee (cocreator of the pantheon of Marvel superheroes), Joe Simon (cocreator of Captain America, the Vision, the Young Allies, and dozens of big-time superheroes), Irwin Hasen (cocreator of Wildcat and Dondi, and artist of Green Lantern, Wonder Woman, and the Justice Society of America), Murphy Anderson (artist extraordinaire of Adam Strange, Hawkman, the Spectre, Dr. Fate and Hourman, Starman, and Black Canary), John Romita (Marvel's great artist of Spider-Man, Daredevil, Captain America, and more), Dick Ayers (artist of Sgt. Fury and inker of many of Jack Kirby's Marvel cocreations), Joe Sinnott (arguably Jack "King" Kirby's best inker), Herb Trimpe (immortalized by his artwork on the Incredible Hulk), Allen Bellman (Marvel's last surviving artist of the Golden Age and its earliest superheroes, Captain America, the Sub-Mariner, and the Human Torch), and so many other superstars. At the end of our "Legends Behind the Comic Books" panel, the New York Comic Con SRO audience gave them all a four-minute standing ovation that still gives me the chills when I recall it.

My love has always been for comic books, not just for superheroes. I read and collected every type imaginable from Classics Illustrated to war, western, mystery, science fiction, and humor comics. The king of the humor comics was undeniably *Archie*.

Today in *Archie* comics, there's a mystical, magical street on the outskirts of Riverdale USA called "Memory Lane." Archie has strolled down Memory Lane on a few occasions, and it has given him a glimpse of his past. He even met himself as he originally looked when he was created in December 1941, a month which will live in infamy, as drawn by his original artist, Bob Montana. But, I rationalized, he has never walked *up* Memory Lane.

In doing so, I would have Archie Andrews walk right into his very own future some four to five years hence. But as Archie arrived at Memory Lane, in walking up, he found it split into two roads diverged in a yellow wood. Archie made a choice and walked down the one that led him to propose to and marry the wealthy debutante, the exotic and erotic Veronica Lodge. With this story of mine premiering in the landmark 600th issue of *Archie Comics* (and very few comic books devoted to one character by name, published continuously, have ever reached issue #600; Archie joined a most elite club consisting of Batman, Superman, and Spider-Man), there was a firestorm in the media on a global basis.

Newspapers, television, and radio were filled with coverage of the stories that Archie was getting married, and then the lightning bolt breaking news that his choice was Veronica, not the heavily favored Betty. Veronica was the rich vamp, Betty the loving, sweet "girl-next-door." A *Today* show poll as to whom Archie should marry had tens of thousands of respondents who favored Betty over Veronica 4–1, with Jughead coming in a surprisingly strong third. The internet was abuzz over this earthshaking development. There must have been at least fifty thousand postings, and I trolled about fifteen thousand of them. Several wonderful things were happening as a result of my story. First, it was getting a strong emotional reaction from three generations, with kids reporting that they were buying these comic book issues to share with their parents and grandparents, and vice versa. Second, thousands upon thousands of people were writing long diatribes on the net or via full-blown blogs (not to mention magazine essays and newspaper op-ed pieces) going on and on about how outraged or happy they were that Archie was getting married at all, and then as to the mistake of his life or good choice he was making by choosing Veronica. At the end of many of these personal outpourings, the writers concluded that they had no idea why they were so emotionally overwrought about this or how they could possibly write so much about it, but that they just really *cared*. Alerted by all the media attention that these characters they grew up with, who symbolized their own childhoods and teen years, were still being published and that the *Archie* comics and digests were still thriving, it was like going to a high school reunion for them. But while we, the readers, have all grown up, Archie, like Peter Pan, stays locked in our hearts forever young as the eternal caretaker of our youth. Thinking of him aging along with us and getting married was traumatic for many. And then for him to pick Veronica was Code Blue for generations of *Archie* readers!

As the fans lined up around me with torches and pitchforks, I had to assuage them. The press coverage in countries like India, China, Canada, Kenya, Australia, and so many more was astounding. Here in America, Archie's marriage made it onto shows including Jay Leno, Stephen Colbert, Katie Couric, *The View*, Rachel Maddow (who covered it like a real ongoing breaking news story), and so many more TV shows and newscasts. I explained to everyone everywhere that as a writer, I had to write the truth. And the truth today is that this story already unfolded in real life. But in real life, we do not call them "Archie" or "Betty" or "Veronica." We say that "Brad" has picked "Angelina" over "Jennifer." I then asked the world, "In this terrible recession, should Archie marry for love or should he marry for money and security?" I had twenty-two-year-old Archie make a choice. But I never said it would be the *best* choice. For Archie and many boy-men at that age, they often have their heads turned by the hot girls walking by and rarely truly see the other girls who may be right under their noses. They don't yet comprehend that perhaps being each other's best friend is the best foundation for a long-term marital relationship. The other thing a lot of young people fail to see is what Nancy's dad said to me at the time Nancy and I got engaged. I think he was trying to make a sage point rather than scare me off when he told me that 90 percent of a person's happiness or unhappiness in life will be due to his or her choice of a mate. And that choice doesn't merely affect the two people making it. It has a huge and permanent butterfly effect on their families and friends too, altering the lives of everyone. And that was an important theme of the "Archie Gets Married" storyline I wanted to explore. If he's marrying Veronica, what about poor Betty . . . and Jughead . . . and Reggie, Moose, Midge, Dilton, Pop Tate, Mr. Weatherbee, Miss Grundy, and Mr. Lodge? There amid the supporting cast in Riverdale was the mother lode of stories and character arcs! And speaking of "poor Betty," I told the press and the fans who were packing the Archie panels at all the big comic book conventions that maybe Betty has some serious self-esteem and self-confidence issues she now needs to deal with. Maybe she deserves someone *better* than Archie, and that had to be examined in our tale as well.

The Betty fans breathed a collective international sigh of relief when they realized Archie had taken another walk through the yellow wood after three issues and now journeyed up the other diverging road, only to see what his future life would be when married to Betty. And it would be a starkly different life for him, as well as for all his family and friends, as concluded in *Archie Comics* #606. Between comic book shops, department stores, supermarkets, bookstores, and chain stores, plus massive foreign sales, millions of copies of these books were sold and then combined into one trade paperback collection, followed by a coffee table hardback book in a die-cut slipcase. I also was honored to write the launch of a trailblazing new Archie color magazine, *Life with Archie*, featuring "Archie Loves Veronica" and "Archie Loves Betty," which continued to follow Archie's two futures, with the understanding that one of these two will come to pass. But which one? That will be up to everything Archie and Betty and Veronica say and do in their soap opera–style relationships, or what they fail to say or fail to do in the years to come. Comic book history had been made, and I finally got to take the road that led me to writing Archie. "The Road Not Taken" was not simply Archie's journey; with crystal clarity, it has been mine too.

Ten years later, I proposed to *Archie* moguls Jon Goldwater and the venerated Victor Gorelick that we celebrate their tenth anniversaries by checking back in to see how Archie and Veronica, and Archie and Betty were faring in their marriages and lives. Now in their thirties, they had to be dealing with growing kids and their cell phones and ear buds and video games and the scary world of internet social connectivity, for better or worse. They surely must be confronting issues of aging parents. What about career and financial struggles? Have they remained close to their high school friends like Jughead, Reggie, Big Moose, Midge, Cheryl, et al., or have they managed to lose contact amid busy lives and day-to-day routines? Writing *Archie: The Married Life—10th Anniversary*, from comic book miniseries to graphic novel, with sterling art by Dan Parent, was a labor of love and a chance to incorporate many of the twists and turns I faced in my own thirties. What a fun sequel!

DC and Marvel were not the only two comic book companies making superhero comics back in the Silver Age I grew up in. In fact, there were at least a dozen companies churning them out. Four of these characters I decided to try to bring to life as movies, starting back in the 1980s with the old MLJ Comics Golden Age character the Web, who predated Marvel's Spider-Man. As a company, MLJ wound up deserting its roster of superheroes in favor of a comedy character who debuted along with Pearl Harbor in December 1941, *Archie*. Archie became so successful that the company changed its name to Archie Comics until superheroes became hot again in the 1960s and brought back the Web as *Mighty Comics*, purposefully designed as . . . let's not call it a "cheaper version" but rather a . . . "less expensive version" of Marvel.

In the Silver Age version, as written by Super-Man's cocreator Jerry Siegel, the Web, whose real name was John Raymond, wound up marrying Rose, his "Lois Lane," who later forced him to give up his superhero crime fighting—due to its lack of income, lack of security, and high risk—and to go out and get a "real" job. Grouchy New Yorker John feels more and more "hen-pecked," to coin the retro word used back then, as Rose asks him to take out the garbage and John whines, "You never asked me to take out the garbage when I was the Web!" Rose always had the last word. "Well, back then I needed my life saved. Now, I need my garbage taken out!" My favorite moment came when John sneaks out one night with his son as he secretly tries to teach him to become a superhero and continue the old family business. Back at home, the Roach, the Web's former archenemy and, unbeknownst to each of them, his hated next-door neighbor for the past twenty years, accidentally turns Rose into a superbeing with the magnified powers of an ant. Now empowered herself and aware of the Roach's plot to destroy her husband and son, Rose throws together her own costume and mask so she can rush out and save them. Her mother, John's less-than-beloved mother-in-law, tells her daughter she can't leave the house without having a superhero name. She rejects Rose's first suggestion of Ant-Woman because it sounds to her like some old monster movie. She disapproves of Rose's second choice, Ant-Girl, believing the feminists would kill her for it. So she just suggests her daughter personalize it and make her debut as Ant-Rose. She loves the idea since everyone in New York has an Aunt Rose and no one would ever be able to track down her secret identity. Pure 1960s silly fun that worked fine for the Web but should never have darkened (or actually, "lightened") Batman's door.

I wrote the two drafts of the screenplay, and we had just gotten the green-light from our financing company, when that company, whose fortune was based on the sales of Betamax and VHS tapes, went belly up.

Our next attempt at another minor league superhero took place when we made a deal with the legendary Joe Simon, cocreator of Captain America, and, once again Archie

Comics, on a character from 1959 known as "the Fly," another cocreation of Joe Simon and Jack Kirby. I had always wanted to produce a movie about the original Captain Marvel, whom today's generation knows better under the nom de plume of "Shazam." Captain Marvel was actually a boy of about twelve or thirteen named Billy Batson. Every time he said his magic word, he turned into an adult superhero. For simplicity's sake, let's just say it's sorta like the movie *Big* meets *Superman*. Back then, I couldn't access the rights, though I did years later, becoming the first and only producer Warner let take a DC property out of Warner Bros. proper, as the originating producer of the *Shazam* movie and its establishment as another franchise spewing *Black Adam* and *Shazam 2*. But back in the 1990s, if I wanted a character who transformed from a child into an adult, the best superhero to bring to cinematic life would be Joe Simon and Jack Kirby's the Fly (first published by Archie Comics), who was more like *Big* meets *Spider-Man*. (Historical note: The original name Simon and Kirby had for the Fly was "Spider-Man," but they were told by the publisher that kids hate spiders and to change the name. They did. When Stan Lee and Steve Ditko created Spider-Man a few years later, Marvel's publisher told them the same thing. Stan did not change it. The only reason he got to use the name was because they were putting that first story in a comic book called *Amazing Fantasy*, which had already been canceled by the publisher, who now could care less what they called the new superhero if it was in the last issue of a comic book and neither marketing nor sales mattered anymore.)

And so, I met with Will Smith, who was super interested in starring, then signed a deal with superdirector Bob Zemeckis to direct, with his respected partner, Jack Rapke, producing with us. Bob brought in a couple of A-list writers, and we set the project up at Dreamworks, feeling highly confident this baby was getting produced. It didn't. The project kept falling into the realm of satire and never earned its wings. I regretted that not only for us, for Joe Simon, for Archie, and for the fans of Simon and Kirby but also because I would now never hear on a TV commercial the words, "*The Fly* opens Friday!"

The third project in the 2000s was Will Eisner's *The Spirit*. The fourth project was *Thunder Agents*. To make it short and sweet, those wounds are still too fresh to talk about, so let's table them till the next book in this trilogy.

Most painful of all was *Black Cat*. This sad tale begins in that magical Bat year of 1989. On Oscar night in 1990, Nancy and I went with our *Batman* production designer, Anton Furst, and his fiancée, Penny. Nancy and I had been getting together with them weekly post *Batman* while they were in New York working on Penny Marshall's film *Awakenings*. I urged Anton to consider taking the leap into directing for the first time, and out of a dozen comic book characters I showed him, he selected a comic book property he loved as the project he would want to do, based on the old Harvey Comics superheroine the Black Cat; eventually, a draft screenplay was written. But in LA on Oscar night, there was true magic in the air. Anton had been nominated for Best Art Direction for our film and won! We yelled and cheered as up he went to collect his statue. As soon as he left the press backstage, he handed the statue to Nancy and said, "This is too heavy for me to carry around all night. *You* carry it." Nancy cradled it like a baby the rest of the evening. We celebrated with a big dinner party at what was then the hot spot on the Sunset Strip, Nicky Blair's, owned by the former actor who knew everyone in Hollywood and whose agent used to be my cousin Hal Gefsky. Nicky went all out and offered all the champagne that night as his personal congratulatory gift. That was the night I met Lucille Ball (and *boy* do "I Love Lucy!"), who was sitting a foot or two away from me. That entire night was simply "the stuff dreams are made of." And that is exactly why I got into this crazy business to begin with!

In the end, Anton was persuaded by the big money to sacrifice his new love for New York and move to LA, where he did not wind up directing or working on passion projects. Tragically, he died in 1991. A creative genius, a friend.

One of the highlights of my work was my association with Stan Lee, who bridged every phase of my life. I met Stan Lee for the first time when I was eleven. My mom had agreed to take me and my friend Bobby to New York City on a day off from school. We would go on the DC Comics tour, and then she would take us to see the Baxter Building, which we knew was the home of the Fantastic Four. *Fantastic Four* #9 had just gone on sale, and we were fascinated by the story in which the group of superheroes doesn't have enough money to pay its rent for its secret headquarters in midtown Manhattan and is evicted from the Baxter Building. When we got to New York, my mom asked everyone, including cops, where the Baxter Building was, but nobody seemed to know. She went into a phone booth (ask your parents about that), then picked up the phone book (also ask your parents about that), and called Marvel Comics. Stan Lee's assistant, Flo Steinberg, answered the call. She was heartbroken for these two eleven-year-old boys who had come to see a building that wasn't real but was only the creation of writer/editor Stan Lee and artist Jack Kirby. Feeling bad, Flo told her to bring the boys up to 655 Madison Avenue and she would see which he could do. When we got there, she greeted us, took us inside, and introduced us to Stan and Jack Kirby. I had with me my oldest comic book from the 1940s, *All-Winners Comics* #18, which Jack and Stan autographed for me. That was it! A Stan Lee fan for life!

Over the years, Stan became my mentor and my friend. My relationship with him as a young adult began on the day he called to congratulate me on the huge media impact of the new college-accredited course on comic books I started teaching at Indiana University in the early 1970s. Once I started working in the movie, TV, and animation industry, our paths crossed often. Finally, we had the chance of a few occasions even to work together creatively. Then in 2015, he and I, along with my son, David, joined forces to design and teach the first ever online course offered by no less than the Smithsonian Institution on "The Rise of the Superheroes." Over 150,000 students from some 160 countries initially signed up for the course. Free, the course is still being offered today via edX. It was paradise working with Stan, capturing and explaining the history of comic books and superheroes from 1938 to today. It's a project that forever will be able to stand the test of time. David and I were honored to be two of the producers of Stan's Hollywood memorial at Grauman's Chinese Theatre following his passing.

Me and David along with fellow producer David Baxter and Chief Paul Cell at the Stan Lee Memorial at Grauman's Chinese Theatre. Stan would have loved this sendoff!

I closed my eyes tight one day, then opened them and the kids had grown up. Life is so fleeting. That's why Nancy and I always followed the advice of her dad and my mom. The sage advice of Dr. Morry Osher was imparted to us in a steady stream. This one particular time, Nancy and I were discussing finances and felt we would have to skip our yearly family vacation with the kids. Her dad said, "Whenever you feel you can't afford to go on a vacation with your family, remember instead that you can't afford *not* to go while your kids are still at home with you. It's a binding experience that creates wonderful memories for everybody." He was right and we always found a way to go. My mom was also right . . . every time, in retrospect. She had a master plan for my brother, Paul, and me. Her dream was that she and my dad would take us to all fifty states and Canada before we left home. Every June, just before the school year ended at Wanamassa School and Ocean Township School, she would visit with teachers from the next grade we were promoted to and ask them what we would be studying that next year in Social Studies. On that basis, she'd figure out where we could go on our summer family trip. So right before I'd be learning about the Jamestown Colony, I was there and walked across it and touched it and it came alive for me. And just before I studied the Battle of Quebec, I was there on the Plains of Abraham and could picture the entire battle in my mind. As a result, I learned to love history and always got an A in it and made it my passion . . . my major in college. When I saw the hundreds of history courses Indiana University was offering (and the fact I didn't have to take math if I went there), I was sold!

And so, as a father, every summer I planned a fun adventure for my family and we flew to a different geographic area of America and rented a minivan and set out on the road for two weeks. By the time the kids went to college, they had, indeed, been in all fifty states and throughout Canada. Sometimes it was a real challenge . . . like finding something interesting to see in Iowa. That's when my love for rock 'n' roll kicked in, and I transported us to Clear Lake and the Surf Ballroom where Buddy Holly, The Big Bopper, and Ritchie Valens gave their last concert before dying in a plane crash in a nearby farmer's field.

As David and Sarah got older, our family trips became more and more adventurous, winding up in Francis Ford Coppola's Blancaneaux Lodge in the jungles of Belize, where scorpions rained down on our beds, vampire bats dive-bombed us, giant spiders crawled next to David's head, a jaguar possibly lurked around the next corner, and something akin to Mothra tried to break into our hut all night long. After enjoying Alaska so much, our next adventure led us to Iceland and then on to an isolated Eskimo village in Greenland that was on the tip of what had to have been the ends of the earth. When we landed in Greenland, the airport terminal was the size of our garage. On each of three walls was the giant skin of a polar bear. I noticed each had a little plaque under it. So I read them: "Shot on runway 1995," "Shot coming through window 1996," and "Shot breaking down door 1997." I had no point of reference in my life for this. While in the comics there had been a "Bat Ape" and "Titano the Super-Ape," there never was a "Super-Bear" in the Legion of Super-Pets. I therefore couldn't relate to polar bears coming through my window. A bubble helicopter jockeyed us two at a time to our inn, where the daily meals were based on the fishermen's catch of the day. Whale was on the menu on day one, seal on day two. I ate rice and old shoes. It wasn't what you'd call an ordinary family trip, perhaps, but how many parents get to land in a helicopter with their kids on August 1 atop a glacier and get out and have a snowball fight? How many parents get to lie in bed with their kids on a night that never gets dark and listen to the baying at the moon of thousands of sled dogs? How many parents get to watch with their kids chunks of ice floes the size of Staten Island broken off from the Arctic and flowing past their mountaintop watch post? How many parents get to go snowmobiling with a guide and their kids up a glacier, experiencing a white-out, where there's no way to determine where the air ends and the ground begins, and all in abject silence? Even when David and Sarah went off to college and beyond, we made the effort each year to have our own special family reunion trip together. Our last was in support of my wife, Nancy's, incredible nonprofit efforts bringing clean water and literacy to Rwanda. Our family trip there and to the Masai Mara in Kenya were life changing for all of us. But, alas, kids grow up and move away from home. I learned that in that great Superman comic book story when his earth parents died and he moved from Smallville to Metropolis and, on the same day, changed his name from "Superboy" to "Superman." He sure figured out the easiest way to deal with puberty. I shoulda changed my name too.

Top left, Nancy and me when we started dating. Here, she meets my mom and dad for the first time.

Top right, Sarah, David, and I fly to Rwanda to support Nancy's incredible nonprofit work providing clean water, literacy, and eye care. Then it was on to Kenya and the Masai Mara.

Right, Nancy working on clean water, literacy, and eye care through her company, NEU Global, LLC.

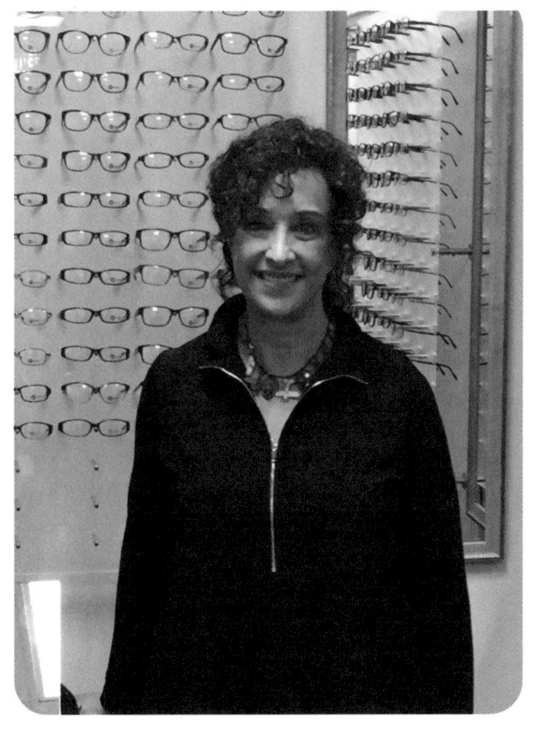

My Batman journey through life is clearly composed of events but is truly all about people. It's the people I've met on my journey who have defined me. People created me, molded me, nurtured me, influenced me, encouraged me, guided me, advised me, supported me, motivated me, challenged me, and loved me. Some people blocked me, frustrated me, deceived me, impeded me, denigrated me, slowed me, but never ever stopped me.

My family, friends, teachers, and mentors stood up for me, stood by me, stood behind me, and stood for the same things I have stood for. They have always been close enough to prop me up when my knees buckled, to hold me up when I was down, to push me forward when I didn't want to take another step, to hold me back from stepping off the next ledge, and to kick my ass when it needed kicking.

I was lucky.

Our parents do for us and give us what they can. But it's up to us as to what we do with that which they have given us. They can bundle us up and pack a lunch for us, but the jour-

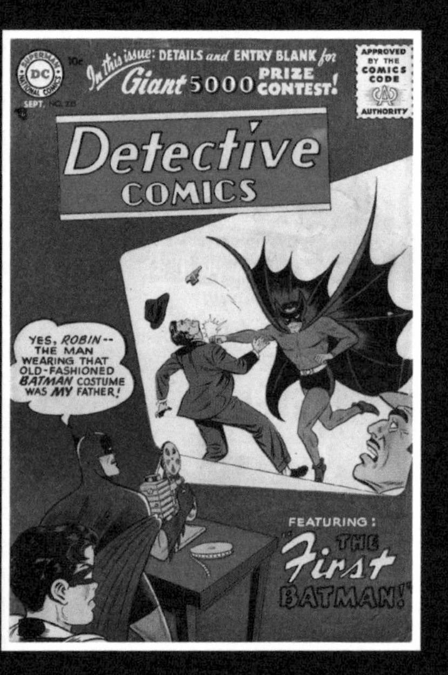
10¢
SEPT.
In this issue: DETAILS and ENTRY BLANK for Giant 5000 PRIZE CONTEST!
APPROVED BY THE COMICS CODE AUTHORITY
Detective COMICS
YES, ROBIN-- THE MAN WEARING THAT OLD-FASHIONED BATMAN COSTUME WAS MY FATHER!
FEATURING: "THE First BATMAN!"

ney we take must be our own. Bruce Wayne finally understood that in *Detective Comics* #235, September 1956. I didn't fully understand that until June 23, 1989, the day *Batman* opened in theaters everywhere. Do the movies and comic books parallel our lives, or do our lives parallel the movies and comic books? In the words of the late Jim Henson, "Life is like a movie. Write your own ending. Keep believing. Keep pretending."

A passion for me since grade school has been creative writing. Books, comic books, graphic novels, screenplays, treatments, essays . . . it doesn't matter. I just love writing. I first dreamed of a career in movies, television, and animation as a writer. But it was only when Irwin Moss of ICM revealed to this naïve kid that I had to be a producer if I had even a prayer of having continuing involvement in a project, that I also became impassioned in this role. One big reason is the way producing allows me to find myself in places and situations no "normal" person would find themselves in, while rubbing elbows with history.

I had just gotten home from a vacation with the family. I turned on my computer and checked the emails I had not checked for days. There I saw an email from Joe Biden's assistant, which, of course, I figured was spam. This was during the closing days of the Obama administration. On a closer examination, I thought there was a slight possibility that this email could be real, so I called the phone number provided, even though it was late. It was real! I was being appointed to Joe Biden's task force on gun violence and the entertainment industry, a subject I and every other Batman fan takes to heart. I was told a meeting would take place the following day at 6:00 p.m. at the White House but they first needed to do a security background check. I had already been working with Homeland Security on certain matters and had spent time at their headquarters on the outskirts of Washington. My clearance came, and quickly I raced to book passage on the morning Acela train from New York to Washington, DC. And since I required a hotel room for that night, I felt the only appropriate hotel for this would be The Watergate Hotel. I then pulled an all-nighter, reading everything I possibly could regarding gun violence in the media and about the Second Amendment itself, even to the point of reading a copy of *The Federalist Papers* that, as a history buff, I actually owned! I did not know if I would have to give an opening statement, as I have seen on C-Span broadcasts of people testifying before the Senate or Congress, so I attempted to prepare for all eventualities. I did not stop taking notes and organizing them until the train pulled into Washington, DC, the following afternoon. I met the good folks from Homeland Security for lunch and went over what the agenda might look like and what my thoughts and ideas were. Satisfied, they sent me over to the White House. I was the first one in the room, which was a historic room, and I saw beautiful nameplates around one long conference table. I would be sitting across from Eric Holder, the attorney general who would be sitting next to Vice President Biden. Next to me would be one of the toppers of the Secret Service and Kathleen Sebelius, Secretary of Health and Human Services. When the vice president arrived, he greeted the motion picture and television luminaries and lobbyists present. Then I walked up to him to introduce myself.

LEFT: Batman reveals his secret identity to the man responsible for the murder of his parents.

THE VICE PRESIDENT

WASHINGTON

January 18, 2013

Mr. Michael Uslan
Branded Entertainment LLC

Dear Michael:

Thank you for taking the time and trouble to meet with me last week at the White House. It meant a great deal to me to talk about the Newtown tragedy with you and what we can all do to help. We discussed a lot of interesting ideas, from ratings to filters to PSAs, and I really appreciated hearing not only what the entertainment industry is already doing to help, but what you can do in the future.

I hope you saw the gun policy recommendations President Obama and I unveiled yesterday at our press conference. I look forward to continuing our conversation and hearing your new ideas as we continue this discussion.

Thank you again for coming.

Sincerely,

Joseph R. Biden, Jr.

One of my greatest honors was being invited by Joe Biden to the White House for his task force meeting on gun violence in the movie and television industry.

He beamed and said, "Michael, I love that story in your memoir about how you were able to teach the first college course on comic books! Eric has to hear it! He's a comic book guy!"

I was stunned. I turned to the attorney general and said I'd like to talk about the history of the Second Amendment with him, but he squelched that.

"Oh no! The only thing you and I are talking about is Batman!"

I was stunned again. As I took my seat at the table, the gentleman from the Secret Service pulled from his briefcase a copy of my memoir, *The Boy Who Loved Batman*, asking me if I would sign it. I was stunned yet again.

"Did they send out an advance copy to everyone here?" I asked incredulously.

"No," he whispered, "I'm a comic book collector. I bought this six months ago!"

The next few hours were awesome! I wouldn't be that stunned again until the day I got the call from my friend from Jordan informing me that the king of Jordan would be in LA the next day and asking if I would have lunch with him and three other people from the movie and television industry. Not only did I have that stunning lunch but also the next morning, my son, David, and I were asked back to breakfast along with a larger number of great industry people. I love my producing work! No day is the same, and when I awaken in the morning, I never really am sure what state or country I'll be in come nightfall.

Todd Phillips is both a genius and a nice guy. I have the greatest respect for him and his work. His masterpiece created with Joaquin Phoenix, *Joker,* was a thinking person's movie and the best commentary on the issue of mental health in this country since *One Flew Over the Cuckoo's Nest.* Todd thanked me for being the first to stand up and support him and his vision for the film when before it even was released, people who hadn't seen it were unfairly criticizing it. My support of Todd was loud and clear, pointing out to the press that when cinema is at its best, it not only entertains but also it acts like a mirror to society, exposing warts and all. Todd's film was an artistic triumph and thematically important commentary on vital issues including the current lack of civility in society, as people talk at each other rather than with each other. Whether on the set, or during the night of the Golden Globes, or during the night at the Oscars when *Joker* received eleven nominations with a Best Actor win for Joaquin, Todd has shown the world a whole new vision for the making of what used to be called "comic book movies." And thus, for the third time in history, a Batman-related film changed Hollywood and changed the world culture's perception of superheroes and supervillains. Jerry Robinson, Bill Finger, and Bob Kane would have been so proud!

And so, in looking back over my lifetime mission promoting everything Batman and the Batman brand through our movies and animation while being the best cheerleader I could be in support of our filmmakers, I can attest that win or lose, it's all about trying your hardest. And if that is the gold standard used to measure a person's success, then on behalf of and along with the creators, writers, artists, colorists, editors, producers, directors, screenwriters, musicians and composers, production designers, creative film crews, executives, animators, voice casters and directors, owners and workers in comic book shops everywhere, and, most importantly, my fellow Bat-Fans globally, I accept today what so long ago my late partner Ben said with a metaphysical tapping on my shoulder with an imaginary mythological sword as he proceeded to Dark Knight me, "Michael . . . You are Batman's Batman."

Meanwhile, my memoir, *The Boy Who Loved Batman*, is in development as a Broadway play in association with The Nederlander Organization and as a live-action feature film, which can only be described as *A Christmas Story* for anyone who grew up loving comic book superheroes. Will these projects take ten years to bring to fruition as our first *Batman* movie did? Will they languish in that development hell enflaming the route from Hollywood all the way to the Great White Way? Will they defy the terrible odds of Hollywood? Will that magical place be my land of milk and honey or, if not, my land of bilk and money? Who knows? Not even the Shadow. But, *ahh*! The journey! That's the thing! My seat belt is fastened. My arms and legs are inside the car at all times. I'm holding on to my possessions. Let's get this show on the road!

Looking back over a lifetime, the choices I made all had consequences . . . serious consequences. For example, choosing not to move to Los Angeles and instead to remain in New Jersey so our children could be raised among my parents and family made so many of my Hollywood projects harder and take longer and, perhaps, made the difference between them ultimately blooming or wilting. But there were far-reaching and more important consequences than that. My children, David and Sarah, are now adults with their own families and soaring careers. And I can proclaim today that I not only love my adult kids, I like my adult kids. They make me proud. Each a dedicated parent, David and Sarah have pursued their own big dreams, found their own passions, their own "Batmans." David is a global entrepreneur as well as my partner on many producing projects. He's also on the advisory board to The Mob Museum in Las Vegas, as the history of organized crime in America is a passion of his. Sarah is a famed editorial and celebrity makeup artist and, after five dedicated years of tireless work, successfully launched her own company, LuLa, introducing her own line of amazing skin-care products at wearelula.com.

In 2020, as the fates would have it, I had long been scheduled to return to Indiana University to do my yearly three weeks of teaching two courses, "The Business of Producing Motion Pictures" and "Live from Hollywood: Experiential Learning with the Pros." Rather suddenly, I had to choose where to be on Oscar night: in Hollywood amid the *Joker* team or living up to my responsibilities as a professor to the students who were already halfway through my courses. Nancy and I talked about it . . . for a minute . . . and knew that our place was in Bloomington with my students, rooting for Todd, Joaquin, producer Emma Koskoff Tillinger, composer Hildur Guonadottir, and the other crew members up for Oscars, from a pizza party we threw that night in the grand atrium of the IU Media School, watching on its prodigious big screen. So as host, I supplied running commentary, including revealing some secrets as to what really goes on during a long Oscar telecast and making my own forecasts amid the endless flow of pizzas. It was a night to remember that neatly tied my life in a bow. "Bloomington to Hollywood—How Do You Get There from Here" and "Hollywood to Bloomington—Why We All Need to Pay It Forward."

ACKNOWLEDGMENTS AND CREDITS

A memoir is only as good as the aging brain cells of its author. Therefore, first and foremost, I must thank my brain trust, who either vetted my manuscript and memory banks or who agreed in the warm and fuzzy spirit of friendship or family connections to allow me to share the memorable antics I had with them from grade school to high school to college to the real world of big business to the ephemeral world of Hollywood: Nancy Uslan; Paul Uslan; Barry Milberg; Marc Caplan; Ronna Berman; Barbara Laufer; Wendy Preville; Candy Hanus; Ellen Genick (etc.); my amazing, fantastic, incredible kids, David and Sarah; Ian Duncan, Paul Hyman, and Bruce Solomon, and my Uslan and Solomon cousins; Dr. Robert Osher; MaisonRK; Steve Huntington; Jeff Mendel; Ira Byock; Indiana University's Lauren Robel and Joel Silver; Chip Cronkite; Jackie Knox; DC Comics' Junior Woodchucks; Marc D. Nadel; my United Artists teammates Michael Klastorin, Lou Castelli, Nan Leonard, Steve Strick, Amy Klein, and Howie Deutch; Scott Maybaum; Brad Finkle; Peeper Freemas; Robbie Skirboll; my frat bros from Sammy; Steve Gorelick; Wade Knowles; Stephen Williams; and the king of Indiana University Press, Gary Dunham.

And now for those of you who pay attention to details:

Prologue: *Detective Comics* #33, story written by Bill Finger with art by Bob Kane and Sheldon Moldoff. Copyright © 1939 DC Comics. All Rights Reserved.

Prologue and Chapters 1–4, 6–8, 10–12: fourteen quotations from various Batman comic books. Copyright © 1989–2021 DC Comics. All Rights Reserved.

Chapters 1 and 3: *Batman: Zero Year*, story written by Scott Snyder and James Tynion IV; art by Greg Capullo, Danny Miki, and Rafael Albuquerque. Copyright © 2013 and 2014 DC Comics. All Rights Reserved.

Chapter 2: Knightfall from *Batman* #497, story written by Doug Moench, art by Kelley Jones. Copyright © 1993 DC Comics. All Rights Reserved.

Chapter 4: *Batgirl: Year One*, story written by Chuck Dixon and Scott Beatty, art by Marcos Martin and Alvaro Lopez. Copyright © 2003 DC Comics. All Rights Reserved.

Chapter 5: *Detective Comics* #38, story written by Bill Finger with art by Bob Kane and Jerry Robinson. Copyright © 1940 DC Comics. All Rights Reserved.

Chapter 6: *Batman: Broken City*, story written by Brian Azzarello, art by Eduardo Risso. Copyright © 2004 DC Comics. All Rights Reserved.

Chapter 7: *Batman and the Outsiders*, story written by Bryan Hill, art by Dexter Soy. Copyright © 2019–2020 DC Comics. All Rights Reserved.

Chapter 8: *Batman: Battle for the Cowl*, story written by and art by Tony Daniel. Copyright © 2009 DC Comics. All Rights Reserved.

Chapter 9: *Arkham Asylum*. Copyright © 2010 DC Comics. All Rights Reserved.

Chapter 10: *Batman* 14–20, story written by Tom King, art by Mitch Gerads. Copyright © 2016 DC Comics. All Rights Reserved.

Chapter 11: *Batman: Absolution,* story written by J. M. DeMatteis, art by Brian Ashmore. Copyright © 2002 DC Comics. All Rights Reserved.

Chapter 12: *The Dark Knight Returns,* story written by and art by Frank Miller. Copyright © 1986 DC Comics. All Rights Reserved.

Chapter 13: *Detective Comics* #439, story written by Steve Engelhart and Vin and Sal Amendola, with input by Neal Adams; art by Sal Amendola. Copyright © 1974 DC Comics. All Rights Reserved.

And . . .

Batman #112, art by Sheldon Moldoff. Copyright © 1957 DC Comics. All Rights Reserved.

World's Finest Comics #30, story written by Bill Finger with art by Bob Kane and Ray Burnley. Copyright © 1947 DC Comics. All Rights Reserved.

John Constantine, Hellblazer #76, story written by Garth Ennis with art by Glenn Fabry. Copyright © 1994 DC Comics. All Rights Reserved.

Mystery in Space #90, art by Carmine Infantino and Murphy Anderson. Copyright © 1964 DC Comics. All Rights Reserved.

Lobo #21, art by Kevin O'Neill. Copyright © 1995 DC Comics. All Rights Reserved.

All-American Comics #16, story written by Bill Finger with art by Martin Nodell. Copyright © 1940 DC Comics. All Rights Reserved.

Adventures of Alan Ladd #7, art by Ruben Moreira. Copyright ©1950 DC Comics. All Rights Reserved.

Just Imagine Stan Lee & John Buscema Creating Superman, story written by Stan Lee with art by John Buscema. Copyright © 2001 DC Comics. All Rights Reserved.

DC Super-Stars of Magic #11, art by Gray Morrow. Copyright © 1976 DC Comics. All Rights Reserved.

Detective Comics #235, art by Sheldon Moldoff. Copyright © 1956 DC Comics. All Rights Reserved.

The Shadow/Green Hornet: Dark Nights, story written by Michael Uslan with art by Alex Ross. The Green Hornet, Black Beauty, Kato, and the hornet logos are trademarks of The Green Hornet, Inc. The Shadow ® and © 2014 Advance Magazine Publishers Inc. dba Conde Nast. All Rights Reserved. Dynamite, Dynamite Entertainment, and its logos are ® and © 2014 Dynamite. All Right Reserved.

Lone Ranger/Green Hornet: Champions of Justice, story written by Michael Uslan with art by John Cassaday. Copyright © 2017 Classic Media, LLC. The Lone Ranger and associated characters, names, images, and other indicia are trademarks of and copyrighted by Classic Media, LLC. All Rights Reserved. Copyright © 2017 The Green Hornet, Inc. The Green Hornet, Black Beauty, Kato, and the hornet logos are trademarks of The Green Hornet, Inc. Dynamite, Dynamite Entertainment, and its logos are ® and © 2014 Dynamite. All Right Reserved.